Career Success Series
Guide 1

JOB SEARCH TIPS FOR RETUR

MW00885599

There is no doubt that Returning Citizens face many challenges in their job some employers have toward formerly incarcerated individuals. How job seekers react to and ... determine how successful they are in securing meaningful employment.

Are You Really Serious?

Are you really serious about getting a job and becoming a productive, self-sufficient member of society once you are released? Nearly every prisoner professes that he/she intends to change their behavior, get a job and become a productive member of society. Unfortunately, the odds are not in your favor to accomplish your goal. Two out of every three released inmates will return to prison within 3 years of their release and three out of four within 5 years. It is your responsibility to remain determined in your resolve to succeed in order to beat the odds.

This and the other Career Success guides are filled with valuable, effective ways that you can obtain and maintain meaningful employment. The process is not going to be easy and you will be confronted with many situations that discourage and perhaps anger you. Whether you are successful or not rests entirely with you. It will not be an easy journey. There will be many people who will want you to succeed, but many that expect you to fail. You are the one who can distinguish between those who are acting in your best interest, truly committed to assisting you to reach your goals and those who are not. Use the Career Success guide, *Resources for Returning Citizens* to obtain additional information and to locate resources that can assist you in your journey.

The Process Is the Same

The process of taking steps to secure meaningful employment is the same for Returning Citizens as it is for non-offenders. This Career Success Guide will focus only on those issues that are unique to the Returning Citizen. The Returning Citizen job seeker is directed to all of the other Career Success Guides for information on the process.

Negative Thoughts

The biggest obstacle to a successful job search is you. You have been in prison and prison is harsh. It has made you feel worthless, paranoid, hopeless and alone. You distrust the system, most people, and yourself. It is easy to convince yourself that the worthlessness you feel is truth. To move forward, you must question the origin and validity of each sabotaging belief. "Am I really not very smart?" "Should I really never trust another person?" "Is it true that everyone is out to get me?" These are all negative thoughts and negative thoughts are cancerous.

Attitude and Desire

Attitude and desire are the two most important factors in your job search. If you really don't want to succeed, you won't, plain and simple. The world is full of talented people who failed because they didn't have the desire to succeed. Conversely, there are millions of stories of average and below average people who accomplished a great deal because they wanted to succeed. Doubt and negativity are killers. You can control your attitude! It takes practice and desire. Successful Returning Citizens turn the negative attitude of *I can't* into *I can*. They constantly affirm that they can and will attain their chosen goal. They exchange the negative talk of prison for the positive mindset of success.

Rebuilding You

It has often been said that incarceration dehumanizes the individual. It is now time to rediscover yourself and the outside world.

- **Family**. Who have been the people who have been good to (and for) you during your incarceration? These are the people you need to remain in contact with. Not only can they provide emotional support, they can be invaluable as contact people during your job search. Don't worry about the fact that you might not have communicated with them for a while. If you are concerned about their reaction, begin your contact with a letter. Most likely they will be glad to hear from you.
- **Forgiveness**. Just as you have felt hurt and anger toward significant others, so have they experienced these same feelings toward you. It is time to move on and put these feelings behind you. In order to accomplish this, it may be necessary for you not only to ask for forgiveness from others, but also to be willing to forgive them.
- **Circle of Friends**. It is critical that your circle of friends support the new you. As hard as it may be, you may have to avoid former friends (and former inmates) who may expect you to engage in activities that are inappropriate and not consistent with your new life.
- **Self-Esteem**. Do you like who you were in the past, who you are today and who you plan to be in the future? The prison experience may have robbed/drained you of your self-esteem. How you re-establish your self-worth will determine your success upon release. Returning Citizens are particularly vulnerable because society will be slow to forget and forgive, and will constantly remind you of your mistakes. You will need to insulate yourself from this negativism with positive affirmation of your worth both by your own self-talk: "I am unique and I add value to society, family, friends and to myself."
- **Know who you are**. You need to know what you have to offer to employers. Review all of the Offender Job Search Guides related to the job search.
- **Clean and Sober**. The same as you want to surround yourself with positive people, so do you want to embrace a positive lifestyle and avoid those lifestyle environments that are troublesome. It is not surprising that a vast number of crimes are committed while under the influence of drugs or alcohol. The message is clear... stay clean and sober. Get support if this is a concern.

The Challenge of Being a Returning Citizen

What makes you different from the average job seeker is the fact that you have a criminal record and you will need to tell the prospective employer about your past. You might be asked on the application or you may be asked about it in the interview. As stated earlier, many people are suspicious and possibly frightened of Returning Citizens. The reasons for these attitudes are many, but usually relate to the fact that they do not trust you. Your challenge is to convince them that you can be trusted.

Employers' Perceptions

It is important that the job-seeker understand that most employers view their company in the same manner that we view our family and home. We are extremely protective of family members and will defend our home and property against any threat. Likewise, employers want to protect the integrity, assets and employees of their company from harm. It is, therefore, incumbent upon the Returning Citizen job seeker to convince the employer that they are not a threat. Remember, usually the only thing an employer knows about the penal system is what they have viewed on television and in movies. They do not have a very realistic viewpoint of the system or the people who have been incarcerated. You have an opportunity to educate them.

Communicating Your Record on the Application

It is legal for an employer to ask if you have ever been convicted of a felony. You do not need to mention any arrest unless there was a conviction, including any pending court action. Any convictions while you were a juvenile are kept confidential and, therefore, do not need to be mentioned.

When asked on the application if you have been convicted of a felony, be honest and say, *yes*. Rather than attempt to explain on the application (even if you have space), write, will explain in the interview. If they require you to explain on the application, be as brief as possible. State your offense, the date it happened, where it happened, the sentence that you received and the date that you were released. Finish the explanation with, *I would welcome the opportunity to provide more details in an interview.* Do not lie about your record.

Communicating Your Record During the Interview

The most difficult question you will be asked in the job interview is the one about your criminal record. Prepare your response well before you enter the interview room. Practice your response with your parole officer or a career counselor.

- **Be honest and direct**. Restate what you wrote on the application. Give the date that the incident happened, charge, conviction date, sentence length and date released.
- **Explain what you did**. Be brief. Don't deny the charge or the conviction. Accept responsibility. Acknowledge that what you did was wrong. Describe what amends you have made to the victims.
- **Explain what you have learned from your mistakes**. This is the most important part of the interview. Since everyone makes mistakes in their lives, the interviewer is interested in what you learned from your mistake and the steps you have taken to prevent it from happening again. How are you different today than you were when you entered prison? Give concrete examples: "Before I was convicted, I drank heavily but since my parole I have been attending AA meetings and have been sober." How have your values changed? "I didn't realize how important my family was to me until I got incarcerated." Talk about your future goals. "Prison gave me an opportunity to get my GED and welding training. I really want to make a career as a welder."
- **Drugs and alcohol**. Be prepared to submit to a drug test as a condition of employment. In fact, offer to submit to such testing as a way of demonstrating being clean and sober.

It's Not So Much What You Say...

It's not always what you say in the interview, but how credible you are that determines whether the interviewer trusts you. The interviewer is looking at your body language, facial expressions and overall appearance. The interviewer is also listening to what you say, your tone of voice and verbal expressions. Do the facial expressions and body language match the words being spoken? If you are sincere, it will show in many ways.

The Outside Is Different

It is not going to be easy to adapt to the real world, but you have to in order to survive. Inside prison you had to be tough, suspicious and aloof. To be successful on the outside you have to be almost the opposite... trustworthy, friendly and flexible. Finally, the language of the real world is different from the language you have adopted while incarcerated. Slang expressions, swear words and phrases, and insider code words may have been acceptable on the inside but are unacceptable on the outside. Watch what you say and how you say it.

RESOURCES FOR RETURNING CITIZENS

Although every guide in the Job Search guides series includes a section listing resources relevant to the guide's topic, this guide lists many more resources available to the re-entering Returning Citizens. Resources include not only websites but also books, videos and pamphlets that Returning Citizens will find helpful as they proceed on their journey to self-sufficiency and employment.

Do Your Own Research

The Internet is an excellent resource for finding almost everything you want and need to know about nearly every subject. Review the Job Search guides How to Use the Internet in Your Job Search. The process is simple. From any of the available web browser programs (like Internet Explorer), go to the www.google.com website. Enter the topic. For example, Jobs for Returning Citizens in Colorado. Google will quickly list all of the websites that have information about the topic. You will need to look at each listing and determine if it is relevant to you. By narrowing your topic (for example, Truck driving jobs for Returning Citizens in Denver Colorado), you can eliminate many non-relevant website.

Whenever you have a question about any part of your journey or you are looking for assistance, use the Internet to locate organizations, agencies and individuals who may be able to help.

Disclaimer

The sites listed below are only a sample of the available sites that can be found on the Internet. Because sites come and go daily, it is critical that you do your own homework (see above). Some of the sites will direct you to other sites. In some instances, be prepared to enter some information about yourself or where you are located. In the latter case, the website may list only sites in your locality. Avoid websites that ask for personal information or ask for a credit card number.

Full Service Organizations and Agencies

There are hundreds of community-based, religious and governmental agencies that are devoted to assisting re-entering felons. Some organizations have a national presence, whereas most are local and only serve people from that community. These agencies usually offer some or all of the following services to Returning Citizens:

- Pre-release Services
- Basic Skills and Literacy Training
- Job Readiness Training
- Occupational Skills Training
- Job Coaching and Counseling
- Job Placement
- Life Skills Training
- Housing Assistance
- Substance Abuse Counseling
- Mentoring
- Financial Counseling
- Family and Psychological Counsel

National Hire Network

www.hirenetwork.org/clearinghouse

This website is a perfect place to begin your search. Once you have identified your state, the site provides email addresses, locations and information about federal, state and local organizations and agencies that provide assistance for reentering felons for that state.

Goodwill Industries

www.goodwill.org

Goodwill Industries has offices in nearly every state in the U.S... This non-profit organization provides a wide variety of services to not only Returning Citizens, but to the disabled and economically disadvantaged. They are an excellent resource for counseling, training and job placement.

Your Local One-stop Career Center

www.careeronestop.org/

You should make visiting your local One-stop Career Center the first step in your job-search process. Review the Job Search Guides How to Use Your Local One-Stop Career Center. One-stop Career Centers provide job counseling, possible job training and placement assistance.

XAMIRE Felon Friendly Network

http://xamire.com/

Established in 2010, this website is devoted to ex-felons wishing to obtain employment, and any other necessary help and information in order to better their lives. You can use the free services to search for local businesses that hire exfelons, find ex-felon federal/state program information, and get support from other members. This site is filled with lots of good information and links to programs available in every state.

Impact Services Corporation

www.impactservices.org/

This organization, which is located in Philadelphia, is an example of the type of community-based agency that offers many services to Returning Citizens including placement assistance.

Returning Citizens .net

http://Returning Citizens.net/

This website has been developed by a Returning Citizens for reentering felons. It is filled with valuable information. The site provides a list of helpful books and other resources and information on your legal rights. Returning Citizens .net also provides a list of employers known to hire Returning Citizens.

Wisconsin Job Center

www.wisconsinjobcenter.org/exo/

This is an example of a state resource for Returning Citizens. The state of Wisconsin has put together an excellent list of resources for Returning Citizens. Resources include tutorials on a variety of subjects (like Federal Bonding) and a series of "fact" sheets covering important topics for the re-entering felon.

The Center for Employment Opportunities (CEO)

www.ncjrs.gov/pdffiles/168102.pdf

This document describes a community-based program that is in New York City which provides transitional services for Returning Citizens immediately following their release.

Job Information and Placement Services

The following websites can be used to not only identify the types of jobs that are available to Returning Citizens, but some sites actually list employers known to hire Returning Citizens.

Your Local One-Stop Career Center

www.careeronestop.org/

One of the primary functions of your local One-Stop Career Center is to provide information about employers and job openings. Every One-Stop Career Center has computers available that link to local as well as national job data banks which list job openings. The staff will provide assistance on locating employers who hire Returning Citizens. Review the Job Search Guides How to Use Your Local One-Stop Career Center.

Exoffenders.net

http://exoffenders.net/

This website has been developed by a Returning Citizens for re-entering felons. Exoffenders.net has compiled a list of employers known to hire Returning Citizens. This list is constantly being updated as fellow Returning Citizens report on friendly (and not so friendly) employers.

Jobsonline™

www.jobsonline.net/

This website is a general website for people looking for employment. You can narrow down your search by indicating that you are looking for a job where the employer will hire a Returning Citizens. In the window JOB, enter Jobs for Convicted. Next enter your zip code. You will be asked to enroll. It is a free site, so do not be concerned with entering your information. You will be given a list of jobs and employers in your areas that hire (and there are openings for) convicted felons.

Ranker

www.ranker.com/list/list-of-companies-that-hire-felons/business-and-company-info

This is a website that ranks a wide variety of things (like the top ten list of movies in 2014). One of the lists is companies that are known to hire Returning Citizens. The information contained in the list comes from Ranker's readership (and in the case of employers who hire Returning Citizens, it would be Returning Citizens who have secured employment from that company). Because employers are added daily, be sure to visit this site often. Currently the site list 134 different companies.

Buzzle

www.buzzle.com/articles/jobs-for-convicted-felons/

Buzzle is a website that compiles information about many things. One section of information they have recorded focuses on the employment of Returning Citizens. They have 14 different sub-topics, all related to the employment of Returning Citizens (Jobs for Returning Citizens, Work Opportunities for Ex-Offenders, Best Jobs for Returning Citizens, are just a few of the topic areas). One of the topics is Companies that Hire Returning Citizens. Check out the growing list of companies that will hire you.

Additional Resources for Returning Citizens

Federal Bonding Program

www.bonds4jobs.com/

In 1966, the U.S. Department of Labor (USDOL) created the Federal Bonding Program (FBP) as an employer job-hire incentive that guarantees the job honesty of at-risk job seekers. Federal financing of Fidelity Bond insurance, issued free-of-charge to employers, enables the delivery of bonding services as a unique job placement tool to assist Returning Citizens, and other at-risk/hard-to-place job applicants (e.g., recovering substance abusers, welfare recipients, poor credits, etc.).

ERE.net

www.ere.net/2012/04/26/what-the-arrestconviction-guidance means-to-you/

This site provides information on how employers can and cannot use arrest and conviction information.

Wisconsin Job Center

www.wisconsinjobcenter.org/exo/eo_criminal_record.pdf

This is an excellent document that addresses the criminal records of Returning Citizen's and what they need to do to get back into the workforce. They list six critical steps that Returning Citizens need to do to get back into the workforce.

Family and Children Network

http://fcnetwork.org

This is a website that provides resources for the families and children of incarcerated and recently released felons.

Joint Fix

www.jointfx.com/

This is a website that has been developed by an-offender, Michael B. Jackson. His blog and publications offer excellent suggestions and advice on how to stay out of jail.

Procon

http://felonvoting.procon.org/view.resource.php?resourceID=00028

A state by state look at the voting rights for Returning Citizens.

Legal Action Committee

www.lac.org/

If you have a legal question, you can ask an attorney for assistance. Located in New York, the Legal Action Committee may be able to assist you even if you are from another state.

Books and Videos for Returning Citizens

Impact Publications

www.impactpublications.com/resourcesforex-offenders.aspx

Impact Publications is a publisher of career and job resources (books and dvds). Several of the publications target Returning Citizens.

Wendy Enelow

www.wendyenelow.com/book-resume-ex-offenders.php

This website is an excellent resource for Returning Citizens. The referenced book may be found in many libraries and at your Local One-Stop Career Center.

Returning Citizens ReEntry

www.exoffenderreentry.com/

This website lists publications that target Returning Citizens and the incarcerated.

ExOffender.Org

www.exoffender.org/up/docs/Exohandbook.pdf

An excellent handbook for Returning Citizens. Covers the job search process and provides links to resources.

I NEED TO CHANGE JOBS

As a Returning Citizen you may find that you need to change careers not only because your previous career excludes convicted felons, but because you no longer enjoy your past occupation. A career/occupation change should be based on a thorough understanding of your workplace needs and wants, and the requirements of the labor market. It cannot be based solely on emotion nor should it be a spur-of-the-moment decision. A career change is more than simply changing jobs or employers. It means going in a new and different direction. This guide focuses on what re-entering job seekers need to do when making a career/occupation change.

Before you are released you need to consider if you need to change your career/occupation.

"My former occupation prohibits convicted felons from participating in the occupation." Are you sure? Before you automatically rule out being able to return to or prepare for an occupation, do your homework. Google the following, "Can a convicted felon be a (enter the occupation) in (enter state)?" Because states have different rules and regulations, you may find that one state prohibits a convicted felon from working in an occupation; whereas, another state may not have such a restriction.

Are there other related occupations that do permit convicted felons? For example, you may be prohibited from practicing as a CPA (Certified Public Accountant), but you could work as a bookkeeper (provided your conviction was not for a fiduciary crime). As you think about related occupations, Google each to determine if you are disqualified from the occupation.

"I do not want to return to any of my former occupation(s)." When you are released you have a choice to either return to the occupation(s) you had before you were incarcerated or to pursue a different occupation. Assuming that you could return to one of your former occupations, but you do not want to, then you need to first identify what you don't like about that career. What are your specific sources of discontent? Some possible reasons are given below. Check those that apply to you. Perhaps you can think of others that are relevant to your situation.

- You have skills you enjoy using, but your former jobs didn't allow you to use them.
- Your jobs didn't give you the monetary benefits that your work deserves. You want to find a job that pays what you believe the job is worth.
- You want to find work that is rewarding.
- You want a change of pace, to slow down and to have more time for yourself, your family and the community.
- You're ready for a new challenge. You want the chance to grow and learn in a direction that your last situation didn't permit.
- You want to enhance your image and prestige.
- You didn't like the work schedule, the hours, the shifts, the overtime or the lack of flexibility.
- You received job training while incarcerated and want to apply these new skills to a different occupation.

AS MANY AS 45 PERCENT OF U.S. WORKERS SAY THEY WOULD CHANGE THEIR CAREER IF THEY COULD.

Are you ready for change?

A successful career transition depends on your Desire for the new career, *Earnings* and the *Needs* of the labor market.

- **Desire**: How badly do you want the career and how passionate are you about it?
- **Earnings**: Will it pay what your work deserves and is it enough to support you?
- **Needs**: What are the needs of the labor market and how much demand is there for this career?

Experts say it's important to clarify the kind of work you find fulfilling before worrying about earnings or the needs of the labor market.

Those making a career change often have the benefit of knowing more about their strengths, limits and preferences than those just starting out in the workforce.

- Review the Career Success Guide: How to Determine Your Skills. Rank skills according to how rewarding they are and how much pleasure you derive in using them.
- Talk with your transition counselor, parole officer or vocational counselor before you are released. Ask the counselor to help you create a Master List of possible careers based on transferable skills on your list.

How to answer questions about your age and legal status.

If you're starting a new career at mid-life (over 50 years old), you may feel uncomfortable if asked to divulge your age on a job application or during a job interview. Although it is illegal to ask an applicant their age, the issue may still arise and is usually related to concerns about your ability to do the job and the reasons why you want to change occupations.

If the occupation or field is new to you, you will need to be able to discuss how your skills are transferable and how you can apply them to the new job. Prepare your narrative well before you are released. Don't wait to think about this until you are faced with a question in an interview. Be prepared!

Other Career Success guides address how and when to reveal information about your incarceration and legal status. Review the Career Success guide: Job Search Tips for Returning Citizens.

You may feel you have a lot to lose if your plan to change careers doesn't succeed.

It's likely that you have more pressure to find a job than someone in their early 20s who is starting their first career. You have a need to immediately support yourself and possibly other family members. Consider this an advantage. You are highly motivated to reduce the risks associated with changing careers and you are, therefore, more likely to succeed.

Investigate careers before taking the plunge.

Increase your chances of finding your best career match by carrying out a thorough investigation before you are released.

The activities below are in the order of easiest first, to get you warmed up. Note that the most effective research strategies are listed last. Several of these activities may be difficult to do while still incarcerated and may need to be postponed until you are released.

- READ anything you can find about potential careers that appears in newspapers, magazine articles, college catalogs and trade journals. Start a file of article clippings on careers that interest you. Use a computer to "google" the career.
- VISIT job fairs, classes, trade shows and conferences. Obviously, you cannot do this while you are incarcerated, but you can do these activities once you are released. Note which types of jobs companies are recruiting for.
- CHAT with friends, former neighbors, acquaintances, parole officers, other prison personnel or anyone you meet who might have information about a career that interests you. Prison personnel will be encouraged by your initiative and interest and will be more than happy to assist you. One of your goals is to seek out those whose outlook and interests are similar to yours and to discuss with them why they chose that career path.
- SCHEDULE AND CARRY OUT informational interviews. An informational interview is an interview that you request with a person who is working in your field of interest. You are not asking for a job, but are simply having the individual discuss the pros and cons of their job. It is best to visit the people at their job site in order to get close to the action. Again, you may not be able to do this until you are released.

Once you've done the research, find a way to test the waters without going in too deep.

- After you are released, find volunteer work, moonlight or do something part-time in the selected field.
- Contact a temporary employment agency and see if you can get a temporary job in the field. Review the Career Success Guide: Pluses and Minuses of Temporary Employment.

Changing occupations versus career transition.

Career transitions typically involve:

- Change in occupation; e.g., from front end loader operator to dump truck driver for an Excavating Contractor.
- Change in the work setting; e.g., from being a front end loader operator at an Excavating Company to being a front end loader operator for a paving contractor.

The riskiest transitions are changing both the occupation and the setting in one step. Experts say you're more likely to be successful if you make the change one step at a time.

For instance, consider a re-entering woman who wants to change both her occupation and her work setting. Before her incarceration she worked as a retail clerk at a convenience store. Now she wants to take advantage of her training while incarcerated and become a cook at a restaurant.

Making changes one step at a time, she has two different paths open to her:

First path: She could change her occupation from being a clerk in a convenience store to being a fast food cook at a convenience store that also serves fast food. Using this experience, she could later become a cook at a family restaurant.

Second path: She changes her work setting from being a clerk at a convenience store to being a cashier at a restaurant. By working in the restaurant, she could later obtain a cooking position in the same restaurant.

Career changes can take a few years if you adopt the 2-Step Switching Strategy.

Do I really need to go back to school?

Going back to school may be the last thing you want to do. If the career you're interested in requires a college degree or other qualifications that you don't have, *find someone who is doing the job without the qualification* – someone who is the exception to the rule. Ask them about the route they took. Community colleges and vocational technical schools frequently offer short, intense and highly specialized courses leading to a certificate that can sometimes serve as a ticket to a new career. Your local One-Stop Career Center can assist you in locating such training.

TRULINCS Friendly! info@ReentryEssentials.org www.ReentryEssentials.org 347.973.0004 2609 East 14 Street, Suite 1018, Brooklyn, NY 11235-3915

Career Success Series
Guide 4

I WAS FIRED FROM MY LAST JOB

If you were working at the time of your conviction, you most likely were involuntarily terminated from that job. As a Returning Citizen you have the added burden of explaining to future employers your legal status as well as any negative work history. Since employers tend to view being terminated from a job as a red flag, it is important that you learn how to turn your termination into an asset rather than a liability.

Some facts about being fired. . .

- It can happen to anyone who has a job.
- It occurs often in today's ever-changing labor market. These days there is no job security. In a sense, every job is a temporary job.
- It can happen for good reasons or silly reasons. In the real world, people are fired for all kinds of reasons that may be justified or unjust. Sometimes employees are fired for immoral, or even illegal, reasons.
- It is not unusual for employers to automatically terminate the employment of an employee whenever the employee has been charged with a crime, even before adjudication occurs.
- It feels worse than being downsized or laid-off because of the embarrassment and shame of being singled out. This is a normal reaction and often leads to anger.

Negative Emotions

Being fired can be one of the most stressful events in a person's life, akin to the breakup of a marriage or the death of a loved one. It can trigger a wide range of negative emotions, including shock, disbelief, anger, fear for the future, guilt and sadness. Often this occurs at the same time that you have had to deal with the legal issues of your arrest, conviction and possible incarceration.

During this difficult period of your life, it is you who must find safe ways to express your emotions, to let out your anger or sorrow without sabotaging your future job search.

Anger is the most frequent emotion that follows being fired. Experts say that although it's better to let it out and not keep it bottled up, it's important to find constructive ways of venting anger. Find a safety valve, a trusted friend who will listen while you fume and who won't feel threatened by your angry demeanor. A pastor, therapist, case worker, parole officer or other trained professional can help you find ways to burn off the anger, so that it doesn't get in the way of your finding another job.

Sometimes people feel intense anger and animosity toward the person who fired them. But there is no future in seeking revenge. In general, avoid saying bad things about your former boss or the last company you worked for.

Take care of your negative feelings before you start talking with potential employers. If you allow negative emotions to spill over into job interviews, your chances of success are greatly reduced.

Illegal Dismissal

There is no law that says an employer has to give a reason for firing an employee. However, in recent decades, laws have been passed at the federal and state levels to protect employees against discrimination. For instance, it is generally illegal to fire employees because of their age, skin color, race, national origin, religious beliefs, handicap, gender or sexual orientation.

Cases alleging discrimination are often reported on television and in the newspapers, but behind the sensationalism such cases are generally lengthy and quite expensive. Be aware that being involved in a lawsuit against your former employer is likely to hinder your job search. Potential employers may be reluctant to hire someone who appears to be a litigious troublemaker and difficult to get along with.

Having said that, there may be times when you should sue. An expert in employment law can help you decide.

- Discuss the facts of your case with a counselor at your local office of the Equal Employment Opportunity Commission.
- The laws governing employment are complex and involved. An attorney who specializes in employment law will be able to advise you on the odds of winning a lawsuit and what the compensation is likely to be.

The National Employment Lawyers Association can refer you to attorneys in your town who specialize in employment law. For information on how to find a lawyer in your area go to www.nela.org.

Before you proceed, keep in mind that nearly every state is an "at will" state. This means that you, the employee, are and remain an employee of the company "at the will of" the employer. The employer is under no obligation to continue to employ you and can terminate your employment without giving a reason as long as the reason is not protected by law.

Before you are released:

Use the time before you are released to create a narrative that explains your work history. Once you actually start the job search you will be frequently asked to explain not only your legal status, but your work history. Because your work history will probably be filled with gaps in employment, involuntary terminations and/or job changes, it is better to have your "story" straight before you start your job search than to "wing it" when asked for this information from a potential employer. Here are some topics to help you plan.

Why did it happen?

Don't just assume that the reason for your dismissal was because you were arrested. It is possible that the employer had a valid reason. Since in your job interview you will need to explain all terminations, don't just focus on your last job termination.

Your chances of finding another job improve greatly if you can:

- Identify the reason(s) you were fired.
- Reassure potential employers that the problem has been fixed.

For instance, suppose an employee was dismissed for being consistently late for work. The employer and employee each have their own point of view of what really happened:

Employer's point of view: "Work was not carried out effectively because the employee's presence at the job site could not be relied upon."

Employee's point of view: "Car continually broke down. It was my transportation that was unreliable."

Regardless of who was right and who was wrong – or who should be blamed – it is to the job seeker's advantage to address the problem and to do everything possible to prevent it from recurring. Figure out what went wrong and fixi it. Your objective is to put your own point of view temporarily on the back burner and see if you can learn the employer's rationale behind the decision to let you go. If you know the employer's reasons, then you are well on the road to fixing the problem.

Often, employers try to explain what the problem was, but there are times when being fired can be as surprising as a lightning bolt from a blue sky. If you're not sure why you were dismissed, it may be worthwhile to contact your former employer. Explain that you're trying to avoid repeating the same mistakes by understanding specific problem areas in which you could do things differently.

Is it time for a whole new start?

Launch yourself toward a successful future by evaluating all the possibilities that are now open to you.

Review the following Career Success Guides:

- How to Determine Your Skills
- How to Relocate to Another Community
- Pluses & Minuses of Temporary Employment. *Sometimes, it's easier to re- establish a good work record by using this route.*

Be open to new ideas and review other Career Success Guides that interest you.

Is it time for a new attitude?

Attitude is an important part of how well we do our work and how others perceive us. The leading reason that people get fired is that they are perceived as having a "bad attitude".

Attitude is among the first things that co-workers and employers notice about you, including whether you are:

- Pleasant to have around
- Enthusiastic
- Interested in others besides yourself
- Positive
- Full of energy

It is particularly important for someone who has been incarcerated not to project an angry, depressed, or whining attitude. Sometimes we are blind to our own attitudes. We may not see how we are sabotaging our lives.

Ask a trusted friend whose opinion you value what they think of:

- Your general attitude
- Your attitude toward your former employer
- Your attitude toward the job-hunt

How to tell others about the dismissal?

Telling future employers:

- The application form is a legal document and it is important to be honest. Do not misrepresent your work history or legal status on your application form, on your résumé or during job interviews.
- When asked about your reasons for leaving a past job, avoid responding with negative words such as "Fired." Use a neutral phrase such as "Let go involuntarily" or "Involuntarily dismissed."
- At interviews, be prepared to answer questions about why you were dismissed. In one sentence, summarize the problem that led to the dismissal; describe how you have solved it and explain why it will not affect your future job performance.
- Do not vent or whine about your former boss or co-workers. Avoid making negative comments about past employers.
- Review the Career Success Guide: How Do I Deal with Negative Information? for hints on how to deal with your criminal record.

TRULINCS Friendly! info@ReentryEssentials.org www.ReentryEssentials.org 347.973.0004 2609 East 14 Street, Suite 1018, Brooklyn, NY 11235-3915

TIPS FOR RETURNING CITIZENS WITH DISABILITIES

There is absolutely no question that Returning Citizens with physical and/or mental disabilities face challenges in their job search that able-bodied offenders do not. You must overcome the temptation to give up on finding a suitable job. Knowing what to expect will greatly enhance your chances for success.

Returning Citizens

Terminology is very important to people with a disabilities. The number of Americans of working age who are disabled is estimated to be more than 32 million. About 36 percent of the disabled men and 30 percent of the disabled women of working age are employed. Surveys have shown that seven out of ten people with disabilities who are not working actually want to work and are actively searching for employment. This represents a sizeable block of potential employees.

No two people with disabilities are alike. Experts describe each disability as a mix of the impairment and how the individual reacts to the impairment. The impairment defines the actual physical or mental limitations of the person. But since individuals react differently to their impairments, the individual's personality, attitude, background and environment must be considered. The work environment includes how fellow employees respond to the disabled individual and how supportive the employer is.

The Americans with Disabilities Amendments Act of 2008

The 2008 Amendments to the Americans with Disabilities Act (ADA) clarifies and reiterates who is covered by the law's civil rights protections. The Amendments revise the definition of "disability" to more broadly include impairments that substantially limit a major life activity. Changes also clarify coverage of impairments that are episodic or in remission that substantially limit a major life activity when active, such as epilepsy or post-traumatic stress disorder. Nothing in the ADA excludes the re-entering population. It also applies to you.

Are you protected by the ADA?

If you have a disability and are qualified to do a job, the ADA protects you from job discrimination on the basis of your disability. Under the ADA, you have a disability if you have a physical or mental impairment that substantially limits a major life activity.

To be protected under the ADA, you must have a record of having a substantial impairment. A substantial impairment is one that significantly limits or restricts a major life activity such as hearing, seeing, speaking, walking, breathing, and performing manual tasks, caring for oneself, learning or working.

In order to be protected from job discrimination by the ADA, you must satisfy the employer's requirements for the job, such as education, employment experience, skills or licenses and you must be able to perform the essential functions of the job with or without reasonable accommodation. Essential functions are the job duties and tasks that must be performed by all employees. An employer cannot refuse to hire you because your disability prevents you from performing duties that are not essential to the job.

What is a Reasonable Accommodation?

Reasonable accommodation is any change or adjustment to a job or work environment that permits a qualified applicant or employee with a disability to participate in the job application process, to perform the essential functions of a job or to enjoy benefits and privileges of employment equal to those enjoyed by employees without disabilities. For example, reasonable accommodation may include: providing or modifying equipment or devices, job restructuring, modified work schedules, adjusting or modifying pre-employment tests and training materials, providing readers and interpreters and making the workplace readily accessible and usable by people with disabilities.

An employer is required to provide a reasonable accommodation to a qualified applicant or employee with a disability unless the employer can show that the accommodation would be an undue hardship.

What employment practices are covered?

The ADA makes it unlawful to discriminate in all employment practices such as: recruitment, hiring, training, job assignments, promotions, pay, benefits, firing, laying off, leave and all other employment related activities.

Can an employer require medical examinations or ask questions about a disability?

If you are applying for a job, an employer cannot ask if you are disabled or ask about the nature or severity of your disability. An employer can ask if you can perform the duties of the job with or without reasonable accommodation. An employer can also ask you to describe or to demonstrate how, with or without reasonable accommodation, you will perform the duties of the job.

An employer cannot require you to take a medical examination before you are offered a job. Following a job offer, an employer can condition the offer on your passing a required medical examination, but only if all entering employees for that job category have to take the examination. However, an employer cannot reject you because of information about your disability that was revealed by the medical examination, unless the reasons for rejection are job-related and necessary for the conduct of the employer's business. The results of all medical examinations must be kept confidential, and maintained in separate medical files.

Do individuals who use illegal drugs have rights under the ADA?

Anyone who is currently using illegal drugs is not protected by the ADA and may be denied employment or fired on the basis of such use. The ADA does not prevent employers from testing applicants or employees for illegal drug use.

Is an employer required to provide reasonable accommodation during the application process?

Yes. For example, an employer may be required to provide a sign language interpreter during a job interview for an applicant who is deaf or hearing impaired, unless to do so would impose an undue hardship.

Should I tell the job interviewer that I have a disability?

If you think you will need a reasonable accommodation in order to participate in the application process or to perform essential job functions, you should inform the employer that an accommodation will be needed. It is the responsibility of the employee to inform the employer that an accommodation is needed. Do this well in advance of the interview.

Do I have to pay for needed reasonable accommodation?

ADA requires that the employer provide the accommodation, unless to do so would impose an undue hardship on the operation of the employer's business. If the cost of providing the needed accommodation would be an undue hardship, the employee must be given the choice of providing the accommodation or paying for the portion of the accommodation that causes the undue hardship.

Can an employer lower my salary or pay me less than other employees doing the same job because I need a reasonable accommodation?

No. An employer cannot make up the cost of providing a reasonable accommodation by lowering your salary or paying you less than other employees in similar positions.

Does an employer have to make non-work areas used by employees, such as cafeterias and rest rooms, accessible to people with disabilities?

Yes. The requirement to provide reasonable accommodation covers all services, programs and non-work facilities provided by the employer.

Is the employer required to select a qualified applicant with a disability over other applicants without a disability?

No. The ADA does not require that an employer hire an applicant with a disability over other applicants.

Can an employer refuse to hire because the employer believes that it would be unsafe?

The ADA permits an employer to refuse to hire an individual if the individual poses a direct threat to the health or safety of the individual or others. A direct threat means a significant risk of substantial harm. The determination that there is a direct threat must be based on objective, factual evidence regarding an individual's present ability to perform essential functions of a job.

Are people with AIDS covered by the ADA?

Yes. ADA also protects persons with AIDS and HIV disease from discrimination.

Job Search Issues for People With Disabilities

The job search process used by offenders with disabilities differs little from that of non-disabled offender job seekers. For that reason disabled job seekers should review all of the Career Success Guides related to the job search process. Although the process to obtain employment is similar, people with disabilities face some unique challenges:

- **Rejection.** Every job seeker (disabled or not) may experience rejection. This rejection, however, can be worse for persons with a disability because they have experienced (and continue to experience) rejection in many areas of their lives. It is easy to become convinced that disabled means unemployable. Disabled job-seekers need to realize that others seeking employment also experience rejection.
- **Focus on what you can do.** Too often people with disabilities have had their limitations emphasized to the point that they have lost sight of their strengths. Employers are interested only in what you can do, and are less concerned with what you cannot do. Be realistic as you list your strengths, recognizing that everyone has marketable skills. Remember, with an effective accommodation, you can enhance a skill that you thought was weak. For example, by using a computer with voice recognition software, a person with finger dexterity limitations can still perform computer-related tasks.
- **Job search resources.** Your particular disability may restrict the types of career and job search resources that you can utilize. Most resources are written, making them difficult to use by people with dyslexia or restricted vision. Your local One-Stop Career Center may have access to Braille, big-print versions or audio versions of popular resources.
- **Speech or hearing limitations.** Since most job interviews are verbal, people with hearing and/or speaking problems need accommodation. Consider asking the interviewer to conduct the interview over the Internet, using TTY or an artificial speech recognition computer program. You could also bring a friend or a professional interpreter (not a family member) to the interview.
- **First impressions.** All people with disabilities are familiar with the reactions of others to their disability. Disarm this reaction by letting the interviewer know in advance. Do this in a casual manner. For example you might say, "I appreciate your building being accessible since I use a wheelchair."
- **Interview Preparation.** You must help the interviewer to conclude that you can do the job. This means that you must have a clear understanding of the job duties and how your limitations will not affect your performance of those duties.
- **Reasonable accommodation.** Employers are concerned about costs. *What will it cost me to hire this individual?* Explore ways to accommodate your limitations that are cost effective for the employer. In many cases you will already have the aid or accommodation, or access to it. Either bring it with you to the interview or describe it to the interviewer.

JOB SEARCH ISSUES FOR WOMEN AND MINORITIES

Employers tend to hire people with whom they feel comfortable. Often, this means they are more likely to hire people who are like themselves. In addition to the prejudice employers often have toward formerly incarcerated individuals, re-entering women and minorities are at a disadvantage, given that historically, positions of power in the business world have been held by white males. This guide focuses just on the unique issues that reentering women and minorities have in addition to being a Returning Citizen.

Many employers consciously or unconsciously bring stereotypes of women and minorities to the selection process. This is in addition to the stereotypes employers have toward formerly incarcerated persons. Although this is unfair and negatively affects the chances of women and minorities to secure employment, it is a fact that must be realized. These stereotypes come from ignorance and usually aren't intended to be harmful. Recognizing that these stereotypes exist means that re-entering women and minorities need to present themselves as being as different from the negative stereotypes as possible.

It is easy to blame others when we don't get the job, especially when it appears to be due to the employer's unfair biases or beliefs. Even when this is the case, it is important to evaluate yourself as well. Is it possible that you went into the interview with the assumption that you would not be hired? Did you fall into the trap of confirming the employer's stereotype?

Discrimination

To determine if you are the victim of discrimination as it is defined by the Equal Employment Opportunity Commission (EEOC), ask yourself the following questions:

- Does my race, gender, religious affiliation, national origin, age, sexual orientation or physical handicap entitle me to protection under the laws of the EEOC?
- Am I being treated differently from other applicants of similar experience, education and skills?
- Is the treatment different because of my race, gender, etc.?

If you can answer yes to all of these questions, you may have a legitimate complaint that may qualify for EEOC action. You, however, need to decide whether you wish to file it. In a complaint to the EEOC, the burden of proof rests with you. Your state Department of Labor can advise and assist you. Remember that businesses with a small number of employees are often exempt from states' civil rights laws.

To Your Advantage

Minority and woman job seekers can use their minority status as a plus in their job search. Often, companies are attempting to establish diversity and seek minority applicants. Check with your local employment service and EEOC office to get a list of these companies.

Fitting In

The job search process, especially the interview, is not the time to make political or ethnic statements. Every company has a culture that reflects the values of the company and the people who work there. Employers are no different than you are. They seek people with whom they are comfortable, who demonstrate similar ideas and values. You will be evaluated against those criteria. If making a statement is important to you, then slowly introduce those values and statements into the work culture after you get hired. Remember that the atmosphere of the company is made up of many people with various views and values, not all of which will agree with your views and values.

It is illegal for employers to ask:

- your nationality
- your ancestry
- your native language
- where you were born
- your sexual preference
- skin, eye, or hair color
- for a photo on an application

It is legal for employers to ask:

- If you are able to work legally in the United States.
- If you want to be identified as a minority for affirmative-action purposes.

Issues Specific to Minorities

As in any job search, networking is the best way to develop job leads. Use your contacts to get your foot in the door at companies. You have a better chance of being hired if you come with a personal recommendation. If you are only comfortable being around people of your own race, confine your job search to just companies that are minority owned. Your local NAACP can assist you in identifying such companies in your community.

Be sure to include non-minorities in your job search network. Look up former classmates or co-workers or join community activities with a large number of non-minority participants. Utilize social networking sites such as www.Linkedin.com and www.facebook.com to find contacts in companies you are targeting for employment. Limiting yourself to minority networking will restrict your opportunities.

Plan ahead. Minorities are often used to a lack of opportunities and, as a result, take the first thing that comes along. Doing this can significantly change the course of your career. Broaden your search, keep an open mind to your options, and do not limit the possibilities.

Gender and Employment

While many jobs are held in equal numbers by men and women, some are still dominated by one gender. It may be more difficult for a woman to find employment in a position or company dominated by men. You will have to make the interviewer feel at ease and convince him or her that you can do the job and that you'll be easy to work with.

Don't assume that if you're being interviewed by a woman she will give you favorable treatment. She will likely have the same concerns a man would.

Learn to Negotiate

Women often are hesitant to negotiate, and they tend to ask for less money than men do. When negotiating a salary, you're looking for a win/win situation, where both parties are happy. Here are some tips to help you settle on a fair salary:

- Do your homework - First, determine how much money and what benefits you need (health insurance, life insurance, retirement, etc.). Second, research typical salaries for similar positions and levels of experience. This will give you a basis for comparison.
- In negotiations, the first person to mention a number usually loses, so try to avoid being the first one to name a salary. If you do have to make the first move, make sure to aim high. You can always come down, but you can't go up later.

Childcare

One major concern of employers of women is whether the employee will need to take a lot of time off to care for her children. Single and married mothers often shoulder the burden of childcare. So even though it's illegal for an employer to ask about this, and even if your partner is the primary caregiver, you may need to address these concerns.

If you have children and are the primary caregiver, of course, you will need to find childcare with which you are comfortable. You should explore options and have a plan prior to submitting a job application. If the issue of childcare comes up during the interview, you can share your plan and assure the employer that you are covered in that department.

This is especially important if the job requires overnight travel or unusual hours. Don't be afraid to address this concern in the interview by stating, "I have excellent childcare, and therefore, I feel that I can devote my time and energies to my work."

Legal vs Illegal

It is illegal for employers to:

- ask whether you are married or ask whether you have a family
- ask your maiden name
- ask whether you are pregnant or whether you plan to have a family
- ask what your daycare arrangements are or ask your spouse's occupation
- list a job as male or female or express a preference in a job advertisement
- hire only unmarried or sterile women
- treat pregnant women differently from any other workers with special needs
- offer benefits, vacations or holidays differently to men and women
- not hire women because of stereotypical characteristics
- hire only one sex based on customer desires

It is legal for employers to:

- Hire based on the gender of the applicant if there is a genuine reason for this basis - as in the case of a model for clothing.
- Ask if there are any reasons why you cannot perform the job as described, including work shifts, work on weekends and other job requirements.

Mother Friendly Employers

Working Mother magazine lists the best companies for working mothers. Look for it at your library or online. The web site is: www.workingmother.com.

Dressing for your interview:

Dress conservatively. Avoid revealing clothes, perfume and very high heels. Carry a purse or briefcase - not both. Your hair and nails should be neat and clean. Remove all piercing-jewelry. Wear clothing that hides any tattoos.

Sexual Harassment

Sexual harassment is defined as any unwelcome sexual advances including any sexual behavior and/or employer promises of a job in return for some kind of sexual favor.

If this happens to you, you may have a viable case for presentation to the EEOC. Again, the burden of proof is on you.

In any case, if the interviewer comments on your appearance in an inappropriate manner, asks you out on a date or has pictures of nude women hanging in his office, you probably won't want to work there.

TRULINCS Friendly! info@ReentryEssentials.org www.ReentryEssentials.org 347.973.0004 2609 East 14 Street, Suite 1018, Brooklyn, NY 11235-3915

HOW TO RELOCATE TO ANOTHER COMMUNITY

Even before the economic downturn in 2009, between five and six million people packed up and moved each year in pursuit of a job, according to the Census Bureau. It may be advantageous for you to locate to another community especially if your community ties you to your offense. Before you consider relocating, however, you will need to discuss the move with your parole officer and other prison officials. For a successful, stress-free move, planning is the key. Figure out your priorities, do your research and develop an action plan.

Can you legally relocate?

Before you begin the process of evaluating other communities, you need to discuss relocating with your parole officer, legal representative and prison officials. It is possible that the terms of your release prohibit your relocating to another community, other state or country. Additionally, the nature of your incarceration may affect where you can live. For example, if you were convicted of a sex related crime, you may be prohibited from living near a school, daycare center or playground. Again, your parole officer can and will detail these limitations to you. It is best that you find out where you can or cannot live months before your scheduled release. This guide assumes that there are no restrictions on your relocating.

The best place to live?

Before making the decision to relocate when you are released, determine what your priorities are in a locale and then research it thoroughly. All of the following can be done while still incarcerated using the Internet and other resources available in most prisons. Consider the following factors:

The Job Market. The new location needs to have a relatively strong and stable economy. This is important to long-term job security and future occupational advancement. So, before considering a new community, do your research. Call, write or email the local Chamber of Commerce and seek answers to the following questions:

- What's the unemployment rate? The rate should be relatively low (less than the national unemployment rate) across all occupations, as well as within your specific field.
- What kind of economic growth is forecasted? Is there growth in your new community? In your industry?
- What kind of business atmosphere exists? Is it a one-company town or is there a healthy diversity of companies, with differences in size and focus?
- Which of these companies utilizes your occupational skills? Ask for a complete list.
- What's the average salary for your occupation? A high salary could mean strong competition among companies for your skills.
- How do average salaries in this area compare nationally? Lower salaries could reflect a low cost of living—or it could indicate a shortage of jobs or an oversupply of workers.
- Are there community-based organizations that cater to re-entering individuals? Are there employers who hire re-entering individuals? Do they have agencies that can provide the support services that you may need?

Cost of Living. Your new residence may possess a substantially higher cost of living than you're used to. Remember, the cost of living may have increased substantially since you last worked. To determine the cost of living, look at the price of basic needs at your future location. Start with the following:

- Food. What's the price of a gallon of milk? A loaf of bread?
- Housing. What's the median price for an apartment?
- Utilities. Talk to the local companies about phone, electric, gas and cable rates. Does the area get extremely cold or hot at certain times of the year? If so, expect higher costs.

Research Help

Not sure where you want to live? Try these sources for ideas.

- *Places Rated Almanac.* This book evaluates nearly 350 metropolitan areas in the U.S. and Canada. http://placesrated.expertchoice.com
- Annual guides put out by magazines like *Money, Time, U.S. News and World Report, Business Week* and *Fortune* rank areas for quality of life and offer up-to-date information.

Job-hunting Long Distance

Locating a job from far away makes a difficult task even more difficult. But the following tips will ease the process:

- Find out the name of the local newspaper. Go online and Google the newspaper's name. Nearly every newspaper has a web site. Within the website they will let you read the "Help Wanted" ads. Also look for news about company expansion and employee promotions and transfers.
- After you are released you can obtain the area's Yellow Pages at your library or by contacting the local phone company. This will save you money on directory calls.
- While still incarcerated you can use any of the online business directories like www.yellowpages.com.
- Obtain the names of all local agencies that assist reentering offenders. Contact them before you are released and obtain information about their services.
- Ask to be assigned a contact person with whom you can correspond via email before and after you are released.
- Contact the local One-Stop Career Center. Indicate that you are about to be released from prison and are interested in relocating to their community. Ask for the procedure for registering and for receiving notifications of job openings in your area. To find the closest One- Stop Career Center, go to www.careeronestop.org.
- Prepare for questions about your reasons for relocating.

These generally will include:

- Why do you want to move to this city?
- How does your family feel about the move?
- How long will it take for you to move?
- Are there legal issues related to your relocation?

The Pitfalls of Relocating

Not having a network of people. It is likely that you will know few if any people in the new community.

- Review the Career Success guide: Using Your Network to Locate Job Openings.
- Create a network when you arrive in the community by joining a church, attending an AA meeting or making other contacts.

Money. Moving is expensive especially in today's economic climate. To ease the blow to your wallet:

- Make a plan. Know exactly what a move is going to cost and how you will cover those costs. Talk to your parole officers about possible sources of assistance.
- Keep records. The IRS allows deductions from your income taxes for certain moving expenses including shipping, storage, fees for disconnecting and connecting utilities and travel outlays related to job interviews and house hunting.

Stress. Moving can cause almost as much anxiety as the death of a loved one or a job loss. Be prepared by educating yourself on how to recognize the signs of stress and how to take care of yourself and your family. Review the Career Success guide: How to Handle the Stress of the Job Search.

Family. If you have a family that will be relocating with you, then you need to be aware of their needs and concerns. Young ones will miss old friends and often feel insecure after a move. You can help them cope if you:

- Involve them in moving plans and house-hunting.
- Take them to visit schools and recreational facilities.
- Watch for signs of loneliness and fear.
- Encourage them to talk about their feelings.
- Allow them to keep in touch with old friends.
- Allow them to make some decisions, like how they arrange or decorate their new rooms.

Hiring a Moving Company

If you have a home and a lot of stuff you might find that having someone do the packing and hauling is often cheaper than the do-it-yourself option, not to mention a lot easier. To ensure the best price and service, take these steps:

1. Five to eight weeks before the move, contact your Better Business Bureau and get a list of reputable movers.
2. Movers generally charge by the pound, so plan to lighten your load by disposing of or donating anything you don't need. These include:
   - Old magazines and books.
   - Clothes that no longer fit, are not in style, or clothes that are not suitable for your new life after release.
   - Furniture and appliances you intend to replace in the near future.
3. Obtain written estimates from three movers. Ask each:
   - To see a copy of their Interstate Commerce Commission Annual Performance Report, which details any past complaints or problems.
   - For a list of references.
   - What types of insurance are available, and the costs.
4. Determine what extra charges will be assessed on top of the given price. These include long distances, carrier's liability and bulky articles. Ask to have these waived or included in the final estimate.
5. Once you make a selection, read the contract carefully. Does it include all your requests? Is the final quote binding?

Ensuring a Successful Move

- Pack carefully. The mover will not accept liability for items you pack. Protect glass items with bubble wrap, put heavy items in small boxes and label all boxes clearly.
- Before the movers arrive, take a complete inventory.
- Carry any sentimental, extremely fragile or irreplaceable items with you, if possible, to ensure their safety.
- After your shipment is unloaded, check and compare your inventory list with the mover's list. Make sure all boxes have arrived and look for damage.

TRULINCS Friendly! info@ReentryEssentials.org www.ReentryEssentials.org 347.973.0004 2609 East 14 Street, Suite 1018, Brooklyn, NY 11235-3915

HOW TO HANDLE THE STRESS OF A JOB SEARCH

It is important to recognize that stress is a normal and inevitable part of the job hunting process. The re-entering job seeker is going through a time of change, moving from something familiar (the routine of prison life) to something unknown. Although job hunting leads to new opportunities and rewards, the job hunting process can create stress.

Stresses Related to The Job Search

- Financial uncertainty
- Increased interaction with new people
- Uncertain direction
- Additional demands on time
- Feelings of isolation
- A sense of lack of control
- Anxiety about the future
- Change in routine
- Telling your story over and over again

The stress of job hunting cannot be avoided, but it can be managed through a variety of techniques. Review the following techniques and then actively use them during your job search to diminish the negative effects of stress.

Stress Management Techniques

- Exercise regularly
- Use support networks
- Get adequate rest
- Limit intake of alcohol
- Involve family and friends
- Eat a balanced diet
- Set realistic goals
- Avoid isolation
- Keep a regular schedule
- Use relaxation techniques

Exercise Regularly

Regular exercise is one of the most important steps in managing stress. Regular exercise will increase your energy, enhance your sense of well-being, help you relax, contribute to better sleep patterns, foster disease resistance and encourage weight management. A regular exercise routine that you choose will give you a sense of control during a time of uncertainty. Exercise will contribute to a healthy and vigorous appearance during job hunting when you want to look and feel your best.

Experts recommend starting with 30 minutes of physical activity three times a week. Work up to the equivalent of 30 minutes a day of moderately intense activity for stress management and significant health benefits. It is a good idea to check with your doctor before beginning any new exercise program. Look into visiting a gym and having an expert develop an exercise plan for you. Pick forms of exercise you enjoy and make exercise a part of your daily routine.

Involve Family and Friends

Involve your family and friends in your job search. Your family may not know what you are going through, so do not wait for them to offer assistance. Ask for help. Most people are more than willing to help if you let them know their help is needed. Remember to:

- Talk to your family - Share your concerns, plans and goals.
- Listen to your family - This is also an uncertain time for them. Listen to their feelings and suggestions.

Ask for help - Family members or friends can offer emotional support and provide feedback. They can assist with practical tasks so that you will have the time you need for job hunting. They can also serve as contacts for networking and informational interviewing.

Use Support Networks

In addition to a support system of friends and family, many job hunters find it useful to participate in job hunter's support groups. People in similar life circumstances can often be very understanding of your experiences. A support group offers opportunities for social interaction, a chance to express a range of emotions (excitement, fear, disappointment, etc.) and a place to relax with others who are in similar situations.

Support groups can be found through local places of worship, libraries, One-Stop Career Centers and United Way directories.

Eat A Balanced Diet

Your health and sense of well-being is affected by your eating habits. Additional time demands and change in routine often lead to snacking on non-nutritious foods, eating at irregular times or skipping meals. Plan time for regular, balanced meals in order to look and feel good during your job search.

Keep Your Parole Officer Informed

One major form of stress for re-entering felons is making sure that you conform to the requirements of your release, which may include your securing a job as soon as possible. You can reduce this stress by keeping your parole officer informed of everything that you are doing to secure employment. Ask for their assistance and involve them in your job search.

Take Care of Yourself While Job Hunting

Prioritize and Set Goals

Effective job hunting takes time. Job hunting can be a full-time job in itself. It is important to organize your time to meet the demands of your job hunt.

Remember that everything cannot be accomplished at once. Setting priorities will help you allocate your time realistically so that time demands do not become overwhelming.

In order to prioritize, make a list of steps in your job hunt which need to be accomplished (include time frames) and other tasks which need your time. Decide which tasks are most important and allocate your time accordingly. Include time for your stress management techniques. Ask your parole officer to assist you in setting these goals.

Your job hunt is placing new and increased demands on your time, so some things you are used to doing may not get done for a while. Let these things go for now or enlist help for these tasks so that you will have the time you need for job hunting and taking care of yourself.

Take Control and Keep A Regular Schedule

Goals will be more effectively accomplished if you keep to a regular schedule of prioritized tasks. A routine which includes job-hunting steps, stress management techniques and family time will give you a sense of balance and accomplishment. Establishing and maintaining a routine will give you a sense of control over your time. Having too much free time can tempt you to return to your former habits and behaviors. Fill your time with meaningful activity.

Use Relaxation Techniques

Relaxation techniques can help manage stress. Begin with simple exercises such as sitting in a chair, breathing deeply and visualizing the tension leaving your body. Other forms of relaxation, such as yoga, Tai Chi, listening to relaxation tapes or doing meditative exercises, can help you release the tension that accumulates in your body and mind during the job-hunting process.

Reduce the Effects Of Stress

Taking time to manage stress is important. If stress is not managed, it can lead to a variety of symptoms, including:

- Irritability
- Insomnia
- Anxiety
- Depression
- Weight fluctuations
- Headaches
- Muscular/skeletal pain
- Chronic fatigue
- Relationship difficulties
- High blood pressure
- Intestinal disorders
- Skin disorders

Avoid Alcohol and Drugs

It is tempting to use alcohol and/or drugs as a way to manage the stress in your life. Don't! Neither alcohol nor drugs are an effective way to reduce stress. In fact the effects of such use will actually create more stress and problems in your life.

Using Stress Management Techniques in Your Job Search Process

- Step 1: Recognize that stress is an inevitable part of not only returning to civilian life but also of the job hunting process.
- Step 2: Make it a priority to take care of yourself during your job search in order to be effective and stay healthy.
- Step 3: Make a list of job hunting tasks which need to be accomplished as well as other demands on your time. Include time for regular exercise, balanced meals, relaxation and family.
- Step 4: Write down tasks that you need help with or tasks that can temporarily be left undone. Discuss these with your parole officer.
- Step 5: Prioritize your list; be realistic about your time and your goals.
- Step 6: Keep a regular schedule in order to accomplish your goals.
- Step 7: Exercise, get adequate rest, communicate with your friends and family, eat well and use relaxation techniques. Avoid the use of alcohol and drugs.
- Step 8: Continue to talk to others and ask for help when needed. Keep your parole officer informed of everything that you are doing to secure a job.
- Step 9: Set realistic goals and make choices that will take you in the right direction.

WHAT DO EMPLOYERS EXPECT FROM EMPLOYEES?

Employers value employees who can do the job well, who are committed to the work and the mission of the organization, and who have a positive attitude toward the job, toward their co-workers and the company. It is possible that it has been years since you last worked in the private sector. It is important, therefore, that you understand what employers expect of you. This way you can communicate in the job interview your willingness to do what the employer expects. Then when you get the job you will need to meet and exceed the employer's expectations.

Employers want employees...

- who want to do the work.
- who can do the job.
- who are willing to do the job.
- whose services they can reasonably afford.

Employers are looking for employees who have a positive attitude.

When there are many experienced applicants for a job, employers are more likely to offer the job to the person who has an outstanding attitude. The applicant's attitude isn't measured objectively by the employer. Rather, it is revealed during the job interview, and the employer weighs it intuitively. Because of the assumption that offenders have a bad attitude, it is critical that you not confirm this expectation in the interview and on the job.

An applicant and employee with a positive attitude are expected to:

- Have a pleasant demeanor.
- Be courteous.
- Have good posture and excellent hygiene and know how to dress appropriately.
- Have an optimistic outlook. They see tasks as potential opportunities, rather than insurmountable problems.
- Show enthusiasm for the job. Even without being hired, they are already engaged in problem-solving tasks related to the job. They listen actively and ask insightful, pertinent questions.
- Be willing to work hard.
- Be reliable, dependable and trustworthy. Employers may check references to confirm the impressions they form from the interview.
- Be a team player who enjoys collaborative efforts and gets along with people.
- Fit in with the organization.

Employers want employees who want to do the job.

During the job interview, employers gauge your enthusiasm for the job by observing your attitude. They look for obvious and subtle signs that you want the job.

What is your body language saying? Do you look as if you are excited to be there? Are you leaning forward at the edge of your seat or are you slumped down as if you wish you were somewhere else? Try not to equate the job interview with an interview with a law enforcement individual. Job interviewers are not trying to trick you or get you to admit something. They are asking questions to determine if you are the right person for the job, not to judge you.

Is the job something that you want to do? Surprisingly, employers find that some job seekers apply for any type of job, even jobs that hold little or no interest to the job seeker. So be prepared to indicate why the job appeals to you and to demonstrate a clear understanding of the job duties and responsibilities.

Employers want employees who can do the job.

Employers look for evidence that an employee can do the job. They assess the employee's past experience, knowledge and skills by:

- Reviewing the employee's job application.
- Reading the résumé.
- Asking interview questions.
- Calling references.

How employers find out if you can do the job:

- They ask questions about your work history.
- They ask you to list your skills. For instance, they may ask whether you're familiar with certain computer programs or whether you have experience using specific kinds of machinery.
- They expect you to have either transferable skills or specific skills that match the job description.
- They may give you a written test to see whether you have the skills and knowledge to do the job. For instance, some jobs require a literacy test.
- They may contact your previous employers that you listed on your application and/or résumé as references.

Employers sometimes hire employees with entry-level skills, if they have a positive attitude and show enthusiasm for the job. Once hired, the employer will provide training to bring the new hire's skills up to standards.

Employers want employees who are willing to do the job.

Employers use the application, résumé and interview to gauge how willing you are to do the job. They look for evidence that:

- Your values are aligned with the values of the organization.
- You are committed to the work involved. For instance, a professional carpenter who is committed to the industry's mission of providing homes may do voluntary work and donate his/her time to Habitat for Humanity.
- You have demonstrated a good work ethic by showing up for work each day and giving the employer 100% effort while at work.

To Hire or Not to Hire?

When making a hiring decision, what is the one quality in the employee that employers consider to be THE MOST IMPORTANT? Assuming that job applicants have the basic skills needed to do the job, the one quality that most employer's value is the willingness to work hard and do whatever it takes to get the job done. Nearly 60 percent of employers surveyed said that they expected employees to have a good work ethic.

Qualities that employers value are:

	Quality	Percent
–	Work Ethic	59 percent
–	Intelligence	23 percent
–	Enthusiasm	12 percent
–	Education	4 percent
–	Other Qualities	2 percent

Employers Want Employees Whose Services They Can Reasonably Afford.

Employers want to keep labor costs low. On the other hand, salaries have to be high enough to attract enthusiastic and competent workers. Employers usually solve the dilemma by investigating the labor market before they negotiate salaries with potential employees.

Employers expect to pay salaries at competitive market rates. They set limits based on:

- The general demand for your skills. For instance, if there is a shortage of skilled employees, salary offers are likely to be higher.
- How badly the company needs someone like you and how long they've been looking.
- The budget of the department or company that is hiring you.
- Your productivity. The amount of money you can generate for the company is often used as a yardstick. For instance, a highly productive sales representative who brings above average revenues into the company is worth more than a sales representative who produces less revenue.

Negotiating Your Starting Salary

Find out what you can do to negotiate a higher starting salary. Carry out market research. For more help, review the Career Success Guide: What Are Your Salary Needs?

Employers Expect Employees to Fit into The Work Environment.

Although employers assume that a person applying for a specific job is familiar with the typical work environment, this may not be the case for re-entering employees. The environment in a work setting is nothing like the environment you have experienced during your incarceration. It is important, therefore, that you spend a lot of time thinking about what it was like working and try to recall how the work environment operated. For example, while incarcerated others controlled your time and dictated what you can or cannot do.

Most work environments are not so rigid and permit the employee freedom to select activities.

- Before you are released try to get as much information as you can about work settings. For example, you want to pursue a job as a cook when you are released. Although you may work in the prison's kitchen, you need to learn about the differences there might be when working in a restaurant. To do this:
    - Talk with prison employees. Ask them about their work experiences outside of the prison.
    - See if the prison library has any books about the occupation you are pursuing.
- After you are released, contact your local One-Stop Career Center. Ask for assistance in making a contact with someone in your selected field. Review the Career Success Guide: How to Use Your Local One-Stop Career Center.
- Consider getting work experience in the occupation by taking a temporary job. Review the Career Success Guide: Pluses & Minuses of Temporary Employment.

Aspects of the work environment are sometimes negotiable. For instance, an employer may accommodate your request for flexible work hours or a desk or office of your own. You are more likely to get what you want if you are valuable to the company.

If you live beyond commuting distance, employers will probably expect you to relocate. Review the Career Success Guide: How to Relocate to Another Community.

Employers Expect Employees to Get Along with Co-Workers.

Employers know that:

- Employees who can collaborate with their co-workers are likely to boost the productivity of the company.
- Employees working together as a team are more effective at meeting goals.
- Successful team efforts lead to high morale and a happy workplace.
- Less time is lost mediating conflicts between employees.

WHERE TO GET JOB TRAINING

It is entirely possible that you will find that you will need to upgrade your skills and knowledge in order to be competitive. Depending upon the length of your incarceration you may discover that your skills are rusty at best or simply obsolete. Training and retraining has become necessary for most re-entering workers. The re-entering job seeker who demonstrates a willingness and ability to learn new skills is in the best position with a prospective employer. With a little exploration you will find training opportunities are plentiful in both the private and public sectors.

Do I need Training? And if so, what kind of training do I need?

Read through each of the statements below. Check those statements that apply to you.

Job-Readiness Training:

- ☐ I have never had a full time job.
- ☐ It has been more than 5 years since I worked at a full time job.
- ☐ When I worked, I was never able to hold a job for more than a few weeks at a time.
- ☐ I was fired from my last job.
- ☐ I do not look forward to going to work.

If you checked any of the five boxes above, you will benefit from Job-Readiness Training.

Basic Education Training:

- ☐ I did not graduate from high school and I do not have a GED.
- ☐ I have difficulty reading, writing and/or doing simple math.

If you checked one or more of the above two boxes, you will benefit from Basic Education Training.

Job Specific Skills:

- ☐ I have had no job training.
- ☐ I have never held a job.
- ☐ It has been more than 5 years since I had a full time job.
- ☐ I am not permitted to return to my former job.
- ☐ I want to do something different from the job that I used to do.
- ☐ I do not have any computer skills.
- ☐ I do not have the skills or training for the job that I want to pursue.

If you checked any of the seven boxes above, then you will benefit from Job-Specific Skills Training.

Job-Readiness Training

There are certain skills, traits and knowledge that every employee in every company needs to have in order to be successful. Some of these "soft" skills include a positive attitude, honesty, dependability, and loyalty, ability to work with others, leadership, good hygiene and the ability to communicate verbally. Employers have identified over 60 such "soft" skills that they want all employees to possess. It has been estimated that over 90% of workers who get fired from their job, are fired because they failed to demonstrate a basic "soft" skill (was continually late to work, for example).

"Soft" skills are generally learned at home and in school. Since some of the skills relate directly to a work situation, these skills are typically learned by the individual on their first several jobs. Even if you have had several positive work experiences before you were incarcerated, you will benefit from learning what behaviors are acceptable or not acceptable in today's work environment by participating in a Job-Readiness Training Class.

Where to get training:

Before you are released ask your prison case manager to assist you in getting this training. Many prisons offer Job-Readiness Training classes for soon-to-be released prisoners. Once you are released you can go to your local One-Stop Career Center and request the training. Most One-Stop Centers offer Job-Readiness training classes on a regular basis. For more information, read the Career Success Guide: How to Use Your Local One-Stop Career Center.

Basic Education Training

Employers want employees who have achieved a level of education that matches the requirements for their job. High school graduates enjoy more employment opportunities and significantly higher wages than non-graduates throughout their lives. If you dropped out of high school, then it is important that you get your GED as soon as possible.

Although you will still be able to find jobs without having a high school diploma or GED, these jobs will be entry level jobs and will be primarily physical or menial labor. You may find yourself frustrated with your lack of advancement and low pay. When filling out applications or during interviews, state that you are working towards your GED. Then do it! Review the Career Success Guide: How to Overcome Challenges to Employment, to learn more about the GED test and where you can obtain the training and take the test.

Job-Specific Skills Training

Nearly every occupation requires the worker to have one or more skills that are used on that job. These skills can be general in nature, like being able to write, to very specific, like how to operate on a heart. There are thousands of different job-specific skills. Some examples are:

- General Job Skills like cooking and driving.
- Self-Management Skills like being creative or diplomatic.
- Data & Analytical like auditing and taking inventory.
- Leadership/Managerial like decision-making & solving problems.
- Technical Skills like manual dexterity and drawing.
- Interpersonal and "People" Skills like comforting and teaching.
- Communicative & Conceptual like being artistic and public speaking.

In order for you to obtain employment in most occupations you have demonstrate that you have the skills required to do that job. Review the Career Success Guide: How to Determine Your Skills.

Where can you get job-specific training?

Many prison facilities offer some job-specific training. You need to take advantage of this free training before you are released. The following suggestions are available only after you have been released. If you are able to pay for your training or can qualify for financial assistance:

- Community colleges. These educational gems are inexpensive and offer academic, vocational and technical courses.
- Vocational and proprietary schools. These schools offer certificate programs, are affordable and have short courses that are frequently offered at night or on weekends.
- Online courses. There are literally thousands of online courses, some are free but for others you have to pay. Courses cover everything from computer skills to cooking. Google your area of interest and note the courses that are available. Caution: You have to be really committed in order to successfully complete the course. Few people do!

If finances are a problem:

- Many employers contract with consultants or community colleges to teach their employees basic and new technology skills. For example, a trucking company may provide free CDL training.
- Government programs. Local, state and federal governments offer job training programs, as well as financial aid to eligible workers. Local One-Stop Career Centers can provide you with a list of low cost training options that are available in your community.
- Community centers. Computer training and courses teaching marketable skills are often available at a minimal cost at libraries, community centers and community based organizations like Goodwill. Check with your local library for a list of these courses.
- Apprenticeship programs. These paid jobs allow you to learn a skill while working under the supervision of a journeyman craftsman.
- Apprenticeships are available in a wide range of skilled trades, including construction trades.
- Internships. These positions are available through a large number of businesses that offer training and experience in exchange for your labor.
- Internships can be paid or non-paid positions. Your local One-Stop Career Center can help you identify employers that offer internships.

Make the Most of Your Training

Before embarking on any training course, whether a company-sponsored course or a full degree program, you need to be able to answer the following questions:

- What do I want or expect to get out of this training? How will it help me achieve my goal?
- What will be the benefits of extra training in my current job? Talk to your boss or an employment counselor about your plans. Find out what long-term changes will be occurring in your job. If you obtain training, will your pay change or will you be given more responsibility?

Basic Computer Training

Employers utilizing computer technology will be more willing to train you in more advanced computer skills if you've got a good foundation. You will benefit from courses in basic computer operations, such as:

- The latest PC or Macintosh operating systems
- Word processing program like Microsoft Word®
- Presentation or graphic programs such as Adobe Acrobat®
- Improved typing skills
- A spreadsheet program like Microsoft Excel®
- A database program
- The Internet and social media programs like Facebook®

Get Help with Training Costs

You may be surprised by how much private and government assistance is available to re-entering citizens for job training. Begin by talking with the Financial Aid Office at your local college or vocational school about these programs:

- Government Gift Aid Federal Pell Grants and the Supplemental Education Opportunity Grant Program are two programs that provide tuition assistance to eligible students. Eligibility is based primarily upon income.
- Scholarships are money grants that can be used for tuition and other expenses. You can find out about thousands of private scholarships and grants in the reference section of your local library or by talking with a Financial Aid Advisor at your local community college. Scholarships are usually based on need, merit, interests or other criteria.
- Federal Loans Stafford Loans, among others, are government-backed student loans. The loans are at a very low interest rate. For more information go to www.staffordloan.com.
- Workforce Investment Act contact your local One-Stop Career Center and ask about training programs. Review the Career Success Guide: How to Use Your Local One-Stop Career Center.

Career Success Series
Guide 11

HOW TO CHOOSE A CAREER

It may have been months or even years since you last worked. You may no longer be eligible to return to your former occupation because of your criminal record or because your skills are no longer in demand. This will require you to pursue a new occupation. Career counselors know that job satisfaction is highest when a person is employed in an occupation that matches the person's values, talents and interests. Identifying which occupations will be satisfying to you requires that you have a clear understanding of yourself and the employment world. This guide provides suggestions on how to identify the occupations that may be satisfying to you.

Career or Job?

A job is an activity, or series of tasks, that a person performs for which they usually get paid. Occupation is another word that means the same as a job. Occupations have names like carpenter, dentist, hair stylist, etc. When we refer to someone as being a carpenter, most people have an understanding of the job that a carpenter performs. A career is an occupation or series of related occupations that occupies a significant period of a person's life. For example a person may have a career in the restaurant industry by working as a waitperson, assistant cook, chef and finally as a restaurant manager.

Misconceptions about Choosing a Career

It is simple.

Although finding a job may be simple, finding a job that is satisfying requires time and thought. Too often ex-offenders take the first job that is offered to them only to find that they do not like the job. This leads to job hopping. It is better to identify what occupations will give you satisfaction before you start your job search. This will not only help you narrow your search, but will increase the probability that you will be happy in your new job.

Money will make me happy.

While money is important, it is only one of the factors that should influence your career decision. Surveys have shown that job satisfaction is more important to workers than money. Before you start your search for a career, you need to identify what your salary needs are. Review the Career Success Guide: What Are Your Salary Needs?

I should pick a career that is in demand.

Every year the U.S. Department of Labor publishes a list of jobs that are in demand. See the Career Success Guide: Resources for Ex-Offenders.

Jobs that are hot this year may not be hot the next. Often these jobs are tied to a trend that becomes quickly saturated. Jobs in the celluar telephone industry are an example. There are some occupational areas that are always in demand. These include the health care industry, hospitality, education, retail sales and public safety. Check with your local One-Stop Career Center for information on occupations that are in demand in your locality.

If a relative likes the job, shouldn't I?

Job satisfaction is related to the match between the talents, interests and values of the person and the characteristics of the occupation. Even though a relative is satisfied in an occupation, it does not mean that you also will be satisfied in that occupation. You may have completely different talents, interests and values than does your relative.

Once I make the decision it will be difficult to change.

This is not true. Studies have shown that people change careers an average of three times before they retire. In a rapidly changing employment environment like we are currently experiencing, workers should expect to change careers even more often. Once you have gone through the process the first time, it will be easier the next time.

I need to make good use of my education.

Studies have shown that fewer than 40 percent of college graduates are working in a field that is directly related to their college major five years after graduation. Since formal education (high school and college) prepares students for work primarily by teaching the student how to learn, graduates are able to easily learn new job skills. Employers are less concerned about the specific major of a graduate and more interested in the graduate's ability to use their education as a foundation to learn new skills.

I will not know if I will like the job until I try it.

Although you can learn a great deal about an occupation by reading about it, you can never know for sure if the occupation is a match until you try it. However, you can maximize the chance that the occupation will be satisfying by going through the process of selecting a career. On the next page you will find suggestions as to ways to get exposure to an occupation before you make a commitment to the career.

Assistance in Making a Career Decision

Although most people can make career decisions without professional assistance, seeking help from a Workforce Development Professional can be beneficial. Workforce Development Professionals can be found in your local One-Stop Career Center.

Making A Career Decision

The process of making a career decision involves gathering information about yourself and information about occupations and matching the two.

Information about Yourself

Since job satisfaction is related to the match between a person's values, skills, talents and interests to the job, it is important that you identify these factors:

Talents. We are born with skills that seem to be natural to us. Because we have a narrow view of talent, it is easy for us to compare our talents to those whose talents are exceptional. Because we do not believe our talents are exceptional, we conclude that we do not have any talent.

The fact is, all of us have talent. Talent is defined as a recurring pattern of thought, feeling or behavior that can be productively applied. All jobs require talent because all jobs require recurring patterns of thought, feeling or behavior. Talents are things that you find yourself doing often. This may be something physical like drawing a picture, rapidly manipulating small objects with your fingers or balancing on a narrow platform. Talents may also be mental such as being able to remember phone numbers and people's names, complete crossword puzzles or easily learn a foreign language. To identify your talents, on a piece of paper list the things that you do that seem effortless. Ask friends and relatives to also list the things that they observe that you do that make you unique. From the list you can identify your talents.

Skills. Skills are things that you have learned to do. For a complete description of skills, review the Career Success Guide: How to Determine Your Skills and SCANS Competencies.

Values. Your personal values are the things that are important or worthwhile to you. Value judgments color a person's priorities and choices in life and at work. Your values are the driving force behind why you behave the way that you do. For more information and a checklist of values, review the Career Success Guide: Identifying Your Job Interests & Values.

Interests. What do you enjoy doing? What activities give you pleasure? What activities cause you to lose track of time because you are so involved in the activity?

These are called interests. For more information on interests and to complete an interest check list, review the Career Success Guide: Identifying Your Job Interests & Values.

Putting It Together

The Job Search Guide Ideal Job Worksheet will help you organize the information on your talents, skills, values and interests. This information will help you describe the type of work setting that will be satisfying to you. Now that you have this description, you need to identify occupations where people have similar talents, skills, values and interests.

Exploring Careers

There are several ways that you can identify occupations that are a match for you. The resources listed below are available at your local One-Stop Career Center or local library. Review the Career Success Guide: How to Use Your Local One-Stop Career Center.

Online resources. The U.S. Department of Labor supports three websites that provide occupational information:

www.onetcenter.org In addition to providing occupational information, O*NET has self-administered assessments of your skills, values and interests.

www.acinet.org/occ_intro.asp America's Career Infonet gives current information about thousands of occupations including job descriptions, working conditions and average salary.

www.quintcareers.com/career_assessment.html this site has several free career assessment tools and tests. The self-assessment tests can help give you a better idea of your aptitudes and interests as they relate to possible career choices.

Professional and trade associations. The websites of professional and trade associations usually have information about the profession or trade. By Googling the name of an occupation, you can find the web address of the appropriate professional or trade association.

Written resources such as the Occupational Outlook Handbook (www.bls.gov/oco/). This publication of the U.S. Department of Labor is updated yearly and is an invaluable tool for people seeking information about occupations. The Handbook gives information on the training and education needed, earnings, expected job prospects, what workers do on the job and the working conditions for each occupation.

Experiencing the Career Field

The following are ways that you can obtain first-hand experience with the occupational field that interests you. For a more complete description of each program, review the Career Success Guide: Where to Get Job Training and How to Acquire Job Information by Interviewing.

Job-Shadowing - If you were permitted to spend an entire day with a person in the occupation that interests you, you would get a clear idea of the tasks that person performs each day, the work environment and the pressures of the job. This is called job-shadowing.

Apprenticeships - Apprenticeship programs are available for many of the skilled trades such as electrician, plumber and pipe fitter. The program involves attending classes, usually at a local community or vocational/technical college part time and working on the job under the guidance of a skilled craftsperson.

Interviewing for information - Talking with a person in the occupation of interest can give you insight into the occupation.

Additional resources - Both volunteering and working as an intern can expose you to the tasks of a given occupation. Review the guides mentioned above for more information.

TRULINCS Friendly! info@ReentryEssentials.org **www.ReentryEssentials.org** **347.973.0004** **2609 East 14 Street, Suite 1018, Brooklyn, NY 11235-3915**

HOW TO DETERMINE YOUR SKILLS

Whether you are a Returning Citizen or not, employers want to know if you have the knowledge, skills and abilities needed to perform the tasks required on the job. When examining your job application and résumé, the employer looks for documentation that you can do the job. In order for you to be able to provide an employer with this critical documentation, it is necessary that you be able to identify your knowledge, skills and abilities.

Knowledge is something you have learned in school, from training or from experience. A skill is something you can do. An ability is a special talent or even a personality quality that you have. Knowing what your knowledge, skills and abilities are will help you:

- Identify jobs that match you
- Properly fill out applications
- Write a better résumé
- Interview more effectively
- Make satisfying career choices
- Increase your self confidence

It is difficult for most people to talk about their skills. In fact, a majority of people who interview for jobs are unable to clearly state what their skills are. It is essential, however, to know specifically what you can offer to an employer. Even though you have the necessary experience and skills for a job, you may not get hired if you cannot communicate to an employer that you have those skills and that you are able to use them well.

Your skills are the foundation on which you build your career. All of us have hundreds of skills. We are average in some skills and excel at others. It will be easier to identify jobs that suit you when you know your unique combination of skills. This combination of skills is called a skill set.

Job-Specific Skills

Job-specific skills are skills that you use when you perform a particular job task. These skills are developed when you participate in specialized training and formal education or they are learned on the job. For example, plumbers need knowledge about how plumbing systems work. They must be familiar with the tools of the trade and have the ability to perform specific tasks, such as cutting pipe, installing fixtures, etc. Most jobs have specific skills that are unique to that job.

Depending upon how long you have been out of the workforce, it is possible that your job-specific skills are rusty or obsolete. You may need to update your skills upon your release. Review the Career Success guide: Where to Get Job Training.

Transferable Skills

Transferable skills are skills that are not unique to a particular task and can be used in more than one job. Some examples of transferable skills are the ability to read and write, do arithmetic, speak in public, supervise people, solve problems and organize events. Unlike job-specific skills which people have or do not have (such as the capability to install a light fixture), transferable skills are measured according to their complexity. The ability to read varies from knowing how to read simple sentences to being able to read complex scientific literature. The more advanced the skill is, the less competition there is for jobs that require that level of skill.

Skills Are Not All or Nothing

Many people believe that either you have or you don't have that skill. Like a light switch, it is either on or off. Experts know that this is not true. People possess skills in varying degrees. Most people are average on a majority of skills, below average on some and above average on others. When you think of skills, don't sell yourself short just because you can name someone who possesses that skill at a higher level than you. There are also people whose skill level is less than yours.

You Are Unique

Possessing a single exceptional skill does not make you special. It is your combination of average and above average skills that makes you special. Being able to accurately shoot the basketball through the net does not make an exceptional basketball player if the player cannot run fast, jump high, dribble the ball or get along with their fellow players. Remember, you are the only person in the world who has your unique set of skills.

Your combination of average and above average skills is your skill set. Emphasize your special combination of skills on your résumé and in your job interviews.

Your Job Objective

If you know what your knowledge, skills and abilities are, you will be able to formulate your job objective. Your job objective is a simple (usually one or two sentence) statement of what you want to do. It is important to define your job objective so that you can focus your job search on jobs that match your objective.

The job objective focuses on what you can do and what you want to do. Your job objective is an important part of your successful job search.

Review the Career Success Guides: How to Complete a Job Application, How to Write a Résumé, and Components of a Résumé.

Discovering Your Skills

Everyone has a variety of skills and abilities. Although most people find it difficult to clearly identify what they do well, it is essential that you do so when looking for a job. There are several ways to identify your skills:

Identifying Your Skills

Complete the Career Success Guide: *SCANS Competencies.* This will help you identify specific skills that you have.

Tell A Story

Tell a story about something you accomplished that you enjoyed and felt was a success. Write the story down. In the story describe what you did and what obstacles you overcame in order to reach your goal. Review the story and note what skills (use the definitions found in the Career Success Guide: SCANS Competencies) you used to accomplish this. Repeat this exercise a number of times and you will begin to have a good inventory of your skills. Remember to be specific.

Review Your Job History

What work have you done in the past? What tasks did you enjoy and feel confident doing? Sit down with someone and explain to them exactly what you did on each job. Break the job down into tasks and list the skills needed to perform each task.

Some employers will overlook a lack of job-specific skills if someone has basic reading, writing and math skills, an ability to listen and speak clearly and a willingness to learn.

Enthusiastically and effectively present to an employer your eagerness to learn. You may be chosen over a candidate who has more credentials than you but does not show a willingness to learn new skills.

Look at Your Life

Outside of work, what do you do in your life that you really enjoy? The skills you use to perform these enjoyable activities are probably things you do well. List these. Be sure to include activities that you perform while incarcerated such as working in the kitchen or laundry.

Use Career Assessments

There are a number of career assessments, available through career counselors and your local One-Stop Career Center and on the Internet, that will help you identify your skills.

What Employers Want

The U.S. Department of Labor has issued a report defining the skills that employers identified as necessary for employment. This was known as the SCANS report. The report divided skills into two areas: competencies and foundations. The competencies and foundation skills defined by SCANS are required for most jobs. A detailed description of each is found in the Career Success Guide: SCANS Competencies and online at www.academicinnovations.com/report.html. They are:

Foundation Skills

- Reading, Writing
- Arithmetic, Mathematics
- Listening, Speaking
- Creative Thinking, Decision Making
- Problem Solving, Self-Esteem
- Reasoning, Responsibility
- Self-Management, Social Abilities
- Knowing How to Learn
- Integrity, Honesty
- Visualizing

Competencies

- Allocates Time
- Allocates Money
- Allocates Material and Facility Resources
- Allocates Human Resources
- Acquires and Evaluates Information

- Organizes and Maintains Information
- Interprets and Communicates Information
- Uses Computers to Process Information
- Participates as a Member of a Team
- Teaches Others

- Serves Clients/Customers
- Exercises Leadership
- Negotiates to Arrive at a Decision
- Works with Cultural Diversity
- Understands Systems

- Monitors and Corrects Performance
- Improves and Designs Systems
- Selects Technology
- Applies Technology to Task
- Maintains and Troubleshoots Technology

SCANS COMPETENCIES

The U.S. Department of Labor issued a report identifying the skills that employers felt were necessary for employment. This report is known as the SCANS (Secretary's Commission on Achieving Necessary Skills) report. Skills are divided into two areas, competencies and foundations. Most jobs require one or more of the competencies and foundation skills that are defined in the SCANS report. Use the exercise below to identify the SCANS competencies that you have.

For more information, review the Career Success guide: How to Determine Your Skills.

Hint: If employers see these skills as important, then be sure to mention that you possess one or more of these skills on your résumé, on your application, in your cover letter and during the interview. This will enhance your chances for employment.

Exercise

Directions: Read the definition of each competency. In the space provided below each definition, write a short sentence describing when and how you used that skill on a job, in school or at home. When you also complete the Career Success guide Ideal Job Worksheet, you will be asked to identify the five skills from this worksheet that you would like to use on a job.

Allocates Time - Manages time well, accurately estimates time needed to complete tasks and is able to prioritize tasks. Avoids wasting time, meets deadlines and adjusts schedule as needed.

____

____

Allocates Money - Prepares and/or uses budgets, tracks budget performances and makes appropriate adjustments.

____

____

Allocates Material and Facility Resources - Acquires, stores, and distributes materials, supplies, parts, equipment, space or final products in order to make the best use of them.

____

____

Allocates Human Resources - Accurately assesses people's knowledge, skills, abilities and potential. Distributes work accordingly, evaluates performance and provides feedback.

____

____

Acquires and Evaluates Information - Identifies need for data, obtains data from existing sources or creates data, and evaluates data relevance and accuracy.

____

____

Organizes and Maintains Information - Keeps systematic records of information.

____

____

Interprets and Communicates Information - Conveys information effectively using oral, written, graphic or multi-media methods.

____

____

Uses Computer to Process Information - Uses computers competently to acquire, organize, analyze and communicate information.

____

____

Understands Systems - Knows how social, organizational and technological systems work and operates effectively within them.

____

____

Monitors and Corrects Performance - Distinguishes trends, predicts impact of actions of system operations and takes necessary action to correct performance of a system.

____

____

Improves and Designs Systems - Suggests modifications to existing systems to improve products or services and develops new or alternative systems.

____

____

Selects Technology - Judges which tools and machines, including computers and software, will produce the desired results.

Applies Technology to Task - Understands how to properly set up and operate machines, including computers.

Maintains and Troubleshoots Technology - Prevents, identifies or solves problems in machines, computers and other technologies.

Participates as a Member of a Team - Works cooperatively with others.

Teaches Others - Helps others learn.

Serves Clients/Customers - Effectively satisfies expectations of customers.

Exercises Leadership - Makes positive use of rules. Justifies a position logically and appropriately. Establishes credibility through competence and integrity and takes minority viewpoints into consideration.

Negotiates to Arrive at a Decision - Works toward an agreement using negotiation.

Works with Cultural Diversity - Works well with men and women and with a variety of ethnic, social or educational backgrounds.

TRULINCS Friendly! info@ReentryEssentials.org 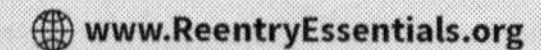 **www.ReentryEssentials.org** **347.973.0004** **2609 East 14 Street, Suite 1018, Brooklyn, NY 11235-3915**

IDENTIFYING YOUR JOB INTERESTS & VALUES

Satisfying work usually includes activities that interest you and that you enjoy doing. Read over the activities listed below and indicate which of the five statements best describe your feelings about that activity. As you conduct your job search, look for positions which will include activities that you rated as 1 or 2 in this exercise. Also go back through your list of high rated interests and circle only five that you believe are your most important. List these five interests on your Career Success guide Ideal Job Worksheet.

1 - I like doing the activity very much.
2 - I like doing the activity.
3 - I neither like or dislike doing the activity. I feel neutral towards it.
4 - I dislike doing the activity.
5 - I dislike doing the activity very much.

_______ Watching TV
_______ Attending Movies
_______ Coordinating Events
_______ Fixing Things
_______ Driving
_______ Helping Others
_______ Gardening
_______ Arguing/Debating
_______ Giving Speeches
_______ Talking To Strangers
_______ Teaching Children
_______ Teaching Adults
_______ Solving Math Problems
_______ Doing Research
_______ Shopping
_______ Eating In Restaurants
_______ Saving Money
_______ Deep Subject Discussions
_______ Playing Computer Games

_______ Cooking
_______ Leading Others
_______ Keeping Records
_______ Thinking/Meditating
_______ Building Things
_______ Sewing/Quilting
_______ Competing In Sports
_______ Hunting/Fishing
_______ Painting/Photography
_______ Preparing Budgets
_______ Investing
_______ Surfing The Internet
_______ Solving Mechanical Problems
_______ Listening To People
_______ Listening To Music
_______ Playing Musical Instruments
_______ Organizing Things
_______ Camping
_______ Going To Amusement Parks

_______ Traveling
_______ Designing Things
_______ Attending Casual Parties
_______ Running For Office
_______ Going To Church
_______ Going To Art Galleries
_______ Writing Poetry
_______ Writing Fiction
_______ Writing Nonfiction
_______ Reading Books
_______ Reading Newspapers
_______ Reading Magazines
_______ Planning Parties
_______ Telling Jokes
_______ Studying
_______ Visiting With Friends
_______ Tending Animals
_______ Selling Things
_______ Talking About Yourself

PERSONAL VALUES AND TRAITS

It is important to find work that matches your personal values and enables you to utilize the traits that are important to you. Below is a list of words that indicate values and traits. Check the ones that best describe you. Go back through the list of checked traits and circle only five that you believe are the most important traits. List these five personal work values on your Career Success guide Ideal Job Worksheet.

I am:

_______ Dignified
_______ Inventive
_______ Punctual
_______ Prudent
_______ Tenacious
_______ Intelligent
_______ Progressive
_______ Zany
_______ Discreet
_______ Kind
_______ Purposeful
_______ Thorough
_______ Intellectual
_______ Precise
_______ Tactful
_______ Witty
_______ Dominant
_______ Capable
_______ Quick
_______ Thoughtful
_______ Informal
_______ Practical
_______ Strong-Minded
_______ Wise
_______ Accurate
_______ Academic
_______ Adventurous
_______ Adaptable

_______ Determined
_______ Eager
_______ Light-Hearted
_______ Quiet
_______ Tolerant
_______ Industrious
_______ Realistic
_______ Trusting
_______ Pleasant
_______ Steady
_______ Versatile
_______ Alert
_______ Daring
_______ Emotional
_______ Loyal
_______ Reflective
_______ Trustworthy
_______ Imaginative
_______ Persevering
_______ Stable
_______ Calm
_______ Tense
_______ Verbal
_______ Ambitious
_______ Curious
_______ Artistic
_______ Courageous
_______ Energetic

_______ Mature
_______ Relaxed
_______ Humorous
_______ Patient
_______ Team Player
_______ Spontaneous
_______ Uninhibited
_______ Fair-Minded
_______ Methodical
_______ Reliable
_______ Unassuming
_______ Far-Sighted
_______ Spunky
_______ Sociable
_______ Forceful
_______ Modest
_______ Retiring
_______ Helpful
_______ Business-Like
_______ Outgoing
_______ Sincere
_______ Formal
_______ Natural
_______ Robust
_______ Healthy
_______ Original
_______ Sharp-Witted
_______ Frank

_______ Obliging
_______ Self-Confident
_______ Friendly
_______ Open-Minded
_______ Self-Controlled
_______ Generous
_______ Opportunistic
_______ Sensible
_______ Gentle
_______ Good-Natured
_______ Optimistic
_______ Organized
_______ Sensitive
_______ Serious
_______ Conservative
_______ Liberal

IDEAL JOB WORKSHEET

In order to prepare a Job Objective for both your résumé and job application, it is important to identify the elements of the ideal job. To complete this worksheet, you will need to have completed the following Career Success guides: Identifying Your Job Interests & Values and SCANS Competencies.

1. List five activities that interest you. An activity should be listed if you would like to do that activity on a job. Use the Career Success guide: Identifying Your Job Interests & Values to help you identify your interests.

    1. ______________________________
    2. ______________________________
    3. ______________________________
    4. ______________________________
    5. ______________________________

2. List five skills that you would like to use on a job. Use the Career Success Series: SCANS Competencies to help you identify your skills.

    1. ______________________________
    2. ______________________________
    3. ______________________________
    4. ______________________________
    5. ______________________________

3. List five personal work values that have meaning to you. Use the Career Success Series: Identifying Your Job Interests & Values to help you identify work-related values.

    1. ______________________________
    2. ______________________________
    3. ______________________________
    4. ______________________________
    5. ______________________________

4. Define the level of responsibility you would like in your ideal job.

____________ Little or no responsibility preferred

____________ Some responsibility

____________ A great deal of responsibility

Supervision of others:

____________ None

____________ Supervise 1 to 5 people

____________ Supervise 6 or more people

5. How much money do you want to make? Use the Career Success Guide: What Are Your Salary Needs?

Range: From $ ______________________ to $ ______________________

6. Where do you want to live? List five geographic preferences

1. ____

2. ____

3. ____

4. ____

5. ____

7. Define your ideal work environment: Check the work environments that appeal to you:

Type of organization:

_______ formal

_______ relaxed

_______ outdoors

_______ indoors

Size of organization:

_______ small

_______ large

_______ established

_______ new

Type of atmosphere:

_______ fast-paced

_______ calm

_______ friendly

_______ work alone

_______ work in teams

_______ sociable office

Work hours:

_______ long

_______ short

_______ flexible

_______ fixed

Supervision:

_______ close supervision

_______ independent

_______ team-oriented

Other:

_______ frequent travel

_______ some travel

_______ no travel

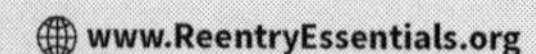

Career Success Series
Guide 17

WHAT ARE YOUR SALARY NEEDS?

Knowing your salary needs can help you focus your job hunt and get a fulfilling job that pays you enough to live comfortably. Understanding the difference between your needs and your wants will help you negotiate a better salary.

Understanding Today's Dollar

If you have been incarcerated for more than three years, you will probably not understand the purchasing power of today's dollar. Because of inflation, what a dollar purchased the year that you were incarcerated is not the same today. Before you can talk about salary needs, you need to equate today's dollar to what it was when you were incarcerated. To do this, make a list of everyday items like milk, coffee, bread, gasoline, rent, tobacco (if you smoke) and anything else you can remember buying on a fairly regular basis. This website provides average costs of some common goods by year (www.anitome.com). If an item is not listed on this website, simply "Google" the following; what was the cost of XXXXX (enter item name) in YYYY (enter year that you were incarcerated). By examining the difference in cost between the year that you were incarcerated and today you will be able to arrive at an amount that you need today that matches what you needed the year that you were incarcerated. For example if the items today average 20% more in cost, and you lived comfortably on $1,200 per month the year that you were incarcerated, then you will need a monthly income of $1,440.

New Ways of Thinking about the Salary You Need

- The salary you need may be different from the salary you want. Estimate the minimum annual salary you need to live comfortably by using the worksheet provided on the back of this guide. The worksheet is also a useful tool for creating a budget.
- The salary you need is often different from the salary offered by the employer. Once you know how much you need to earn, you can negotiate more effectively with a potential employer.
- The salary you need may be different from the market value of the job that interests you. Target only those jobs in the market that meet your salary needs.

Benefits of Identifying Your Salary Target

- Knowing your salary needs helps you find the right job faster. It saves you from wasting time and effort trying to get jobs that may not cover your financial needs. It helps you focus your efforts on jobs that pay enough for you to live comfortably.
- Identifying your salary needs is just as important as identifying your knowledge, skills and abilities.
- Estimating the minimum salary you are willing to accept is the first step to negotiating a higher starting salary when you are offered a job.

What If the Job That Interests You Doesn't Pay The Salary You Need?

If a higher salary can't be negotiated, then you can:

- Lower your monetary needs. Cut back or make arrangements to postpone as many expenses as you can. Prioritize your needs. Review the Career Success Guide: How to Negotiate a Fair Salary.
- Raise your job sights. Often, you can earn a higher salary by doing a similar job at a higher level of responsibility. Contact professional associations to find out more about industry certification that may make you eligible for a higher pay-scale.

What Is A Fair Salary?

It is understandable that employees want as high a salary as they can get, and employers want to pay as low a salary as they can. As a job seeker you want to know what you can expect in the way of salary. You need to determine what is the average wage for the job you seek. The U.S. Department of Labor compiles and publishes this information. Contact your local One-Stop Career Center and request Labor Market Information for your geographic area and your targeted job.

You can also go to www.indeed.com/salary and insert the job title and location. This site will give you the average wage for the job title in a specific location.

How to Discuss Your Salary Needs

If you have done your homework and your expectations are reasonable for the job and the company, then you are prepared to discuss the minimum salary that you will accept. However, if you're still seeking information, don't specify a salary:

- On the job application: If asked to specify the salary you need, write "negotiable."
- On your résumé: Do not mention salary requirements anywhere on the résumé.
- At the interview: Let the interviewer be the first to bring up the topic. For negotiating strategies, review the Career Success Series Guides *How to Negotiate a Fair Salary.*

Don't Waste Your Time

If the salary offered by the employer is less than what you believe to be fair for the job you seek, save yourself (and the prospective employer) time. Withdraw your application. Only pursue the job if you are comfortable with the offered salary.

How to Make the Most of the Worksheet

You may not be able to complete the Worksheet until you have been released. If you intend to live with someone else after your release, you may ask for their assistance in completing the worksheet.

Record you're spending habits. Even if you think you know where all your money goes, you need to keep track of all you're spending for a two-week period. You can then double the figures to obtain an estimate of the monthly amount for each category. Examine your monthly check stubs and bank statements. Total the amount that you spent last month for each of the budget categories.

Other expenses not on the worksheet.

Customize the worksheet by adding categories that are not listed. These are expenses that are unique to your situation, e.g., alimony, child support, educational loans, children's daycare expenses, etc.

When should you do the worksheet?

Plan to complete the worksheet in the early stages of your job hunt. By completing it before you start looking at jobs, you can target only those jobs that pay at or above your needed amount. Don't start interviewing without a clear idea of the monthly salary that you will accept.

Create a spending plan for all your desires and dreams.

After completing the worksheet and obtaining a realistic estimate of your annual salary needs, go through the exercise a second time and increase the spending for fun items. Add money for a better car, a new home, a bigger clothing allowance, an annual trip to a holiday resort or anything else you want. Use this new budget amount as a target. Plan your future based on this amount. With additional training, experience and responsibility, how quickly can you reach your target salary?

Worksheet to Estimate Your Monthly Salary Needs

HOUSING:	Mortgage or Rent Payment	________
	Maintenance and Repairs	________
	Furnishings and Improvement	________
	Gas, Electricity and Water	________
	Telephone/Cell/Internet/Cable	________
	Garbage Collection	________
FOOD:	Groceries, Etc.	________
	Restaurants, Fast Food	________
CLOTHES:	For You and Your Dependents	________
	Grooming, Haircuts	________
	Health Club	________
PET EXPENSES:	Food and Veterinarian	________
TRANSPORTATION:	Car Loan Payments	________
	Gas	________
	Regular Maintenance	________
	Other Regular Travel Costs	________
INSURANCE:	(Divide Annual Premiums By 12)	________
	House and Its Contents	________
	Life Insurance*	________
	Car	________
	Medical*	________
CHARITY:	Church and Other	________
TAXES:	Federal	________
(Monthly estimates)	State	________
	Personal Property and Real Estate	________
INVESTMENTS:	Monthly Savings	________
	Retirement Contribution	________
MONTHLY DEBTS:	Credit Cards	________
	Store Cards	________
	Other	________
SPENDING FOR FUN:	Movie Tickets, Video, Etc.	________
	Other Regular Entertainment	________
	Books, Magazines, Hobbies	________
	Vacations	________
	Christmas, Birthday Gifts, Etc.	________

Add it all up to calculate the sub-total.

SUB-TOTAL; ________

Now, add 15-20 percent to the sub-total, to create a buffer zone to cover unexpected monthly expenses.

Plus Buffer Amount; ________

TOTAL MONTHLY SALARY NEEDED; ________

Multiply this figure by 12 to estimate your annual salary.

TOTAL ANNUAL SALARY NEEDED; ________

*Your employer(s) may provide these.

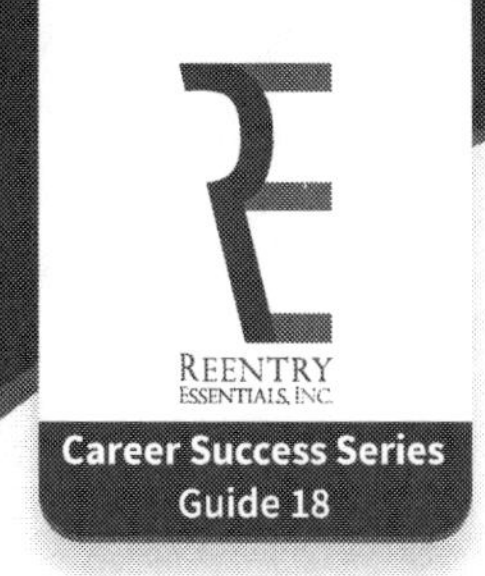

HOW TO USE YOUR LOCAL ONE-STOP CAREER CENTER

Federal law established local One-Stop Career Centers in 1998. One-Stop Career Centers are designed to provide a full range of assistance to job seekers, including re-entering individuals, under one roof. These Centers usually include the state employment office and other agencies charged with assisting the unemployed. Centers record job openings from employers, refer qualified applicants to those positions, and provide job counseling and job training.

One-Stop Career Center

One-Stop Career Centers are a single point-of-entry to services and programs that assist you to prepare for and obtain employment in your community. The Center brings together various organizations and agencies, both public and private, in one place for the benefit of both employers and job seekers. These agencies include the state employment service, welfare offices, rehabilitation, veterans' services, job training programs and community college programs. Some centers may also have a representative from the court system available. The goal of the Center is to provide individuals seeking employment with whatever assistance necessary for them to obtain employment self-sufficiency. Services include counseling, a career resource center, labor market information, access to electronic job information and openings, basic education, job search assistance and short-term job training. These programs are provided free to the general public.

The following are a few of the services and programs offered by most local One-Stop Career Centers. Note that not all Centers offer all of these programs and services.

- Programs authorized by the Workforce Investment Act (WIA) of 1998. These include adult and youth services, dislocated workers, Job Corps, Native American programs and veteran services. Each of these programs has specific eligibility requirements. The One-Stop Career Center intake staff will determine your eligibility for each program.
- Job Service programs include assistance for job-seekers in finding employment and to employers in finding workers.
- Adult and Education Literacy programs assist adults to obtain basic knowledge and skills necessary for employment. Programs include English as a Second Language.
- Vocational Rehabilitation programs assist people with disabilities.
- Older Worker programs target individuals 55 and older. Programs include part-time employment and volunteer work.
- Veterans Employment and Training Services focus on unique training, services and placement for qualified veterans.
- Other targeted groups include those in subsidized housing and low income families.

Services Available to Formerly Incarcerated Individuals

Some One-Stop Career Centers offer programs specifically for the re-entering population. These services include:

Federal Bonding Program. The Federal Bonding Program is a job hiring incentive program that protects employers from loss resulting from any dishonest acts performed by "at-risk" employees that they hire. The Federal Bonding Program issues bonds for "at-risk" job seekers who are not bondable by private insurers, thereby removing one barrier to employment. Go to www.bonds4jobs.com/ for more information.

Work Opportunity Tax Credit Program (WOTC). This program is a Federal tax credit available to employers for hiring individuals from certain target groups who have consistently faced significant barriers to employment. Go to www.doleta.gov/business/incentives/opptax/ for additional information about this program.

CORI Report Assistance. The One-Stop Career Center can assist you in obtaining a copy of your Criminal Offender Record Information report. Finding employers willing to hire ex-offenders. One-Stop Career Center resources will include a list of employers who have in the past hired people impacted by the criminal justice system.

Referrals to Support Services. There are a number of agencies that can assist you in your journey toward self-sufficiency. Staff at the One-Stop Career Center can refer you to the agency that most matches your needs.

Explaining Legal Issues Related to Criminal Records. You need to fully understand the legal issues related to your employment. The staff at the One-Stop Career Center can provide you with this important information.

One-Stop Career Center Programs and Services

Labor market information

In order to make an informed decision about an occupation, you need information about that occupation. The state and federal government publishes information that can assist you such as: How many people in my geographic area are working in that occupation? Can an ex-felon be employed in that field? And, what is the average income for that occupation?

This information is very important for a job seeker. This valuable information is available in all One-stop Career Centers or you can visit the Bureau of Labor Statistics (BLS) at www.bls.gov.

Unemployment Insurance

Although many states have gone to call centers to take applications for unemployment over the telephone, all One-Stop Career Centers have access to the call center and can help applicants register.

What is unemployment insurance?

Employers contribute a percentage of their monthly payroll to a state and federally administered insurance program. These funds are made available to eligible citizens who have been displaced from their employment. Eligible workers receive a weekly check.

Who is eligible to receive unemployment compensation?

You are eligible to receive unemployment if your employer has paid unemployment taxes, if you were employed by the organization for at least thirty days, it has been less than one year since your employment and you meet the criteria established by the state. Since most ex-offenders do not meet this criteria, it is doubtful that you would be eligible to receive unemployment insurance payments.

How do I apply?

Most states have gone to a call center arrangement for taking applications. Ask your local One-Stop Career Center for the telephone number. Be sure to have information about your last places of employment when you apply. Obtain further information on benefits that are available from your state at www.servicelocator.org/UI_Filing_Search.asp

Services for the job seeker

One of the partners in most One-Stop Career Centers is the State Employment Service, sometimes called Job Service. It is the division within the Center which assists job seekers in obtaining employment. To use the free service, you must:

- Complete a Registration/Intake form that gives the Career Center staff and potential employers' information about you.
- Pay attention to the work history section of the Registration/Intake form, as it will represent your special skills and accomplishments to an employer. Note that this can work against you if you desire to change occupations or you have not listed all of the skills you possess.

The information provided will allow the Job Service staff to match your education and experience with job opportunities as they become available. Most (but not all) job openings received by the Career Center office are added to the state computerized database. (See the Career Success Guide: How to Use The Internet In Your Job Search.) Job information listed in the database includes:

- Job title
- Years of education or experience required
- Hours per week
- Starting salary
- Special qualification and duties
- How to contact the employer

How can information be accessed?

Information can be accessed by using the on-site computer terminals at the employment office or at home. When you visit the One-Stop Career Center, find out how to access this information on the Internet.

Who lists jobs with the Employment Service?

- Employers
- State government agencies
- Federal government
- Almost anyone with a job opening

Career Resources

In order to make an informed vocational decision, you need to have accurate and current information about yourself and the world of work. There are many resources that can aid you in your search. These resources can be found in the Career Resource library. Do not be afraid to ask for assistance. A One-Stop Career Center staff person will be happy to help you find the information you want.

Most Resource Centers have the following types of references:

- Labor Exchange Information Lists of companies in the area and those that are hiring.
- Résumé Writing Software that will help you write, format and print your résumé.
- Career Exploration Software that will guide you through the career decision-making process.
- Self-Assessment Tools for self-administered skills and interests inventories.
- Labor Market Information about salaries, projected openings and demographics.
- Career Planning Books and videos on planning your future.
- Job Search Information Books and videos on how to find and secure a job.
- Interviewing Books and videos on how to ace the job interview.
- Books and videos on how to write résumés and cover letters.
- Job Retention Books and videos on how to keep your job.
- Written Business Directories and computer generated directories of businesses.
- Local and national newspapers and other periodicals.
- General Information on child care, housing, medical facilities and other important information.

Training

If you meet certain eligibility requirements you may be eligible for free job training. Speak with your One-Stop Career Center counselor about training offered by your local community college, vocational technical school, college or university or special classes. See the Career Success Guide: Where to Get Job Training.

USING YOUR NETWORK TO LOCATE JOB OPENINGS

It has been estimated that 70% of the people who secure a job get the job as the result of some form of personal contact and referral. The primary referral comes from current employees of the potential employer. Learning how to use personal contacts effectively, therefore, is crucial in your job search. Networking is the process of contacting individuals who can help you in your job search by either suggesting job leads or giving you a referral to people who may know of job openings.

Networking Allows You To:

- Find out about job openings.
- Get names of other people to contact.
- Inform many people that you are looking for work.
- Have a "foot-in-the-door" for job openings.
- Discover job openings before they are advertised.
- Face less competition for jobs.
- Be more familiar to the hiring authority.
- Let people know what your skills and interests are.

Some Networking Facts

- Over 80% of jobs are never advertised in the newspaper or listed on any job posting service. Most jobs are filled before they need to be advertised or listed with an employment agency. These never-advertised job openings are referred to as the "hidden" job market. Networking is the best way to gain information about these job openings.
- Networking is a simple process that enables you to gather information about job leads. It gives you access to potential employers that you could not gain by any other method. Not everyone you contact will be willing or able to be part of your network, but many people will. Networking is one of the most effective methods of gathering information about job openings and gaining access to employers.
- Employers generally feel more comfortable interviewing and hiring someone they know or someone who has been referred to them by someone they know. Networking will give you the advantage of being "known" by the employer before the interview.

Begin Networking Before You Are Released.

You need to start the networking process long before you receive a release date from the courts. Start by creating a list of people and organizations in your former community, or new community if you are electing to relocate after your release. Later in this guide you will find a list of types of contacts. Activate your list as soon as you receive the date of your possible release. Also included in this guide are suggested ways to make your contacts and what information you want to share with them.

Do Your Homework First

Before you start contacting your network for the specific purpose of finding job leads, you need to prepare yourself. You need to know:

- What your skills and interests are.
- The type of work you want.
- The kind of place where you want to work.
- The employers who employ people with your skills.

Do not expect your networking contacts to make career decisions for you. To be effective at networking you need to know what you are looking for. Be specific when you ask about job leads. Do not say, "...if you hear of anything." Instead, identify the job you want. "I am looking for a job as a finish carpenter." Contacts cannot help you if you are not clear about what you want.

Networking Basics

- Before you are released you should contact people by either snail mail or email if you are permitted to send emails from prison.
- Be aware that your contacts may be reticent to recommend you to potential employers. It is important that you reassure them that you are ready to move on in your life and that the issues that caused you to be incarcerated are no longer issues.
- Be polite and friendly.
- After you are released, contact people by phone or email. If you call, ask if it is a good time to talk. If not, ask when would be a good time to call back.
- If someone sounds reticent talking with you, thank them for their time and move on to another person.
- Do not ask your networking contacts to give you a job. Ask them if they know of any available openings for the type of job you are seeking. Ask for referrals to other contacts.
- Do not use your networking contacts as your emotional support system. Reserve discussions of your feelings for conversations with your family or friends.
- Listen - be interested in what your contacts have to say.

Make a Networking Contact List

While still incarcerated, start making a list of people to contact once you start your job search process. Start with people you know. The following are examples of people to add to your list:

- Relatives
- Members of your church or synagogue
- Former school classmates and teachers
- Doctors, dentists, hairdressers, shopkeepers, etc.
- Former supervisors
- Professional associates
- Work colleagues
- Members of social or sport groups
- Neighbors
- Friends

You will probably be surprised at the number of names on your list. You do not need to know everyone on your list personally. If you have some association through your former work, a social or religious organization, school, etc., put them on your list. Most people are willing to help if you are friendly, ask politely and are clear about what you need from them.

Get a list of agencies in your community that cater to re-entering persons. Your parole officer can assist you with preparing this list. Try to obtain a name of a contact at each agency and include their email address and telephone number. Once you have an initial list of people with whom you are familiar, their telephone numbers and/or email addresses, you are ready to begin the process of contacting them and building your job-hunting network.

Helpful Hints

Get Organized

Your network of contacts will quickly expand as you contact people and obtain referrals. You will be gathering lots of information, so it is important to be organized. Be prepared to take notes as you talk with or meet with someone. Get names, phone numbers and email addresses of all referrals. Write down the information you gather in an organized way, rather than on scattered pieces of paper that will get misplaced or lost. You will find that you will often need to refer back to the information.

Systematically Contact People

Once you have developed your initial list of names and contact information, begin contacting people systematically. It is often difficult to make the first couple of contacts, so start with people you know well. Once you become familiar with talking to people about your job-hunt, the contacts will get easier. Continue contacting those on your list. Write down any pertinent information from your contacts.

Calls or Meetings

Most networking can be done with phone calls or through email. If you have the name of someone who you think has valuable information, contact them and ask if they have the time to meet with you in person. Decide on relevant questions ahead of time in order to use the meeting time productively.

Questions to Ask

It is important to be brief and to the point when you contact people on your networking list. Remember that your purpose is to gather information about job leads and referrals that will lead you to a person who has the authority to hire you. If someone wants to talk about other things, be polite and listen, but try to keep the conversation directed toward your goals.

Begin your contacts by introducing yourself. Tell the person that you are in the process of looking for a job as (state your goal). Then ask:

- Do you know of any openings for a person with my skills? (Identify what your skills are.)
- Do you know of anyone else I might contact about openings? (Get names and phone numbers, if possible.)
- Do you know of anyone else who might know of someone who could help me locate openings?
- May I use your name when I contact...? Be sure to thank the person and say, "If you hear of any openings, please let me know. My telephone number and email address are..."

Contact Referrals

When someone on your list gives you the name and number of other people to call, follow up and contact those people. Mention the name of the person who gave you their name when you make the call. Employers are often more willing to speak to a "friend of a friend" than to someone with whom they have no connection. Gradually, you will build your network of people. Your goal is to continue contacting people until you reach a person who has the authority to hire you.

Present Yourself Well

Be polite and gracious with each contact. They are doing you a favor by talking with you. Let them know what you are looking for. Be persistent but not pushy. You want them to be comfortable referring you to someone they know. Because most people have pre-conceived ideas about Returning Citizens, it is important that you present yourself as being different from what they expect. Be prepared to speak openly about your offense and to persuade the listener that you are moving on.

Follow Up

Thank each person verbally. If someone has been especially helpful, a written thank you note is appropriate. During your contacts, ask if you may send them a résumé in case they hear of any job openings in your field. If they agree, follow up by sending your résumé with a thank you note attached. Review the Career Success Guide: How to Write a Thank You Note.

TRULINCS Friendly! info@ReentryEssentials.org **www.ReentryEssentials.org** **347.973.0004** **2609 East 14 Street, Suite 1018, Brooklyn, NY 11235-3915**

GOVERNMENT JOBS

Working for the government is attractive because it can offer competitive pay, job security and excellent benefits. Government jobs also emphasize training and other career advancement opportunities. The official job website of the United States Federal Government is www.usajobs.gov. Job seekers need to start their search at this website.

Can I Work for The Government If I Was Formerly Incarcerated?

The following is a quote from the government website, www.usajobs.gov.

> *Being an ex-offender does not prevent you from obtaining Federal Employment. OPM or the hiring agency considers your criminal conduct in determining your suitability but there are no general prohibitions against hiring you. We consider a number of relevant factors such as the duties of the positions you have applied for, the nature and regency of the misconduct, and any evidence of rehabilitation.*

Although there are no general prohibitions against employing you in the Federal Government, there are some regulations which will prohibit you from working in certain positions if you have a specific conviction. The most common situation involves being convicted of misdemeanor domestic violence crimes under Federal or State law. These persons are "prohibited from employment in any position requiring the individual: to ship, transport, possess, or receive firearms or ammunition" (Public Law 1-4-208 Omnibus Consolidated Appropriations Act of 1997.)

Other statutory or regulatory debarments exist, but are rarely applicable. They cover debarment from Federal employment from such offenses as treason, inciting rebellion against the U.S., willful and unlawful destruction of public records, or knowingly and willfully advocating the overthrow of the U.S. Government.

It is important for you to provide all the required information about your criminal record when you apply for Federal employment. Then, either OPM or the employing agency can determine early if a specific prohibition exists.

Since each federal and state agency has their own hiring restrictions, it is imperative that you find out what the restrictions are for the agency with whom you seek employment.

Federal Government Jobs

The Federal Government employs over 1.8 million people (not including those in the armed forces). Federal government jobs are located not only in this country, but in nearly every foreign country. Hiring departments include the Departments of Agriculture, Justice, the Treasury, Veterans' Affairs, Defense, Health and Human Services, Transportation, Labor, Energy, Housing and Urban Development, Education and others. The Social Security Administration, General Services Administration and the Environmental Protection Agency are independent Federal employers.

How Federal Jobs Are Filled

Most Federal agencies have hiring procedures similar to those in the private sector. Applicants will need to contact the specific agency directly for application requirements and to receive an application. Federal employment is subject to many specific laws, executive orders, and regulations. These laws are in place to ensure that applicants and employees receive fair and equal treatment throughout the hiring process. There are two classes of jobs in the Federal Government: competitive service jobs and excepted service jobs.

Competitive Service

Competitive Service jobs are under the jurisdiction of the Office of Personnel Management (OPM). Employers have authority to review many applicants before selecting the best-qualified candidate. Candidates are selected based on stated job-related criteria. The employee must meet the minimum qualification requirements listed for the position. Competitive service job wages are regulated in order to ensure equitable compensation for workers.

The Federal hiring authority must choose from three groups of candidates:

1. New applicants who meet the qualification requirements for the job,
2. Applicants who have civil service status (are currently working or previously worked for the U.S. government), or
3. Applicants who are part of certain appointing authorities like the Peace Corps and veterans.

Excepted Service

Excepted Service jobs are not subject to the same pay, classification, and appointment rules as competitive service jobs. These agencies are permitted to set their own qualification requirements. They are still bound to certain hiring practices, such as preferential treatment for disabled veterans. Some Federal agencies, such as the Federal Bureau of Investigation (FBI) and the Central Intelligence Agency (CIA) have only excepted service jobs. Other agencies may have some competitive and some excepted service positions.

Job Posting

While laws require all competitive service jobs to be listed on the Federal government's job search website – www.usajobs.gov, excepted service employing agencies are not required to post announcements there. Candidates will need to visit the excepted agency's independent website to search for job listings and submit an application. For further information about how to access information on job banks, review the Career Success Guide: How to Use the Internet in Your Job Search.

Pay Scales: Wage Jobs vs. General Schedule Jobs

Most trade, craft, and laboring employees are paid under the Federal Wage System (FWS). Most professional, technical, administrative and clerical positions use the General Schedule (GS) pay scale. These standardized pay scale systems ensure that Federal employees are paid amounts comparable to the prevailing wage or salary in a particular area. Under these grades and pay scales, compensation is based on qualifications (education and experience), and on comparable wages and salaries for similar work in the geographic area. The salaries of employees of quasi-government agencies like the Postal Service, legislative workers, and private contract workers do not follow either FWS or GS pay scales, but rather are determined by the agency.

How to Apply for a Federal Government Job

- Visit www.jobsearch.usajobs.gov on your computer, at the library, or at your local One-Stop Career Center. In addition to listing job openings, this website has applications, forms, and other useful information about federal employment.
- When you first access this website, you will be asked to set up an account. Fill in the requested fields in the online form. Be sure to make a note of the user name and password that you select. Although you do not need an account to search for jobs, you will need one to set up and submit your application and résumé.
- You will be able to search for job openings by location, agency, or occupation using the "Search Jobs" tab. You can save your search, and the site will retrieve job listings matching your criteria and email them to you. Review the "Qualifications and Evaluations" section of the announcement carefully to be sure that you qualify for the job you have highlighted. This is where the announcement will list ex-offenders as an exclusion.
- Carefully follow the directions in the "How to Apply" section, if you qualify for the position. You may be directed to another website to obtain information about the job or to fill out an online form.
- Some agencies require applicants to provide information not normally supplied on an application or in a résumé. This information is usually provided on a Supplemental Form which is available on the website.
- It is possible that you will be asked to create a résumé on the site. If asked to create a résumé online, you will be providing the same information you have on your paper résumé. You will be asked to input your name, experience, education, training, other skills, and references. For information about creating a résumé online, refer to the Career Success Guide: How to Write an Internet Résumé.
- The website has excellent tutorials. Highlight the "Resource Center" tab. Here you will find tutorials to help you use the www.usajobs.gov website most effectively. For more information about internet job applications, refer to the Career Success Guide: How to Apply for a Job Online.

Areas of Consideration

The area of consideration is the source from which the agency will consider candidates. It is often listed in the job announcement as "Who May Apply". The agency may designate whatever area of consideration it considers appropriate. A candidate who is outside the area of consideration will not be considered.

Veterans and Other Special Groups

All agencies give preferential treatment to qualifying veterans and some family members to compensate them for economic loss due to their service and to acknowledge the obligation the government owes to its disabled veterans and their families. You will need to fill out a form (listed in the job application) and submit it with your application to receive this preference.

Other Targeted Groups

See the following web sites for information targeted to the following groups:

- Veterans and family of veterans – www.fedshirevets.gov
- Students – my.usajobs.gov/studentjobs
- Senior Executives – my.usajobs.gov/seniorexecutives
- Individuals with disabilities – my.usajobs.gov/individualswithdisabilities

State and Local Government Jobs

Consider looking for jobs working for your state or local government. Application and search processes vary by state, but a complete list of state job websites and links can be found at http://50statejobs.com/gov.html. This site also lists government employment web sites for many of the larger cities in the US. Keep in mind that states have different rules and restrictions when it comes to hiring ex-offenders. Whereas one state may prohibit the hiring of an ex-offender for a specific job, another state may not have such a restriction.

Quasi-Government Jobs

Check out the following quasi-government agencies for additional job openings:

- The US Postal Service (USPS) – www.usps.com/employment
- Department of Homeland Security (DHS) – www.dhs.gov/xabout/careers
- Transportation Security Administration (TSA) – www.tsa.gov/careers
- Amtrak – www.amtrak.com/careers

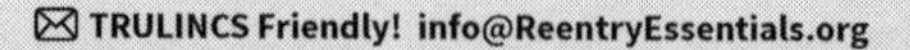

TRULINCS Friendly! info@ReentryEssentials.org **www.ReentryEssentials.org** **347.973.0004** **2609 East 14 Street, Suite 1018, Brooklyn, NY 11235-3915**

PLUSES & MINUSES OF TEMPORARY EMPLOYMENT

Temping, or performing a short- or long-term work assignment, is a viable option for re-entering job seekers. Not only can temporary employment provide an income, it can help you gain job experience and employer references. Temporary assignments permit the job seeker to check out different companies and, best of all, open the door to a permanent job. About 5% of all new hires come from the company's temporary pool. You need to identify which temp agencies that specialize in placing reentering citizens. Not all agencies consider ex-offenders for temporary employment.

Temping: The Stats

- In this recession, temping is on the rise. 26.2 percent of all jobs added by private sector employers in 2010 were temporary jobs.
- Currently there are about 20,000 offices placing temps nationwide.
- 18 to 20 percent of temps find permanent work through their assignments.
- Nearly 3 out of 4 companies use staffing companies to help find qualified employees.
- Temps are now found in almost every career field including IT, healthcare and manufacturing.

The Temp Agency Is Your Employer

The temp agency is your employer. You will, therefore, need to reveal your record to them at the time that you apply for employment. The temp agency may or may not reveal your past to the company where they assign you. Be sure to ask if that is the agency's policy so you do not find yourself having to reveal any information during your assignment. Follow the policy of the temp agency.

Know Your Rights

Temporary employees are protected by the same laws that protect other workers and enjoy the same rights to minimum wage, overtime, worker's compensation and unemployment as do other, non-temp workers.

Warning!

Temps are not independent contractors!

If your temp company is not withholding income or social security taxes from your paycheck call them immediately. Although you'll have more short-term cash as a contract employee, if taxes are not withheld, you'll owe more at tax time, including a 15.3 percent self-employment tax. Resolve the situation or move to another agency.

Getting Your Foot in the Side Door

If there's a particular company that you want to work for, but they have no openings, find out which temporary staffing company they use. Then, sign up with that agency and ask that they assign you with that company. It's likely that the company's hiring authority will be impressed with your initiative and persistence.

Finance Basics

- You are an employee of the temp services firm and not the company where you are assigned.
- The hiring company in almost all cases pays a fee to the temp company for your services. If the temp company expects you to pay for their services, go elsewhere.
- Your paycheck, whether weekly or biweekly, will come from the temp serices company.

Advantages to you:

- Show off your skills and personality to a potential employer.
- Try out a variety of positions and companies without a long-term commitment.
- Determine what line of work is best for you.
- Opportunity to evaluate a company and decide whether it's the right fit for you.
- Gain an inside track on unadvertised positions within a company.
- Learn new marketable job skills while looking for permanent work.
- Expand your network of job search contacts.
- Build your résumé and gather valuable employer references.
- Have an income while looking for a permanent job or relocating.
- Control your work schedule. You work when you want to work.

The Downside:

- For those in it for the long-term, temping can be insecure.
- No temp agency can guarantee that an assignment will meet your requirements or that you will ever receive a permanent job offer from an employer.
- There might be downtime between assignments. Again, there are no guarantees that you'll get as much work as you want.
- Many temp companies do not offer benefits to employees. However, this has been changing, as some agencies now offer health insurance and other benefits to temps after they've worked for a certain period of time.

Before you sign anything...

- Decide whether temping is the best course for your situation. Temping is an excellent bridge to full-time work for those who:
  - have never had a job
  - have few marketable job skills
  - are reentering the work force
  - are older workers
  - want to change careers but lack market skills
- But it's not for everyone. The best temps generally:
  - are flexible
  - enjoy working in new situations
  - are comfortable with people they don't know very well
  - are quick studies and eager to upgrade skills
  - can work independently
- Know what kind of schedule you want to work.

Selecting a Temp Agency

- Look for a temp company that meets your specific requirements. Don't just sign with the first company that interviews you. Interview with several.
  - Is the agency a member of a national trade association? This indicates that they are up-to-date in their policies.
  - Do they specialize in one type of career field like manufacturing or are they a general temp company? What type of industries do they serve?
  - Will they accept re-entering applicants?
  - Do they offer temp-to-permanent opportunities?
  - Do they have a policy against your accepting a full-time job offer after you complete an assignment?
  - What happens if you turn down an assignment? Are they then less willing to call you the next time?
- Be up front about what your goals are. If you are temping to land a full-time job, say so during the initial interview.
- If you plan to temp for an extended period of time, consider signing with more than one company. Be sure to check for any company policies against this before you sign anything.
- Ask about benefits. Health insurance, vacation time and other benefits are rare for beginning temps, but may be available after you've worked for a certain length of time.

Temping and Unemployment Compensation

Unemployment checks will vary if you work a short-term or part-time position. As a result, temping while collecting unemployment can be tricky. Unemployment agencies generally encourage temp work because they recognize that it improves a person's marketability and chances for a full-time job. However, you should protect yourself by doing your homework first. Talk with both your unemployment agency representative and your temping coordinator. Get the answers to the following questions:

- If I take an occasional temporary position, how will my claim be affected? Will it be interrupted? Will I have to reapply again after the assignment ends?
- If I turn down a temping assignment, will I be seen as having turned down work?
- What if I turn down a full-time position that's not right for me? What are the consequences of turning down work?

Employee Leasing

Don't confuse temping with employee leasing. Employee leasing is a strategy used by small companies to help provide their employees with benefits. The company in effect fires all of its employees, who are then immediately hired by the leasing company.

The employee receives all paychecks and benefits from the leasing company, who handles enough employees to qualify for low insurance premiums.

Temp to Permanent Employment

You're offered a permanent job with the company. Now what?

- Feel flattered, but don't jump at the offer. Make sure that this is the job you really want. You can quit later, of course, but that can jeopardize your future with the temp company.
- Will they hire a formerly incarcerated individual? It is possible that the company does not know your criminal justice system history. You need to find out what the company's policy is concerning hiring re-entering employees. Don't risk not letting them know about your past.
- First, evaluate the company.
  - What is the management style? Is it a match for your work style?
  - Is the company viable for your long-term goals? Is it in the right industry? Is it a leading edge company? Is it financially stable? Have there been recent layoffs?
  - What about the company's employment policies? Ask about health benefits, retirement plans and vacation and holiday pay.
- Next, evaluate the job.
  - Does it meet all of your goals and requirements? If it's not exactly the job you've always dreamed of, is the position going to get you where you want to be? If not, continue temping until you get the right offer.
  - What kind of job performance and results does the employer expect of you? Will there be a probation period? What are the chances for advancement within the company? Is the offered salary adequate?
- Accept or reject the offer first by phone, then by letter.
  - If you accept the position, be enthusiastic, but reiterate in writing all of the details that you and the hiring authority have agreed to.
  - If you reject the position, detail why the position is not right for you at this time, but don't burn your bridges. If you like the company, ask that they keep you in mind for additional temping assignments.

HOW TO USE THE INTERNET IN YOUR JOB SEARCH

In the new millennium the Internet has become an important resource for all job seekers. Nearly every public and private organization and company both large and small are listing job openings on the Internet. Large Internet databases daily list in excess of a million job openings, including jobs for re-entering individuals. Savvy re-entering job seekers are posting their résumé on the net and with résumé services both before and after their release. It is critical, therefore, that you understand how to use this resource. It is observed that some jails and prisons are now allowing inmates to access the Internet especially to aid them in their job search.

New To the Internet?

If you are new to the Internet, you need to ask for assistance. If you want to access the Internet before your release, ask for assistance from the monitor overseeing the computer room. If seeking assistance after your release, go to your local One-Stop Career Center. They can train you on the use of the Internet. This familiarity with the Internet is necessary in order for you to benefit from this valuable resource.

Disclaimer

Be aware that the information provided in this guide was current as of the date that the guide was written. The Internet is constantly changing. Websites change names and addresses. New sites are added and old sites may vanish. All websites are updated almost daily so the information you obtain today will most likely change tomorrow. The sites, www.rileyguide.com and www.job-hunt.org should be your starting points for current web names and addresses. Both sites stay current on web names and addresses that are of interest to job seekers.

Note that nearly every guide in this series lists websites that are relevant to the topic of the guide. Special attention should be paid to the websites listed in the Career Success Guide: Resources for Ex-Offenders.

Search Engines

Search engines are Internet companies that compile and reference information posted on the Internet. You ask a search engine to list all web sites that mention a selected word or phrase. In a matter of seconds the search engine lists all known sites that use that word or phrase. Depending upon the word or phrase, you can get as few as no "hits" to several million. For example, use the search engine, Google and enter the phrase, "Job openings for ex-felons." Google will return over ½ million "hits." A "hit" is a website that includes some to all of the words that you entered. Be mindful, though, that the first group of websites listed are "paid" listings, meaning that the website paid the search engine company to list their website near the top of the listing. Also, it is not unusual for a website to be listed more than once.

Search engine companies are not all alike. Their methods of searching the World Wide Web differ so you may find one engine more responsive than another. Also, the more sophisticated you become in using a search engine, the more targeted your search becomes. The following are popular search engines:

- Google www.google.com
- Yahoo www.yahoo.com
- AOL www.aol.com
- Bing www.bing.com
- Ask www.ask.com

Job Seekers Use The Internet To:

Identify resources to be used in their career and job search.

- Find information on companies.
- Locate job openings.
- Post their résumé so potential employers can see it.
- Network job openings. The Internet helps the job seeker to identify people who may help them identify job openings. You can find people and organizations in your home town that aid re-entering ex-offenders. You would search, *"Offender resources in (enter your town's name)."*

General Information

Job Search Information - The following are a few sites that provide both general "how to..."information on job searches, but also specific job search tips. Note that each of these sites will also provide other web sites where you can obtain additional information.

- www.careermag.com
- www.theworksite.com
- www.rileyguide.com
- www.job-hunt.com
- www.jobhuntersbible.com
- www.careeronestop.org
- www.mindtools.com

Moving/relocating - Check these sites for information about cities, states, homes, taxes and cost of living:

- www.statelocalgov.net
- www.realtor.com
- www.homefair.com

Salary Information - These sites provide information on average salaries for selected occupations.

- www.jobstar.org/tools/salary
- www.bls.gov

Information on Companies

These sites will assist you to identify companies, get their address, telephone numbers and often employee names and titles. Many sites provide information about the company, including annual reports and recent news articles.

www.bizweb.com, www.superpages.com, www.sec.gov, www.bbb.org, www.businesswire.com, www.businessweek.com, www.bloomberg.com

Job Opening Data Bases

There are literally thousands of sites that list job openings. Some are industry or occupation specific, whereas others are local or regional. To narrow your search, use a search engine and target your search. For example, search on *brick layer Oklahoma job* to get a listing of jobs for brick layers in the state of Oklahoma. In addition to the list of Mega job banks listed below, Internet providers and newspapers have job banks. If you belong to AOL, EarthLink, etc., check their sites for job listings.

Be aware that some sites require you to provide information about yourself and the type of job you seek before they will allow you access to the job listings. You may or may not want to provide this information before you look at the job information. Also, avoid sites that require you to subscribe and pay a fee before you can access the job information. The following are a few of the Mega job banks:

- Each state has a job bank that is managed by the state employment department. Follow the on-screen directions to select your state or the state of interest. www.Jobbankinfo.org
- CareerBuilder searches the databases of many job sites. www.careerbuilder.com
- Indeed allows you to search for jobs by location. www.indeed.com
- Monster is a Mega site that offers many services as well as a large job database. www.monster.com

Posting Your Résumé

More and more companies are asking candidates to submit electronic résumés. These résumés differ significantly from traditional paper résumés. How you plan to make your electronic résumé available to employers dictates the format of the résumé:

- Do you plan to post your résumé on-line to commercial résumé posting services?
- Do you plan to send your electronic résumé directly to company web sites?
- Do you plan to e-mail your résumé to individuals in response to advertisements?

There are essentially three types of electronic résumés: plain text, formatted and web based. Review the Career Success Guide: How to Write an Internet Résumé for more details.

E-Mail

If you want to participate in the Internet revolution, it is imperative that you have an e-mail account. You don't have to have a computer, only access to a computer. Check with your prison officials to see if they will allow you to obtain an email address and to send and receive emails. It appears that only federally run prisons allow inmate email. After you are released you can secure access at most local One-Stop Career Centers and local libraries. Web- based e-mail accounts allow you to get your mail from any computer and are generally free. Three popular sites allow you to set up an e-mail account. You will be required to "register" in order to set up an account at each of the following sites:

www.hotmail.com www.yahoo.com www.gmail.com

Again, check with your prison official if still incarcerated, or your local One-Stop Career Center or librarian if released. They can help you. You will need to select a unique "name" and a password so others cannot access your mail. Selecting a unique name with any of the above sites can be difficult since most common names are already taken. Once you have succeeded in selecting a username and password, never give out that information.

Internet and Privacy

The Internet has been described as a giant party line. In other words, information that is transmitted over the Internet can be intercepted by hackers. Unless an encrypting program is used, information is generally not secure. Therefore, do not send any information that you want to keep private. Strangers, in addition to the people to whom you are sending the information, may also have access to it.

Using Your Work E-Mail Address

If you are working, do not use your work e-mail address in your job search unless you have permission from your employer. Your e-mail account at work technically belongs to your employer who has the legal right to monitor your communications. It is better to use your home e-mail address when job-searching.

Caution: Not All Ads Are Legitimate!

Although most job listings are legitimate, especially those on the large job banks, some unscrupulous people use the Internet job banks as a way to get information about people. They use information garnered from your résumé for identity theft purposes. To protect yourself, check out the company posting the ad by making a telephone call to their office. Make sure that they have posted the opening and that the web address is legitimate. Be wary if no company name is given in the job listing.

Do's and Don'ts

- Do become familiar with a company before you contact them. If they have a web site, they expect you to have read it.
- Don't send attachments to e-mails unless the receiver knows you. Most companies have a policy (because of the threat of a computer virus that could be embedded in a file) against opening attachments from non-company e-mails. If you want to include your résumé, paste it within your e-mail.
- Do keep all correspondence short and to the point.
- Don't send e-mails to the company president or vice-president unless directed to do so. If they don't know you, your e-mail and résumé will be sent to Personnel, often with a note, Don't Hire!
- Don't spend more than 50% of your job search time using the Internet.

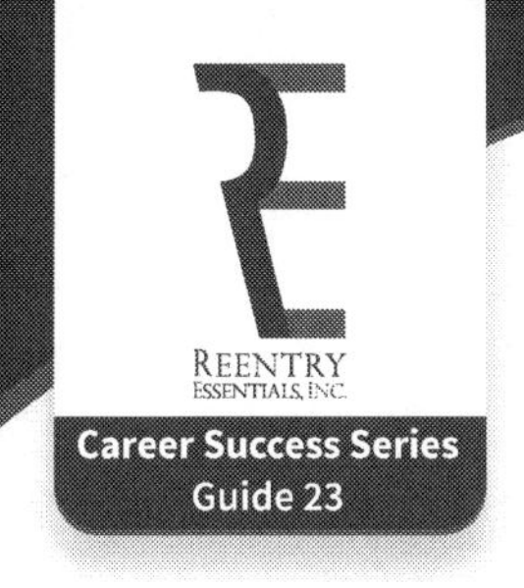

HOW TO APPLY FOR A JOB ONLINE

Since the beginning of the 21st century, medium to large companies have changed the way that they recruit candidates, capture and evaluate information about applicants, and select possible employees. Companies have begun using computer programs to assist in all phases of the hiring process. Since even small companies are using this technology for recruiting new employees, the re-entering job-seeker must be familiar with these procedures in order to successfully secure employment. Because most incarcerated people do not have access to the Internet while still in prison, you may need to wait until you are released to use this procedure to locate and apply for jobs.

Manual Versus Electronic Applications

Manually Processed Applications

Before the development of employee recruitment computer software in the early 1990's, all employers manually processed submitted job applications and résumés. Today, employers who do not rely on a recruitment computer program recruit using the following process:

- They usually recruit prospective employees by placing an ad in a local newspaper or registering the job opening with the local state employment office.
- They require all applicants to complete a company supplied paper job application or have the applicant submit a written résumé.
- They have a company employee (usually in the Human Resources Department) evaluate every application and résumé. That employee determines if the applicant, based on the applicant's submitted application or résumé, qualifies for the job opening(s).
- Rejected applications and résumés are either discarded or filed. If filed, the application or résumé is usually filed in a file folder with all the other submitted applications and résumés, and is labeled with the name of the open job.
- Employers rarely have a system to permit applicants to update their application or résumé. They require the applicant to resubmit either a new application or an updated résumé.
- Employers also rarely have a way to retrieve previously submitted applications that might match a new job opening.
- Employers rarely accept unsolicited applications and résumés.

Electronically Processed Applications

Recruitment computer software is used by most employers with more than 100 employees. Recruitment computer software permits the employer to:

- Recruit nationally. By placing an ad either on a Mega Job Board or on the company website, employers can reach potential applicants from wherever applicants have computer access.
- Standardize the information that they receive from all applicants. Applicants usually are required to complete the employer-designed online application. The application focuses on the information that the employer needs from the applicant. Additionally, the employer can embed in the application, or ask in a separate questionnaire, questions that assess the applicant's skills, abilities, values and integrity.
- Have the computer program select only those applicants who meet the specific job requirements. The employer has the computer program identify only those applicants that match the selected skills, abilities, values, etc. of the job. The program reviews each application and résumé and notes if and how often the applicant mentions the selected phrases and words. See Key words on the next page.
- Select out applications and résumés that do not meet the selection criteria. These documents are then electronically stored and can be easily retrieved.
- Easily retrieve a submitted application and résumé. This permits the applicant to update and make changes to their application or résumé.
- Retrieve previously submitted applications based on the criteria of a new job opening.
- Accept, evaluate and store electronically unsolicited applications and résumés. These applications or résumés can be retrieved when a job opening occurs that calls for the applicant's skills.

Note: Although most employers with fewer than 100 employees continue to recruit and process new employees manually, recently available computer software for small businesses has made this process more appealing. Since approximately 95% of all employers have fewer than 100 employees, it is critical that job seekers be familiar with both the manual and the electronic recruitment methods.

Before You Begin

Before you begin applying for any job online, it is critical that you:

- Review the Career Success Guide: How to Complete a Job Application. After reviewing this guide, complete a blank application within the Career Success Guide: Sample Blank Employment Application. Make sure that all information is current and accurate. Check all dates of employment. Identify people who can serve as references. Double check all spelling and grammar.
- Review the Career Success Guide: How to Write an Internet Résumé. Prepare a résumé that can be submitted electronically.

The Importance of Key Words

The power of electronic recruitment software lies in the key words. The computer permits the employer to quickly evaluate every submitted application and résumé to determine if the candidate possesses a set of specific skills and/or traits that are required on the job. The employer provides the computer program with a list of words and phrases that describe the skills and traits critical to the job. The computer program then compares this list to the phrases and words mentioned by the candidate in the application or résumé. Those candidates that mention the specific words and phrases in their application or résumé may be selected for an interview. Applications and résumés that do not mention enough skills and traits are kept on file but probably will not get selected.

Hint: Not sure what key words or phrases you need to include? Key words are the words and phrases that describe the job.

- Google "Job Description for [insert the job title]." Review several of the listed web sites that give job descriptions. Jot down key phrases and words that describe the skills and traits of people in that occupation. These are key words!
- Check the company's web site. The company may publish a job description. Closely review the job announcement. Pay special attention to the words and phrases that the company uses to describe the job. These are key words!

You need to load your application or résumé with key words. They should be nouns and noun phrases, and industry specific. Try not to repeat key words and phrases since the computer only counts the inclusion once. Try to mention at least 20 different key words in your application or résumé. This is one time that more is better.

Where should I insert the key words? If you are submitting an online application, use key words to describe your past work experiences. If submitting a résumé, load the description of your work duties for your past employment with key words. Consider submitting a Skills (Functional) résumé. Review the Career Success Guide: Components of a Résumé.

Ways to Apply For a Job Online

Job Boards

A job board is an electronic bulletin board where employers can post job openings and job seekers can post their résumé. There are hundreds of job boards listed on the Internet. Some are large (Mega Boards) like www.careerbuilder.com and www.monster.com. Other boards are small and focus on a specific occupational or geographic area. Google the title of the job you seek. You will likely find several job boards that focus on that occupational area.

Job Boards typically permit a job seeker to post their résumé on the board's site. Employers frequently search the list of résumés for ones that match the company's job opening. Many companies have computer software that permits them to access most job boards and identify potential candidates.

All job boards require the applicant to register with the board; some charge a fee for this service. When you register, be sure to write down the user name and password that you selected. Follow the board's instructions for how to post your résumé or to respond to a company ad. Review the Career Success Guide: How to Write an Internet Résumé.

Company Web Sites

Company web sites are an excellent source of information about job openings. You will have to know, however, which companies employ people in your occupation. Most company web sites post job openings on their web site.

Many companies permit you to submit a résumé. Be sure to carefully follow the instructions for submission. You will be asked to register. Be sure to note the User Name and Password you selected. If you are asked to submit your résumé as an attachment, be sure to name it [your name] resume (for example, JohnDoeResume) and not simply, "resume."

There are many advantages to applying directly to the company rather than going through a Job Board. Studies have shown that as many as 10 times more people apply for a specific job using a job board than do people applying directly to the company. Better yet, network and find someone in that company who will refer your name and résumé to the personnel office. See the Career Success Guide: How to Use Your Network to Locate Job Openings.

On-Site Computer Kiosks

Many retail establishments are using self-service employment kiosks to obtain applications. Kiosks consist of a desk, computer screen and keyboard. Once applicants log on to the program, they simply follow the program's instructions. Applicants essentially complete an online application and often are asked to respond to questions that assess skills and traits required for the job position sought.

Most applications take approximately 30 minutes to complete and require a minimum amount of computer knowledge. Do not start the process unless you have time to complete it. Because you will be supplying information about your work history and references, be sure to bring your completed Career Success Guide: Sample Blank Employment Application with you.

Practice Online Application

If you have access to a computer, go to www.nicic.gov/library/022996 and download the Simulated Online/Kiosk Application program. This program walks you through the process of completing an online or kiosk application. Click on each of the "help" buttons for information on how to respond to each question.

HOW TO RESPOND TO NEWSPAPER WANT ADS

Used correctly, newspaper want ads can be a good source for job leads. Knowing which ads to answer and how to respond can help in your search for employment. Your goal in responding to a Help Wanted ad is to make the employer interested enough in you to call you for an interview. Because you must be available for an interview, you will not want to start this job search procedure until you are released.

Finding and Selecting Ads

Where to Look:

Your local paper - Usually contains hourly positions, jobs that are hard to fill and low-paying jobs. Sunday and Wednesday papers typically contain the most ads, but it's worth looking every day.

Trade magazines - Good for searching for jobs related to a particular trade.

The Internet - Major newspapers place their ads on the Internet. Google the name of your local newspaper to identify the newspapers website.

Old papers - Look at the help wanted ads for the past month. This will give you an idea of who is hiring. If an ad is still in the paper, then it may mean that there are problems with the employer filling the position. Your library will have back issues.

What to Look For:

- You are looking for ads that describe employment that is of interest to you and for which you are qualified.
- Don't take want ads at face value. As in any other form of advertising, the product (the job) may not be as wonderful as it sounds.
- The ad will describe the ideal candidate. Don't worry if you don't meet all the qualifications. The more qualifications you do have, the better will be your chances of getting an interview.

Beware of Blind Ads!

A blind ad does not mention the name of the company in the ad. Many companies do not mention their name in the ad for fear that they will be overwhelmed with telephone calls. With a little sleuthing you can often find out who placed the ad, even if it isn't listed.

There are several Internet web sites that have reverse phone listings which allow you to identify the owner. If it's a local ad, you can also identify the employer by going through the yellow pages under the type of business to match the phone number or address to a business name.

Due to privacy laws the name of the person who rents a post office box is not public knowledge. Newspaper box numbers are also not traceable.

Typical newspaper ad

(1) FRAMING CARPENTERS ABC CONSTRUCTION, a leader in the (2) residential construction industry with over 200 employees is seeking (3) Framing Carpenters. Applicants should be able to immediately join a team of framing carpenters. The (4) ideal applicant must possess excellent carpentry skills, be able to read blue prints and work in a team atmosphere. (5) Candidates must demonstrate an excellent work ethic, have reliable transportation and communication skills. (6) Good salary and benefits for full-time position.

Apply in person to:

(7) Mark Smith
ABC Construction
123 Main Street
Anywhere, USA 00000

Ads typically include:

1. Job title
2. Company name
3. 3Description of company
4. Responsibilities
5. Qualifications
6. Salary/benefits
7. Application information

Harmless Reasons Businesses Place Blind Ads...

- To avoid getting calls about the job.
- They think it will draw more applicants.
- To keep their competition from learning about company expansions or relocations.
- To keep their own employees from learning that they're hiring from the outside.
- Headhunting companies are looking for a pool of applicants for future job openings.

Not So Harmless Reasons Businesses or People Place Blind Ads...

- Scam artists sometimes use blind ads to get people to send them personal information.
- To see if the company's current employees are looking for work outside the company.
- Recruiters and employment agencies run ads to expand their pool of applicants.
- Some blind ads are really advertisements for products to "go into business for yourself" - products that are seldom worth the money.

How Want Ads Usually Work:

Many want ads are placed by the Personnel Department of large companies that typically have a large turnover of employees. Small companies that do not have personnel offices also place want ads since they have no other means to recruit employees. These companies receive hundreds of responses, weed out unqualified applicants and pass along promising ones to the person in charge of hiring. The personnel office may interview applicants prior to turning over the top few candidates to the people who make the hiring decision. It's best if you can avoid this screening process altogether (see next column), but if you can't, here's what to do:

- Send a cover letter and a résumé, unless other information or action is requested in the ad.
- In the first paragraph of the cover letter, state where you saw the ad and your interest in the position. Review the Career Success Guide: How to Write a Cover Letter.
- In the following paragraphs, list each qualification in the ad and state next to it exactly how you meet that qualification. Do not leave out any information. You do not need to mention that you were formerly incarcerated in the letter.
- Use bullet points for each qualification, so the person can quickly see that you meet all of the requirements.
- At the end of the letter, summarize why you are a great candidate for the position. Repeat your interest in working for the company and your desire for an interview.
- Keep your letter short, one or two pages.
- Your résumé should support the information you give in the cover letter. If you have one, make sure the job objective given on your résumé matches the job title listed in the ad.
- Don't respond to salary requirements. If it's absolutely necessary, give a range and indicate that you're willing to negotiate.
- NEVER give out your Social Security Number, birth date, driver's license number, account numbers, utility bill information or other personal information when answering a want ad, either via the Internet or mail.

A Better Way To Use Want Ads:

One way to avoid the crowd of applicants answering the ad is to write directly to the person in charge of hiring for the position. Find this person by asking contacts, calling the company or any other way you can.

- Review the Career Success Guides: How to Make Cold Calls and Using Your Network to Locate Job Openings.
- If you write to someone other than the person listed in the ad, do not mention the ad. Simply state your interest in working for the company or say that you heard that there was an opening. Mentioning the ad might send your response back to the personnel office.
- Describe your qualifications, making sure that they match fairly closely to those described in the ad. Don't make it as obvious, however, as you would in your letter to personnel.
- Your résumé should reflect those qualifications.
- Your letter will stand out from other applicants because it is going directly to the hiring person and because you won't sound as if you are merely trying to make your qualifications fit the ad.
- Use your networking to get an introduction. If you know someone at the company, use them to find out who's in charge of the position and how best to approach them. They might even give you a personal referral. The social networking site: www.linkedin.com can be useful in finding contacts at a specific company. Ask for assistance at your local One-Stop Career Center. They should be able to help you find a name at the selected company.
- Feel free to write to several people at the company.

In Your Job Search...

- While want ads aren't the most effective job search method, they do work for some people. Most job search consultants recommend that from 10% to 15% of the time allocated to job searching be spent finding and responding to want ads.
- Don't just read the classifieds section; read articles with an eye to jobs. News of a company expansion or a branch opening in your town might mean a job for you.
- Most experts agree that placing your own ad seeking employment is not worth the money.
- Remember, most jobs aren't listed in the want ads. Be sure to spend time on more effective job search methods, such as networking and contacting employers directly.

TRULINCS Friendly! info@ReentryEssentials.org www.ReentryEssentials.org 347.973.0004 2609 East 14 Street, Suite 1018, Brooklyn, NY 11235-3915

HOW TO WORK A JOB FAIR

Job Fairs are organized events at which a sponsor brings together employers and job candidates. They are usually held in a large auditorium, convention center, community center or large hotel. In recent years Job Fairs have become popular recruitment methods for employers. In a single day, an employer can obtain hundreds of résumés. As a job seeker, you need to know how to "work" a Job Fair; otherwise, it will be a waste of your time and effort. Since these events are typically held in public settings outside of the prison, you will only be using this procedure after you have been released.

What Is A Job Fair?

A Job Fair is like a Flea Market. Rather than merchants, companies occupy the booths or stalls. A booth may be as simple as a table and two chairs or it may be elaborately decorated with posters and other display materials. Each participating company purports to have job openings and is interested in getting résumés and talking to prospective employees. Job Fairs have become a common method for companies to recruit and screen applicants. Often the job openings are primarily entry level jobs. The booths are usually staffed by trained Human Resource recruiters rather than by the persons who make hiring decisions.

Job Fairs are an excellent opportunity for savvy job seekers to identify potential employers. Some job seekers view a Job Fair as an opportunity to window shop the employers. Job seekers should, however, view each employer contact as a mini-interview. Even though the contact is brief, employers are evaluating each candidate based upon appearance, communication skills and first impressions. These 30-second encounters can result in rejection or can result in further interest by the employer. Your goal is to convince the recruiter that you are an ideal candidate and that they need to give you a complete interview.

Types of Job Fairs

When you see an announcement that a Job Fair is scheduled in your community, you need to determine what type of fair it is. Attending a Job Fair where the employers represent industries that do not have your desired positions is a waste of your time. Explore in advance the companies who are scheduled to attend. Do they offer the type of jobs you seek?

Community Job Fairs

Community Job Fairs are usually sponsored by an organization in the community such as the local newspaper, Chamber of Commerce or One-Stop Career Center. These fairs are open to any local company and are usually large. Often the employers are recruited by the sponsor and may or may not have job openings. They may have a booth simply to give support to the sponsor and the fair. Because these fairs are open to any type of employer, it is important that job seekers do their homework before stepping into the arena. You will find that most of the jobs are sales oriented and/or entry level. If you seek a more skilled job, you may find the fair a waste of your time.

Specialty Job Fairs

These fairs concentrate on jobs that are related to a specific field such as medical or computer technical jobs, or for specific populations of job-seekers like re-entering individuals, veterans and youth. Businesses that are opening a new locations often hold a Job Fair to recruit new employees. In this case the only employer is the sponsor and the only jobs are the jobs that the sponsor has. Retail establishments and hotel/motel properties often recruit using a Job Fair.

Savvy job seekers check to see if the sponsoring company also hires people in their field even though the job is not listed in the announcement. For example, although a Hospital is recruiting primarily nursing staff, the hospital also has maintenance personnel. When you approach the Job Fair recruiter, indicate that you are not seeking a nursing position, but rather you would like information on how you would apply for a maintenance position.

Professional Job Fairs

These Job Fairs are usually sponsored by a local professional association and often target professional jobs such as engineering, accounting or computer programming. There will be many employers. The jobs that are sought are usually high-level jobs and the employers are looking for people with training and experience. If you are looking for a high level job in a professional field, this type of Job Fair is ideal. Your goal is to get names and numbers of people with whom you will make direct contact after the fair. Do not expect to be contacted by companies after the fair.

What to Bring To a Job Fair?

The following are items you need to bring to the Job Fair:

- Résumés. Bring at least twenty copies. Make sure that your résumé stands out.
- Portfolio. You need something to hold your résumés, pens and pencils and a place to store the materials and business cards that you will pick up.
- Note Pad. Bring a pad of paper, pencils, pens and your business cards.

Types of Interviews

There are essentially three different types of interviews that take place at a Job Fair. Some employers will only conduct screening interviews. These interviews may be as short as 30 seconds or last up to ten minutes. Following the screening interview the recruiter may hand you to another person who will conduct a full interview. Be prepared for all three types of interviews.

Screening Interview

Because of limited time and the large number of applicants, most interviews are extremely short, sometimes less than 30 seconds. The employer is interested in gathering résumés and getting a quick look at the candidate. As a candidate, you have to make your case quickly. Be prepared for the first question or a variation of this question, "What kind of position are you looking for?" Tell the interviewer what your goal is. Do not say, "I am looking for a job." If you have done your homework, you will have identified the positions for which the employer is recruiting. Only approach those employers whose positions match your employment goals.

Give recruiters a copy of your résumé and ask what the next step will be. Get business cards and other literature employers may have. Thank them for their time and immediately record on the business cards what you remember about the meeting.

Screening Plus Interview

If the initial screener wants to gather additional information from you, the screener may invite you to sit or may turn you over to another recruiter for a more in-depth interview. These mini interviews last approximately 10 minutes. Be prepared to answer typical job interview questions and to expand on what you have written in your résumé. Conclude the interview in the same way that you would a screening interview. Ask for a business card and literature on the company. Be sure to find out what happens next in the process. Immediately after the interview, write down the name of the company, position sought and other information.

Full Interview

Occasionally employers will have a private interview room somewhere in the building. Applicants who pass the screening and the screening plus interviews are invited to participate in a full job interview. Treat these interviews like any job interview. Often you will be asked the same or similar questions that were asked in the screening interview. Be prepared to give a similar response, because the recruiters will compare notes. Because both you and the employer consider this type of contact a job interview, it is acceptable to ask them questions about the job and the company. Do not ask about salary or benefits, as these questions are reserved for an onsite interview. Conclude the interview in the same way that you concluded the screening plus interview.

How to Work a Job Fair?

Attending a Job Fair can be overwhelming. You will see long lines in front of each employer's booth and you will wonder how you can be noticed. Here are some suggestions to make the Job Fair work for you.

- When you first arrive at the Job Fair take at least the first hour to just walk around.
  - Note where each employer is located. If you were given a program by the sponsor, circle the employers who may have positions of interest to you.
  - As you pass by the booth of each employer, note which employers are conducting just screening interviews and which are conducting screening plus interviews. You may also be able to see if an employer has a separate interviewing room.
  - Rather than get in line for the employers that interest you, simply walk up, or approach from the side, and gather the literature that is on the table. Do not leave your résumé.
- Because the encounter between you and the recruiter is short, you need to leave a positive first impression. This impression will be based primarily on your appearance. Review the Career Success Guide: How to Make a Good First Impression.
- Many Job Fairs offer free seminars which are sometimes conducted by the recruiters. Look in your program and identify those seminars that either may be of interest to you or are being taught by a recruiter from one of the companies that interest you. Go to that seminar and, at the seminar's conclusion, make a point to say something to the instructor/recruiter.
- Armed with the information that you have, exit the Job Fair room and find a quiet place to sit and review your materials. Identify no more than five employers that interest you. Read the literature from each and make notes as to how you can benefit the company.
- It is best to return to the fair after lunch. Most of the applicants will have completed their trek around the hall and will have left.
  - Target the five employers of interest. Go ahead and get in line. As you stand in line note how the recruiter deals with the applicants in front of you.
  - Rehearse your opening line. Link it to something you read in the literature. For example, "Good afternoon. My name is John Doe. I am interested in seeing how my skills and experience in bookkeeping would fit into your new computer accounting system. When I read about it in your brochure, I wanted to learn more about it." Remember, like a TV commercial, you have 30 seconds to convince the recruiter to want to learn more about you.
  - If the recruiter appears to dismiss you, ask, "What is the next step in the process?" Often recruiters will say that they will review the résumés that they receive and get back in touch with those candidates that appear to match their company's requirements.
  - Without being pushy, say to the recruiter, "As you can see from my résumé I am looking for a position in bookkeeping. Who would you suggest that I talk to in your company who is knowledgeable about the bookkeeping positions?"
- Expect no more from a Job Fair than the opportunity to get a list of employers in your community who may have job openings. Add the names to your network list. Review the Career Success Guide: Using Your Network to Locate Job Openings.
- When you get home, take time to write each recruiter a thank you note. It may be the only one they receive. It may also be all that is needed to get them to review your résumé a second time.

HELP WANTED RESPONSE FORM

A comprehensive job search will include responding to help wanted ads and making cold calls. It is important for you to keep track of the ads you respond to and the cold calls that you make by recording the information on the form below.

Be sure to attach to this form:

- A copy of the ad, and
- A copy of the cover letter that you send in response to the ad.

Make as many copies of this form as you need. Review the Career Success guides: How to Respond to Newspaper Want Ads and How To Make Cold Calls.

Help Wanted Response Form

Name of the publication in which the ad appeared: ____________________ Date: ____________

Name of the company (if available): ________________________________

Address to which the response was sent: ________________________________

Name and title (if available): ________________________________

Phone number of company: ____________ Fax number: ____________

Date of your response: ____________ How did you respond (phone, fax,& letter in person): ____________

What materials were submitted with your response (letter, résumé, references, etc.)? ____________

____

What response have you received from the company? ________________________________

Date of Company's response: ________________________________

What follow-up steps are necessary with this employer? ________________________________

____

Help Wanted Response Form

Name of the publication in which the ad appeared: ______________________ Date: ______________

Name of the company (if available): ______________________

Address to which the response was sent: ______________________

Name and title (if available): ______________________

Phone number of company: ______________ Fax number : ______________

Date of your response: ______________ How did you respond (phone, fax,& letter in person): ______________

What materials were submitted with your response (letter, résumé, references, etc.)? ______________

____

What response have you received from the company? ______________________

Date of Company's response: ______________________

What follow-up steps are necessary with this employer? ______________________

____

HOW TO MAKE COLD CALLS

Many job openings are never published or advertised. As a job seeker you are challenged with trying to locate these "hidden" job openings. One of the most effective methods is "cold calling." Cold calling involves contacting an employer without knowing if the employer is hiring or not. The goal in making cold calls is to get an interview. This guide provides information on how to make these contacts.

Steps to Making Cold Calls

Find A Company You Want To Work For

Start by targeting employers who may need your skills and are known to hire reentering persons. Use a computer keyword search or contact your local Chamber of Commerce or local One-Stop Career Center to create a list of employers. From this list of employers identify those who may be interested in you. Review the Career Success guide: Resources for Returning Citizens to learn how to identify potential employers. See if each employer has a web site by "Googling" the name of the company. Then check to see if they have posted job openings and note the contact information.

Your local One-Stop Career Center will be able to help you to identify employers in your area of interest, to research web site information and to check if the employer has any job listings. Review the Career Success Guide: How to Use Your Local One-Stop Career Center.

Find The Person Who Has The Power To Hire You

This requires you to call the company. Do not ask for the Human Resources Department. Unless you are seeking a job in the Human Resources Department, they are not the final hiring authority. In a small company you can simply ask for the person in charge. In a larger company ask for the person in charge of the department in which you want to work.

If you can't get past the receptionist, call back in a couple of days and tell the receptionist that you wish to mail some information to the person in charge of the department where you would like to work. Ask for the name of the individual, the correct spelling of the name and the correct address of the company. With this information send the person a letter stating that you will be calling them within the next week. Then when you speak to the receptionist the next time, you can tell the receptionist the person is expecting your call.

Script Your Call

Write exactly what you will say, but be sure to write it as you would naturally speak. Keep it fairly short, about thirty seconds. Practice reading your script out loud. Here's one possible format:

- Introduce yourself.
- State what you want.
- Explain why they should hire you.
- Ask for an interview.

You may have to ask for the interview several times. Be persistent. It usually pays off. If, however, you aren't successful in getting an interview, try to get another good lead.

Sample Scripts for Different Occasions

- May I please speak to the person in charge of the engineering department?
- I would like to send some information to the person in charge of the engineering department. Could you please tell me their name and address? How is the name spelled?
- Hello, Ms. Jones, my name is Joe Smith. I am interested in a position as a machinist.
- I worked as a machinist for the Wilson Company for three years. Prior to that, I ran my own small engine repair shop for five years. I went to Samuels Technology Institute and graduated at the top of my class. I am hard-working and reliable. I would like to talk to you about the Widget Company. When would be a good time to meet? Or Could I set a time to meet with you?
- I understand that you won't be hiring in the foreseeable future. Do you, however, know of anyone who is? Do you have their phone number? Can I tell them you suggested that I call?

When you're Nervous.

Many people are nervous about making cold calls. This is because we don't like immediate rejection. It is estimated that it takes between ten and fifteen cold calls to get one interview. It sounds like a lot of failure, but it shouldn't take more than a couple of hours to make those calls. If you are nervous, try some of the following:

- Remember, you're not asking for a job, but offering the potential employer something they need - you!
- Try to make your voice lower than it usually is, and speak more slowly too. We tend to speak faster and at a higher pitch when we're nervous.
- Keep to your script and practice it before you call.

Calling Someone You Know.

Most people are more comfortable calling someone they know. If you know the person with the power to hire you, you're very lucky and should definitely use your connection with that person to get yourself an interview. Review the Career Success Guide: Using Your Network to Locate Job Openings.

You Should Still Use Your Script.

Before you start your script, talk informally with the person about whatever common links you have. If you are only an acquaintance, explain how you know the person so they can place your name.

If You Are Calling On A Referral, This Is The Time To Mention The Person Who Suggested You Call Them.

This will make the person you're calling more likely to listen to you. Having someone they know endorse you is a big selling point for most employers. In addition, they will feel like they are doing that person a favor by talking to you and will be more willing to spend time talking with you.

Once You Have Established A Connection With The Person, Go Back To Your Script.

As you are more familiar with someone you know than with a stranger, you might need to alter it beforehand to make sure the wording isn't too formal or stiff. Hello, Ms. Jones, this is Joe Smith. Our children play soccer together.

Sample Scripts

- Hello, Ms. Jones, my name is Joe Smith. Mary Williams suggested that I call you.
- I would like to talk to you about a position as a machinist with the Widget Company. Do you have a few minutes?
- Ms. Jones? My name is Joe Smith. I wrote you a letter about setting up a meeting with you to talk about a position as a machinist with the Widget Company.

Keep Track Of Your Calls.

Do not rely on your memory. Immediately after you complete the cold call make a note of the person's name, company name, date that you called and a summary of the call.

Using Cold Calls, Letters and E-Mails

Sending a "cold letter" prior to making your call can give you your introduction.

In your letter, state what positions you are interested in and why you would be a good hire for those positions - the same points you put in your script. Include your résumé, if you like, and state that you will be calling them in a few days.

Sending cold e-mails.

If you are able to obtain the hiring person's e-mail address, you may send them an e-mail. Make the message short and to the point. Be sure to include your e-mail address, as many workers today use this medium for most of their correspondence. Be aware that some companies do not accept e-mails from unknown addresses, so don't be offended if your e-mail gets rejected by the company's computer.

When you call, mention the letter and again highlight the information you wrote in your letter.

Remember, your goal is to get an interview!

You should send a letter after you call someone.

In the "thank you note," thank them for their time and confirm the e date and time of your interview. If you didn't get an interview, you should send a letter anyway, thanking them for taking the time to talk to you. Be sure to enclose a copy of your résumé. Review the Career Success Guide: How to Write a Thank You Note.

In your job search...

- Cold calling may be the only way for you to approach companies where you would like to work but where you don't have a contact. It is much more effective than simply sending your résumé to the personnel department.
- Research target employers before you call. Consider the type of job you're looking for and only call companies who would be likely to hire people into those positions. A fast food restaurant wouldn't be a good choice for a sales job. You'll be more successful calling a retail store.
- Don't forget to network! Once you have identified companies you want to call, ask around to see if you have any connections you can use to avoid making a completely cold call. Review the Career Success Guide: Using Your Network to Locate Job Openings.
- Use your local One-Stop Career Center as a resource. It can provide lists of companies in the area, information on the companies and give you suggestions on companies that employ workers with your skills and background. Review the Career Success Guide: How to Use Your Local One-Stop Career Center.

COLD CALL TELEPHONE LOG

Prepare yourself before you make a telephone call to a potential employer. Use a computer record, card or log similar to the format below to write down the points you want to make before you make the call. Have your form in front of you when you make the call. Record the information you get from the call on the form. You will be more effective and less nervous during your calls if you are prepared. Review the Career Success guide: How to Make Cold Calls. After you have completed the form, file the form in a folder. Arrange the forms alphabetically in the folder by the company's name so that you will be able to retrieve the form quickly.

Cold Call Log

Name of Employer: ______________________ Phone Number: ______________

Address: ______________________

Contact Person: ______________________ Title: ______________

Receptionist's or Secretary's Name: ______________________

Referred by: ______________________

Position I am interested in: ______________________

Reason for calling: ______________________

____

____

____

Key points to make:

____

____

____

____

Date of call: ______________________

If contact was unavailable, date to call back: ______________________

Results of call: ______________________

____

____

____

Follow-up steps needed: ______________________

____

____

____

Cold Call Log

Name of Employer: ______________________ Phone Number: ______________

Address: ______________________

Contact Person: ______________________ Title: ______________

Receptionist's or Secretary's Name: ______________________

Referred by: ______________________

Position I am interested in: ______________________

Reason for calling: ______________________

____

____

____

Key points to make:

____

____

____

____

Date of call: ______________________

If contact was unavailable, date to call back: ______________________

Results of call: ______________________

____

____

____

Follow-up steps needed: ______________________

____

____

____

HOW TO GET INFORMATION ABOUT JOBS IN YOUR AREA

In order to make appropriate career and job decisions, it is important to become knowledgeable about the world of work. As a Returning Citizens it is critical that you have a clear understanding of the job market in your local community. This will be extremely beneficial during your job search. Labor market information includes data about unemployment and employment, salary information, employment trends, industry trends and where the possible job openings exist. Returning Citizens may also find that there are organizations in their community that specialize in locating jobs for Returning Citizens.

Population Trends

The growth or decline of population in a certain geographic area is an indicator of the level of economic health of the area. Steady increases in population usually indicate the availability of employment in an area. If the population is steadily decreasing, the major employers may be declining and jobs may be scarce.

Researching population levels, age ranges of the population and distribution of the population will also help you evaluate which industries and services will be in demand.

Education Levels

The education and training that are necessary for particular jobs are influenced by the educational levels of the available workforce. If there is a generally high level of advanced education among the resident population, the educational levels required for even entry-level jobs may increase. It is important, therefore to compare your level of education or training to that of the available workforce of the area.

Major Employers

Research who the major employers are, the number of people they employ, the type of product or service they offer, their growth or decline, salaries, benefits, working environment, their history on hiring ex-offenders and a contact person.

If possible, find out the number of job openings in your field compared to the number of residents who also work in that field, in order to assess the availability of jobs that use your skills.

National labor market trends indicate that most of the job growth is with small companies, companies with fewer than 100 employees. Therefore, it is valuable to also gather information about the smaller businesses in an area.

Salary Levels

Analyze the local salary ranges that are available in your career field. It will help you determine the feasibility of meeting your economic goals while living in that location.

Growth by Industries and Occupational Areas

The major industries of an area will indicate the occupational categories where the majority of employment opportunities are. These industries also help determine the economic health of an area. If the major industries are in occupational areas that are presently growing and projected to grow in the future, it is likely that the economic health of an area will remain strong and jobs will be available. If, however, these industries are in decline, new employers will need to become available in order to maintain high employment rates.

Cost Of Living

The cost of living in a particular area will determine the salary that is necessary to maintain your lifestyle in that area. Cost of living can be based on many factors, but the most important living expenses to consider are: state income taxes, state and local sales taxes, property taxes, rent or mortgage, utilities, transportation, food, health care and recreation.

Employment/Unemployment Statistics

The unemployment rate for a town is a useful guideline of the economic health of an area, the demand for services, the availability of jobs and the competition for available jobs. Unemployment is affected by a variety of factors and occurs in different ways. The Department of Labor divides unemployment into four categories:

1) Seasonal Unemployment is very regular and predictable. It occurs at the same time each year. Employees who work in jobs specific to a season (ski resort workers, migrant farm laborers, swimming coaches, etc.) often experience seasonal unemployment. If your career is specific to a season, you may need to find another seasonal job during your period of unemployment or you may need to relocate each season. For example, if you are a landscape worker, you will find jobs available in the northern states in the summer and in the southern states in the winter.
2) Cyclical Unemployment occurs as a result of fluctuations in the economic activity of businesses. When an industry is growing and its products or services are in demand, employment in that industry will be high. If demand decreases, employment also decreases. Check the major industries of an area in order to project the possibility of cyclical unemployment.
3) Structural Unemployment occurs when the basic nature of the economy changes and the skills that workers have are no longer in demand. Labor market trends project that many workers will need to upgrade their skills and/or education in order not to experience structural unemployment. Evaluate the education and training levels of the population of an area in comparison to your own in order to determine your likelihood of structural unemployment. Be willing to upgrade your education or training if necessary.
4) Frictional Unemployment is the largest single cause of unemployment. Frictional unemployment is largely due to inefficiencies in the labor market. Job openings exist, workers have the necessary skills, but the jobs remain unfilled due to the length of time it takes job seekers to find out about openings, apply and be hired. The most effective way to avoid frictional unemployment is to become skilled at job-hunting techniques, particularly networking. The process of gathering local labor market information is an ideal way to begin networking in an area.

Where to Find Local Labor Market Information

The library

Your local library is an excellent source of information about the local labor market. Libraries usually have Internet access, career information centers and computer terminals set up specifically to access economic development information and the web sites of local employers. There are a variety of books and periodicals that are useful in gathering information about the areas labor market. General information is available through books such as: Career Guide to America's Top Industries, the U.S. Reference librarians can be very helpful in assisting you.

Industrial Outlook and Places Rated Almanac. Industry-specific and local information is available through trade magazines, guides to individual employers and articles in local newspapers and Associations lists thousands of specialized professional associations with addresses. The ones that are relevant to your industry can provide newsletters and/or other information that will be useful.

One-Stop Career Centers

Your local One-Stop Career Center has information about job openings, local unemployment rates, population data, area wages, Bureau of Labor statistics and other information. Career Centers will have computer terminals available to access information and people to offer assistance. Review the Career Success Guide: How to Use Your Local One-Stop Career Center.

Chambers of Commerce

The local Chamber of Commerce can provide information about major employers in the area, web site addresses for employers, population trends, economic development plans and general information about an area. Information is usually free or available at a nominal charge.

Economic Development offices

Many cities and county governments have offices of economic development which can provide information about an area, including population statistics, educational levels, cost of living, major employers, focal industries, employment trends, unemployment rates, salary levels, transportation and the economic development plans for an area.

Information for the formerly incarcerated

There are many organizations that provide job information specifically for ex-offenders. These organizations are listed in the Career Success Guide: Job Search Tips for Returning Citizens.

People

Local residents are often one of the greatest resources for information about the labor market of an area. People who work in the industry in which you are interested, for the employer you are investigating, in city and county government, in placement offices, or in any organization that assists people with employment, are good contacts.

While gathering information from local residents, begin the process of networking. People are generally glad to share information if you approach them politely. Asking for information provides you with an opportunity to discuss your skills and interests and leave a positive impression.

Review the Career Success Guides: How to Use Your Network to Locate Job Openings and How to Acquire Job Information by Interviewing, for more information about the process of building a network and asking for help with your employment needs.

On-Line Resources for Labor Market Information

Much of the information about occupations, specific industries, companies and local labor markets is available through computer on-line services. Many employers have web sites that provide information about their company and list available job openings. If you do not have access to a computer and the Internet, most libraries and One-Stop Career Centers provide free access. Review the Career Success Guide: How to Use the Internet in Your Job Search for addresses of useful on-line career resources.

Some useful World Wide Web sites to review are:

- Department of Labor www.dol.gov
- Bureau of Labor Statistics www.bls.gov
- Career Builder www.careerbuilder.com
- Online Career Center www.monster.com
- Career Web www.employmentguide.com
- Internet job search www.rileyguide.com

Information on the Internet changes daily. In order to gather the most up-to-date information and to research new web sites, consider doing an on-line search using such key words as: jobs, career, salaries, and jobs for ex-offenders and the name of the companies that interest you, etc.

HOW TO ACQUIRE JOB INFORMATION BY INTERVIEWING

An information interview is a meeting between you and someone whose career field or occupation interests you. Talking to people in order to gain information can be one of the most effective ways to learn what you need to know about an occupation or career field. There are important differences between a job interview and an information interview: During the information interview you ask questions in order to evaluate the job or company. In a job interview, the company representative asks you questions to determine whether or not you are appropriate for the job. Obviously you will only be able to have an informational interview after you have been released.

Information Interviews Are Valuable Because:

- They are powerful investigative tools to help you find out more about the labor market.
- They reveal up-to-date information about careers from someone who is in the field.
- You can use them to evaluate possible careers and eliminate those that are unsuitable. Information interviews increase your chances of finding a career that is right for you.
- They help you to evaluate companies and learn what they do and who they hire. You can get the latest information about the future of the field and the company.
- They help you become familiar with the field, its jargon and the important issues.
- They help you expand your network. After you've done several information interviews and you're sure this career is for you, you can come back to your contacts and turn them into networking opportunities.
- They a low-pressure way of practicing self-marketing skills. It gives you the chance to practice presenting yourself professionally in the field that interests you.
- They can give you a sense of how employers will react to you as a re-entering citizen.

You're Ready to Do an Information Interview When:

- You've read books and articles about the occupation or field and you feel it might be the career for you.
- You've found that trade or professional journals hold your interest.
- You've gone to trade shows or conferences and the people you've met there seemed to share many of your views or interests.
- You've met someone informally who told you about their job and it sounds like the job for you.

The Golden Rule for Information Interviews

You must never go into an information interview secretly hoping to turn it into a job interview. Be honest with yourself and the person you are interviewing. You're there just to gather information.

Where Do I Find Potential Contacts?

Job seekers often find it difficult to identify a person with whom they can talk to about the job they seek. The first step is to identify the career field of interest. You need to be specific; *I want to talk to someone who is a foreign car mechanic.* Here are some ways to identify potential people to contact:

- Ask family members, friends, neighbors and former employers if they know someone in the selected occupation.
- Contact former teachers and guidance counselors. They may have a list of former students who are working in your selected occupation.
- Use the telephone or email to contact trade and professional associations that are related to your selected occupation. Ask them for a name of a person who would be willing to talk to you about the field.
- Talk to a counselor at your local One-Stop Career Center.

How Do I Set Up The Meeting?

1. Telephone or write (e-mail is acceptable) the person and explain your request. Ask for a 15-minute appointment. Indicate clearly that you are seeking information and help and that you are not requesting a job interview. Follow the letter or e-mail with a telephone call five days after sending the letter or e-mail to confirm your appointment date and time.
2. Introduce yourself, citing that the referral person provided his or her name.
3. Again explain the purpose of the information interview. Try to schedule a 20- 30 minute appointment. The interview can be conducted in person or by telephone. If the contact is unable or unwilling to schedule the appointment, ask if there might be someone else in the company who would be able to talk to you about the career field.
4. It is possible that the contact person will want to conduct the interview at that time over the telephone. It is critical, then, that you be prepared by having your questions ready.
5. If you are scheduling an on-site visit be sure to find out the location of the person's office and where you should park.

Use the Opportunity

Use the opportunity to assess how employers will react to your having been incarcerated. Ask the person with whom you are interviewing to give you counsel on how you should approach employers. If you are open about discussing your incarceration and are sincere in wanting to move forward with your life, they will sense this and give you an honest answer.

The Information Interview

- Remember that you are conducting the interview to get information that will help you make decisions concerning your career and occupation. You are not there to ask for a job.
- Be very mindful of the time. You asked for 15-20 minutes of the person's time. Do not exceed this time limit unless the interviewee offers to continue the interview.
- You'll know the interview is going well when the other person is doing most of the talking, while you're steering the course of conversation. To encourage the other person to relax and open up, do what journalists and investigative reporters do: Make your questions open- ended. Frame questions so that they begin with one of 7 key words: What, when, why, who, where, which and how. Questions that start with one of these words cannot be answered by yes or no.
- Don't interrogate. Maintain a conversational style. Use subtle prompts, such as an occasional nod of the head, while maintaining eye contact to indicate that you're listening and want to know more.
- Create a list of questions before you arrive for the interview. Below are some questions you could ask. You will probably want to modify them to fit your particular situation.
- During the interview, your questions may come in any order as the conversation unfolds. The best interviews can seem haphazard, but by the end you should have answers to all the questions on your list.

Sample Questions If You Are Seeking Information About A Career:

- How did you get into this field?
- What do you like most about your job? What do you like least?
- What is your typical day like?
- What are the responsibilities of your job?
- Are these duties the same for everyone with this job title?
- In terms of talent and personality, what kind of individual would be best suited for this kind of job?
- What are the prospects for someone entering your field today?
- What advice would you give me for locating and obtaining a job in this field?
- What sources of information would you recommend (magazines, journals, etc.?)
- What kind of programs or activities does your office perform?
- What is the median salary in your occupation?
- What seem to be recurring problems for people in your field?
- What kind of education do you need?
- What rewards does your job offer?
- What are other related career fields?
- What are some other settings in which people in this occupation are found?
- What kind of training is required? Are any license or other qualifications required?
- What is the employment outlook?
- What would be a typical career path in this field?

Sample Questions If You Are Seeking Information About A Company:

- For what position would this company hire someone with my qualifications?
- If I were hired by this company, what might I expect to be doing over the next three to five years?
- How much freedom do employees have to determine their own job movement and responsibilities?
- How does the company facilitate employees staying current in their fields? How are employees encouraged to continue their professional development over an extended period of time?
- What kind of training is provided for each level of employee? Do you have or sponsor any continuing education programs for employees?
- What are management's basic philosophies in managing the business and employees?
- What are the company's values? What does the company stand for?
- What is the company's mission statement?
- How are the company's values reflected in everyday activities?
- Why is the work environment what it is (formal/casual, elegant/simple)?
- What kind of people are most successful or satisfied at your company?
- Who do you consider to be your major competitors? How would you evaluate your success in the competition?
- What is your company's compensation philosophy compared with other companies? How are individual salary increases determined?

After The Interview:

Ask yourself:

- Do I understand what people do on this job?
- Does this person use the skills that I have?
- If I want to work in this field, what do I need to do to become qualified?
- If it is not the field for me, where do I go next?
- Would I enjoy working for this company?
- How do my skills meet the needs of the company?
- If I want to work here, who do I contact next?
- If I don't want to work for this company, where do I go next?

Send the interviewee a thank you note. In the note, express your appreciation again for their time. Emphasize that they have assisted you in making important career decisions. See the Career Success Guide: How to Write a Thank You Note.

TRULINCS Friendly! info@ReentryEssentials.org www.ReentryEssentials.org 347.973.0004 2609 East 14 Street, Suite 1018, Brooklyn, NY 11235-3915

HOW TO RESEARCH THE JOB & THE EMPLOYER

Finding out everything you can about a job and a company before you apply can save you a lot of wasted time. Deciding whether a job is worth applying for will help you focus on only those job openings that will work best for you. Your goal is to make the best use of your time during your job search. One way to do this is to decide before you apply whether the job and the company are a good fit for you. If you do this, you will spend your time in high-value activities that give you a greater payoff for the time and energy that you invest. The Internet has made this task simple and easy.

Why Do Research?

- To spend your time wisely.
- To find out about job openings.
- To learn about the job.
- To learn about benefits.
- To show interest and initiative.
- To learn about the company.
- To prepare for the interview.

Get Organized

- To keep a paper record, make copies of both sides of this guide. Use the forms to help you organize your information. Set up a simple filing system, using a separate folder for each potential job.
- If you are proficient with a computer spreadsheet software program, record the information by setting up columns for each desired data element like company name. This will allow you to sort and filter your data as you wish.
- Whichever method you use, keep your information close to the telephone.

1. What does the person do each day?
2. Usual starting salary.
3. Which benefits are included?
4. Are there opportunities for advancement?
5. Is the work inside or outside? Noisy or quiet? Office or shop floor?
6. To whom will you report?
7. From whom did you obtain this information?

THE JOB

Job Title ____________ Date Completed ____________

(1) Job Duty ______________________________

____

____

(2) Salary/Wage $ ________ Month or $ ________ /Hour

Hours of Work Days: Sun Mon Tues Wed Thur Fri Sat Hours ________

(3) Benefits:

________ Health Insurance ________ Sick Leave (Days per ________

________ Life Insurance ________ Training Provided by the Employer

________ Disability Insurance ________ Vacation (Days per) ________

________ Other ________ ________ Other ________

(4) Promotion Opportunities ______________________________

(5) Work Environment ______________________________

(6) Supervisor's Name ______________________________

(7) Source of Information ______________________________

1. Mailing address for sending correspondence.
2. Important for quick access, and to fax résumés, letters, references, etc.
3. Manufacturing, construction, legal services, retail, etc.
4. The primary products produced or services delivered.
5. Where you will be working (if different from address above).
6. Knowing the competition shows the interviewer that you've done your homework.
7. If employees leave the company on a regular basis, this may not be a good place to work.
8. Find out the reasons why they leave.

THE COMPANY

Company Name ______________________

(1) Address ______________________

____

City ____________ State ____________ Zip ____________

(2) Telephone ____________ Fax ____________

Web Site ______________________

Contact Person ______________________

Email Address of Contact Person ______________________

(3) Industry or Type of Business ______________________

(4) Products or Services ______________________

(5) Location of other Plants/Offices/Facilities ______________________

(6) Competitors ______________________

(7) Employee Turnover ______________________

Source of Information ______________________

Contact Dates ____________ ____________ ____________

Where to Find This Information

Internet (Company website, Facebook page, etc.) See Internet resources below.

- Local One-Stop Career Center
- Libraries
- Company annual reports
- Company visits
- Informational interviews
- Observation of employees leaving work
- Current and former employees
- Newspapers
- Business organizations (Chamber of Commerce, etc.)
- Industry directories

Using the Information in Your Job Search

- Decide which job openings interest you.
- Complete an information sheet for each job opening and company that interests you.
- Compare this information with your interests, knowledge, skills, abilities, salary/fringe requirements and other needs.
- Decide whether it is worth your time to apply for this job.
  - If the answer is "no," don't waste your time.
  - If the answer is "yes," go for it!

WHAT ARE EMPLOYEE BENEFITS?

Employee benefits are called fringe benefits because they are compensation that is provided by the employer that is in addition to your salary. Benefit packages vary from employer to employer and can be as much as 35% of the employee's wages.

Typical Employee Benefits

Retirement/Pension Plans

Social Security is a federally mandated retirement program. The federal government requires all employers to withhold 6.2% of an employee's salary and deposit the amount with the Social Security Administration. Your employer is also required to match your contribution for a total contribution of 12.4% of your salary. Social Security retirement benefits are available to anyone who has worked under the system for at least 10 years. A retiree can currently receive the highest benefit starting at approximately age 66. Check with the Social Security Administration for the current age when a person can become eligible for full benefits. Reduced benefits are available as early as age 62.

Employers are also required to withhold 1.45% of your salary as a contribution to the federal Medicare program. Medicare is a government-sponsored medical plan for retirees over 65 years old.

Pensions are sums of money paid regularly to retired workers by the company as a retirement benefit. Pensions are generated from contributions to a pension fund made by the employer during the employee's working years. The amount of a pension is usually figured as a percentage of an employee's salary.

401(k) and 403(b) plans enable a portion of an employee's salary, and the income tax that would have been paid on that amount, to be contributed to a retirement plan. All taxes on the earnings from the plan are deferred until the person withdraws funds from the account. Employers may or may not make matching contributions to these types of plans. These plans have many rules and restrictions. It is important, therefore, that the employee discuss these rules and restrictions with the employer before making any withdrawals.

Many types of pension, retirement and tax-deferred savings plans are available from employers. The best way to find out about your employer's retirement benefits is to speak with a benefits officer. Some questions to ask are:

- What type of pension or retirement plans are available?
- How is the money from my plan distributed when I leave?
- How long does it take for me to become vested? When do you become vested (when you own the funds) in the account?
- What types of tax-deferred savings/pension plans are available to me as an employee?
- Does my employer match my contributions to a tax-deferred savings/pension plan?

Health Insurance

Employers often offer access to group health insurance plans as a benefit for their employees and their families. Participation in a group health insurance plan, particularly if the premiums are paid by the employer, allows an employee significant savings toward the cost of health care.

> The Affordable Health Care Act of 2010 (sometimes called Obamacare) will change many provisions of company provided health care plans. Because the rules and regulations are evolving, it is critical that employees check with their employer concerning their health care benefits and cost.

Many group health insurance plans now offered by employers are "managed care" plans. These types of plans define the health services that are covered. Managed care plans also designate the providers that are qualified to be used by the participants in the plan. The plans usually have a deductible that an individual must pay before coverage begins, and/or an amount of co-payment that is required for a given service. It is important to be aware of the type of health insurance plan that your employer offers as a benefit and how the plan works.

Employee health insurance plans can cover such services as: hospital and medical services, dental services, vision services and mental health services. Employers may cover the cost of health insurance premiums for the employee, the employee and one family member or the employee's entire family. The option of participating in a group plan may also be available for a certain length of time after an employee has terminated employment.

Additional types of insurance that may be offered by an employer as an employee benefit are: life insurance, accidental death insurance, disability insurance, long-term care insurance and major medical.

Information about an employer's insurance plans can be obtained from a benefits officer or a representative of the insurance companies that provide the plans. Often the plans are explained in the Employee's Handbook which is provided at the new hire orientation meeting. Some important questions to ask are:

- What services are covered by my health insurance plan?
- Does the employer cover the cost of the premium for family members? If so, which family members? If not, what is the cost of insuring additional family members?
- What is the deductible or co-payment designated by my health insurance?
- Am I eligible to participate in the health insurance plan after I leave employment? If so, for how long?
- Is long-term-care insurance available to employees?
- What amount and type of life insurance is available to employees?

Worker's Compensation

Employers are required to purchase Worker's Compensation Insurance for all of their employees. If employees are injured on the job, they may be eligible for paid leave, compensation and medical payments until they are able to return to work.

Paid Leave

The most common employee benefit is paid leave. There are a number of types of paid leave. These benefits are optional and will vary from employer to employer. Your benefits officer can explain the company's policy for each of type of paid absence from work.

Annual/Vacation Leave

Annual or vacation leave is the number of days designated per year that an employee may take off without providing a reason for their absence. The number of annual leave days is often determined by the length of time an employee has worked for the company.

Sick Leave

Sick leave days are designated for use when an employee is unable to work for health reasons. Sick leave usually accrues on a monthly basis.

Family Sick Leave

Family sick leave days can be used to care for family members who are ill. An individual's sick leave may be considered separate from or included with family sick leave.

Holidays

Employers usually have certain days (such as Christmas or New Year's Day) designated as paid holidays. Retail businesses are the least likely to offer this benefit as they frequently operate during holidays.

Maternity Leave / Family Leave

Maternity leave is time designated to be used by a worker during the birth and early infancy of a child. Family leave may be available to both parents and may or may not be fully compensated by an employer.

Compensatory Time

Compensatory or "comp" time is leave time that is given instead of additional salary. Comp time is usually given in exchange for working more than the required hours in a designated time period.

The number of leave days usually is calculated by an employer at the beginning of each year of employment. It is important to be aware of what leave is available, the type of leave that is designated and whether leave days that are unused are carried over and available to be used in subsequent years. It is also important to determine whether compensation is provided for annual or sick leave that is unused when an employee leaves employment.

Additional Benefits Offered By Some Employers

Education

Some employers cover the cost of work related course work and educational degree programs.

Professional Development

The cost of seminars, conferences and training that are relevant to one's work may be covered by employers.

Travel

The cost of business-related travel, meals, accommodations and vehicles is sometimes paid as a benefit.

Child care

Child care is a significant cost for working parents. Some employers contribute toward the cost of child care or offer access to subsidized on-site child care facilities.

Employee Discounts

Employees may be eligible for discounts on the products that their employer sells or manufactures. This is a common benefit offered by employers in retail businesses.

Stock Options

Stock in the company is sometimes given as an item of compensation to employees. Some employers will match the number of their company's stock purchased by an employee.

Flexible Scheduling

More employers are beginning to offer employees scheduling options other than the standard five-day, forty-hour week. A growing number of employers are also allowing employees to work from their home using the computer.

As an individual's and family's needs change, employers are developing various benefit packages to respond to these needs. Some employers are willing to respond to valued employees' needs with creative benefit packages. It is important to ask about, understand and evaluate what benefits are available from an employer. If a certain benefit that is important to you is not identified as available (i.e., a flexible schedule), it may be worth discussing this with your employer to determine whether you can negotiate for it.

Although part-time work is an option for many employees, employers are slow to offer benefits to part-time workers. Some companies offer reduced benefits to part-time employees. If you are considering part-time employment, it is important to inquire what, if any, benefits are available to you.

HOW TO COMPLETE A JOB APPLICATION

The job application is a written, structured one-way form of communication between the job applicant and the employer. The completed application will often make the crucial difference in whether or not an applicant is seriously considered for an interview and employment by the employer. When an employer reviews an application, four things are looked at: (1) the information given by the applicant, (2) the skills that the applicant claims to possess, (3) how clearly the applicant answered the questions, and (4) the appearance of the application. Since you may be completing applications even before you are released, it is important that you understand how to complete a job application.

The Job Application Is Used By:

The employer . . .

- To see if the applicant is right for the company and the job.
- To screen out applicants.
- To identify applicants who (1) match possible job openings, (2) have the ability to perform the tasks required on the job, and (3) demonstrate that they will do the job.

The applicant . . .

- To make a good first impression.
- To communicate to the employer (1) the type of job they desire, (2) their educational background and skills possessed, and (3) their employment history.
- To get an interview.

Since employers use the application to screen out applicants, and applicants want to be screened-in (get an interview), it is critical that the applicant provides information that helps get the application placed in the "To-Be-Interviewed" pile.

To Complete An Application You Will Need To Provide The Following Information About Yourself:

- Personal Information
- Education and Training History
- References
- Employment History
- Military Experience

Questions You Do Not Want To Answer

All of us have experienced one or more events in our work and/or personal lives that we would just as soon keep to ourselves. Occasionally, the application forces us to reveal that event. Remember, the job application is a legal document. Falsifying information or failing to reveal requested information either on the application or in the interview can be grounds for dismissal.

Review the Career Success Guide: How Do I Deal With Negative Information.

Questions about Your Conviction(s)

A common question on job application forms is "Have you ever been convicted of a crime?" You need to be honest about this fact, but you also don't want to give more detail than is being asked for. If you do not answer this question truthfully, an employer will have reason to question your honesty and may end the hiring process.

If asked about your criminal background, write "Will discuss at interview." Work with a career advisor or your parole officer to rehearse your explanation. Read each question on the application carefully and only give the information requested. For instance, if an application asks you to list all convictions or all offenses, you should list both criminal (felony and misdemeanor) and non-criminal (violations) convictions. Do not list any arrest that was not followed by a conviction.

Another approach to dealing with this question is to submit a Summary Statement with your application. Review the Career Success Guide: How Do I Deal with Negative Information, for more information on what to include in the statement.

Illegal Questions

Laws are specific about what factors an employer cannot use in making hiring decisions. These factors are not supposed to be addressed on the application or in the interview. However, out-of-date job applications are used by some employers. These applications may still request this information. If such information is requested, it is best to leave the response blank. Questions that address age, race, gender, sexual orientation, religion, national origin, handicaps or other personal information are generally illegal.

There are situations, however, where asking one or more of these questions is legal and expected. For example, it is acceptable to ask an applicant their sex if the job is to model women's clothing. Also, some employers may request this information on a separate form. In these cases, the employer is required to state that the information is for data-gathering purposes only. If in doubt, indicate that you will complete the information after you have been offered employment.

References

Employers contact references usually only after they have completed the interview, in order to document the information supplied by the applicant in their application and during the interview. Since the employer is seeking to confirm the information given in the application, it is critical that the applicant list references who can and will supply that information. Employers are interested in information that can be given by former supervisors and/or teachers. Before listing a person as a reference, you need to contact that person and ask their permission.

- When you talk to the reference, make sure you will get a favorable recommendation. Ask what they might say to the employer when the employer calls or writes.
- If you know someone who is employed with the employer, be sure to ask if you can list that person as a personal reference. Employers like to hire people who are known by their employees.

Before proceeding further, locate the four-page Career Success Guides: Sample Blank Employment Application and the Sample Completed Employment Application. Complete one of the blank sample applications using the completed application as a guide. Fill out the application in pencil so you will be able to make changes and refine your answers. Be sure to answer every question.

Helpful Hints for Completing Your Job Application

- Print your responses carefully. Appearance counts! When completing a real application use a ballpoint pen (not a pencil).
- You must enter a telephone number when requested. This needs to be a phone that is answered during the day, because this is when employers call. If you have a cell phone, be sure to provide that number on the application. If you don't have a telephone, ask a relative or friend if you can use their number. Make sure they agree and will take messages. This may present a problem if you are still incarcerated. Ask a prison official for assistance and suggestions on how you can stay in contact with prospective employers.
- If asked to provide an expected pay rate or salary, respond with either "negotiable" or your last pay rate. If you know what the job pays, and are willing to accept that rate, enter that amount.
- Provide accurate information on your prior employment. Get current and former employer addresses and telephone numbers from the phone book or by looking them up on the Internet.
- Give employment information on all jobs during the past twenty years, beginning with your current or last job. If you have a gap in your employment, place an asterisk (*) between the two jobs and explain the time-gap at the bottom of the page or in the space provided for Additional Information.
- Always give a positive reason why you left your jobs. Don't put "the boss was a jerk", or "I got fired for missing too much work." It is better to say that "I wanted a job with more security", or "I was laid off because of my lack of seniority."
- You can explain terminations during the interview.
- If asked to list job duties and/or skills, be specific and relate them to the job that you are seeking.

Employers make inferences (that are not always accurate) from the information supplied by the applicant. Therefore, think through every response, putting yourself in the employer's shoes. Ask yourself, "What impression will this response give the employer?"

Using the Application in Your Job Search

Nearly every employer requires a completed application as a condition of employment, even if they have a résumé on file. Many employers require a completed application before they will schedule an interview.

Step 1: Complete the Career Success Guide: Sample Blank Employment Application. Answer every question by entering the response or N/A if not applicable to you. Use a pencil so that you can correct mistakes and refine your answers. Review your completed application with a spouse and/or friend to double check for accuracy, spelling, grammar and wording.

Step 2: If you have access to a typewriter (or you have a friend who does), type your responses on a second Sample Blank Employment Application. If you don't have access to a typewriter, then legibly print the responses on a blank Sample Blank Employment Application using a ballpoint pen. Make at least ten copies of your completed application.

Step 3: Have at least five copies of your completed Sample Blank Employment Application with you at all times. Place the applications in a folder so that they do not get wrinkled or smudged. A generic application can often substitute for a résumé.

Step 4: When an employer asks you to complete an application, use your completed Sample Blank Employment Application as a guide. Carefully transfer the information from your application to the employer's application. Take your time completing the application. If you are pushed for time, ask to take the application home and return it the next day. If you make a mistake, and the mistake cannot be neatly corrected, ask for a new application and start over. Completing a sloppy, inaccurate application will result in your being screened out 99% of the time! Use the opportunity to tell the employer why you are the ideal person for the job. Tell them what they want to know about you; specifically, tell them what kind of job you want, the skills and training that you have to support that job and that you will be a good employee (honest, dependable, willing to learn and able to get along with others).

Step 5: When you give the completed application to the employer, ask for the next step in the process. Get the name and telephone number of the person who takes your completed application (get a business card, if available). Ask how often you need to update your application.

Step 6: If you have not heard from the employer in 30 days, return and ask if you can update your application. When a job opens up, employers usually review only applications filed within the last 30 days, so you want your application put into the "To-Be-Interviewed" pile.

Step 7: Review your completed Sample Blank Employment Application every week. Make corrections, additions and subtractions as needed.

SAMPLE BLANK EMPLOYMENT APPLICATION

Sample Company is an equal opportunity employer and fully subscribes to the principles of equal employment. All applicants and employees are considered for hire and promotion without regard to race, color, religion, gender, national origin, age, handicap or status as a veteran.

Directions: Complete all questions. Print or type responses. If unable to complete a response in the space provided, complete your answer in the space provided in item 30 on page 4.

1. Kind of position or job for which you are applying (give the job title or job announcement number)

2. Other positions for which you would like to be considered

3. Name (Last, First, Middle)

4. Street address (No P.O. Box Numbers)	5. Apartment number	
6. City	7. State	8. Zip
9. If mailing address is different, provide address	10. E-mail address	
11. Telephone number	12. Cell phone number	

13. Have you ever been employed by this company? ☐ Yes ☐ No

If yes, provide dates of employment: From: Month ________ Yr ________ to Month ________ Yr________

14. What starting salary would be acceptable to you? Per hour ________ Per month ________

15. When would be the earliest date that you would be available to start work?

Month ________ Day________ Yr ________

16. Are you available for:	Yes	No
Part-time work	☐	☐
To relocate	☐	☐
Overnight travel	☐	☐

17. Would you consider temporary work of:	Yes	No
Less than 3 months	☐	☐
3 - 6 months	☐	☐
9 - 12 months	☐	☐

18. Hours preferred: No preference ☐ or Start work at ________ (enter time of day).
Days of the week: No preference ☐ or Circle the days of the week that you prefer to work:
Sun Mon Tues Wed Thur Fri Sat

19. Military experience: ☐ Yes ☐ No

If yes, List branch of service:

Dates of active duty: From ________ to ________

Primary duties: ________

20. Experience. *Begin with current or most recent job. List each job separately even though it may have been with the same employer. Account for all jobs during the past ten years. Use additional sheets, if necessary.*

Name of employer	Immediate supervisor	
Address of employer	Telephone number	
City	State	Zip code
Type of business	Your job title	

Dates of employment
From Month ______________________ Yr ________ to Month ______________________ Yr ________

Reason for leaving

Salary range
Beginning wage $ ______________ per ________ Ending wage $ ______________ per ________

Duties (be specific)

Special training that you received

Name of employer	Immediate supervisor	
Address of employer	Telephone number	
City	State	Zip code
Type of business	Your job title	

Dates of employment
From Month ______________________ Yr ________ to Month ______________________ Yr ________

Reason for leaving

Salary range
Beginning wage $ ______________ per ________ Ending wage $ ______________ per ________

Duties (be specific)

Special training that you received

Name of employer	Immediate supervisor	
Address of employer	Telephone number	
City	State	Zip code
Type of business	Your job title	

Dates of employment
From Month ______________________ Yr ________ to Month ______________________ Yr ________

Reason for leaving

Salary range
Beginning wage $ ______________ per ________ Ending wage $ ______________ per ________

Duties (be specific)

Special training that you received

21. Explain all gaps in your employment that were 3 months or greater:

From: Month __________ Yr ________ to Month __________ Yr __________ Reason ____

From: Month __________ Yr ________ to Month __________ Yr __________ Reason ____

From: Month __________ Yr ________ to Month __________ Yr __________ Reason ____

22. List special qualifications and skills that you have

23. List professional association memberships

24. List licenses or certifications (list state and expiration date, if applicable)

25. If currently employed, may we contact your employer and/or supervisor? G Yes G No

26. Education: Indicate highest level of education. ________________________

List, beginning with high school, all schools attended. Indicate city and state of school, degree (if any) and major subject

School name	City and State	Degree	Major Subject

Other training. Describe any other formal or informal training received in the past ten years. Provide dates of attendance, course length, location and certificate received.

27. List honors, awards, etc., received

28. References: List three persons not related to you who are able to verify the information provided in this application. Do not list supervisors mentioned above.

Name	Mailing Address	Telephone Number
	Street Address	
	City, State and Zip	
	Street Address	
	City, State and Zip	
	Street Address	
	City, State and Zip	

29. Respond to the following questions:	Yes	No
a. Are you eligible to work in the U.S.?	☐	☐
b. Have you ever been convicted of a felony? *	☐	☐
c. Have you ever been convicted of a drug-related crime? *	☐	☐
d. Do you have a valid driver's license?	☐	☐
e. Do you have any blood relatives employed by this company?	☐	☐

If yes, name of relative: ____

Relation to you: ____

(Company may have a nepotism policy that prohibits close relatives from working in the same department or division.)

f. Have you applied for employment with this company before? ☐ ☐

If yes, when Month ______________________ Year __________

** Conviction will not necessarily disqualify the applicant from employment.*

30. Additional information. Use this space to expand upon your answers to questions. Indicate item number.

Item Number

____________	______________________________
____________	______________________________
____________	______________________________
____________	______________________________
____________	______________________________
____________	______________________________
____________	______________________________
____________	______________________________
____________	______________________________

31. Candidate statement: Use this space to communicate to the company any special information not listed in the application.

Notice: All information supplied by the applicant is subject to review and verification by the employer. Inaccurate information may result in rejection of the application or dismissal from employment.

"I certify that all of the statements made by me are true, complete and correct to the best of my knowledge and belief."

______________________ ______________________

Applicant Signature Date

SAMPLE COMPLETED EMPLOYMENT APPLICATION

Sample Company is an equal opportunity employer and fully subscribes to the principles of equal employment. All applicants and employees are considered for hire and promotion without regard to race, color, religion, gender, national origin, age, handicap or status as a veteran.

Directions: Complete all questions. Print or type responses. If unable to complete a response in the space provided, complete your answer in the space provided in item 30 on page 4.

1. Kind of position or job for which you are applying (give the job title or job announcement number)
   Truck Driver

2. Other positions for which you would like to be considered
   Material Handler

3. Name (Last, First, Middle)
   Simmons, Carl J.

4. Street address (No P.O. Box Numbers) *127 Blackrock Drive*	5. Apartment number *#105*	
6. City *Anytown*	7. State *Virginia*	8. Zip *99999*
9. If mailing address is different, provide address *P.O. Box 199, Anytown, VA 99999*	10. E-mail address *Carl123@Internet.com*	
11. Telephone number *(999) 555-0010*	12. Cell phone number *(999) 555-9919*	

13. Have you ever been employed by this company? ☐ Yes ☒ No

If yes, provide dates of employment: From: Month ________ Yr ________ to Month ________ Yr ________

14. What starting salary would be acceptable to you? Per hour *Negotiable* Per month ________

15. When would be the earliest date that you would be available to start work?
Month *march* Day *1st* Yr *2014*

16. Are you available for:	Yes	No
Part-time work	☒	☐
To relocate	☒	☐
Overnight travel	☒	☐

17. Would you consider temporary work of:	Yes	No
Less than 3 months	☐	☒
3 - 6 months	☐	☒
9 - 12 months	☒	☐

18. Hours preferred: No preference ☐ or Start work at *7 a.m.* (enter time of day).
Days of the week: No preference ☒ or Circle the days of the week that you prefer to work:
Sun Mon Tues Wed Thur Fri Sat

19. Military experience: ☐ Yes ☒ No

If yes, List branch of service:

Dates of active duty: From ________ to ________

Primary duties: ________

20. Experience. *Begin with current or most recent job. List each job separately even though it may have been with the same employer. Account for all jobs during the past ten years. Use additional sheets, if necessary.*

Name of employer *Henry Construction*	Immediate supervisor *John Henry*	
Address of employer *916 Main Street*	Telephone number *(999) 555-6565*	
City *Anytown*	State *Virginia*	Zip code *999999*
Type of business *Home Remodeling*	Your job title *Material Handler/Helper*	
Dates of employment From Month *September* Yr *2006* to Month *March* Yr *2007*		
Reason for leaving *Incarcerated*		
Salary range Beginning wage $ *10.50* per hour Ending wage $ *11.50* per hour		
Duties (be specific) : *Was general laborer for construction company. Carried materials, unloaded trucks, mixed concrete, operated backhoe when needed.*		
Special training that you received *On-the-job training for operating a fork lift and back hoe*		

Name of employer *Home Town Construction*	Immediate supervisor *Bill Smith*	
Address of employer *19 South Street*	Telephone number *(999) 555-1000*	
City *Anytown*	State *Virginia*	Zip code *99999*
Type of business *Commercial Construction*	Your job title *Laborer*	
Dates of employment From Month *June* Yr *2002* to Month *July* Yr *2006*		
Reason for leaving *Laid off when job was completed.*		
Salary range Beginning wage $ *9.50* per hour Ending wage $ *10.00* per *hour*		
Duties (be specific) *Helped carpenters. Carried materials. Unloaded trucks. Cleaned up work site.*		
Special training that you received *None.*		

Name of employer *Yourtown Fast Food*	Immediate supervisor *Mary Jones*	
Address of employer *2695 North Main Street*	Telephone number *(999) 555-2005*	
City *Anytown*	State *Virginia*	Zip code *99999*
Type of business *Fast Food Hamburger Restaurant*	Your job title *Assistant cook*	
Dates of employment From Month *July* Yr *2000* to Month *June* Yr *2002*		
Reason for leaving *Got job with Home Town Construction.*		
Salary range Beginning wage $ *6.50* per *hour* Ending wage $ *8.50* per *hour*		
Duties (be specific) *Cook the various foods like hamburgers, fries. Cleaned up.*		
Special training that you received *In store training on cooking.*		

21. Explain all gaps in your employment that were 3 months or greater:

From: Month *March* Yr *2007* to Month *Present* Yr ______ Reason *See #30*

From: Month ______ Yr ______ to Month ______ Yr ______ Reason ______

From: Month ______ Yr ______ to Month ______ Yr ______ Reason ______

22. List special qualifications and skills that you have

I received truck driving training while incarcerated. Obtained CDL.

23. List professional association memberships *None*

24. List licenses or certifications (list state and expiration date, if applicable) *Virginia CDL License - Expires April, 2017.*

25. If currently employed, may we contact your employer and/or supervisor? ☐ Yes ☐ No *N/A*

26. Education: Indicate highest level of education. ______

List, beginning with high school, all schools attended. Indicate city and state of school, degree (if any) and major subject

School Name	City and State	Degree	Major Subject
Anytown High School	*Anytown, VA*	*None*	*General*
State Community College	*Southville, VA*	*GED*	*General*

Other training. Describe any other formal or informal training received in the past ten years. Provide dates of attendance, course length, location and certificate received.

Obtained GED and CDL Training from State Community College while incarcerated.

27. List honors, awards, etc., received

None

28. References: List three persons not related to you who are able to verify the information provided in this application. Do not list supervisors mentioned above.

Name	Mailing Address	Telephone Number
Mary Samuel	*P.O. Box 19* Street Address *North, VA 99998* City, State and Zip	*(999) 555-2626*
Rev. Martin Bolles	*2620 Main Street* Street Address *South, VA 99997* City, State and Zip	*(999) 555-2727*
Frank Gibbs	*970 Smyth* Street Address *Anytown, VA 99999* City, State and Zip	*(999) 555-6999*

29. Respond to the following questions:

	Yes	No
a. Are you eligible to work in the U.S.?	☒	☐
b. Have you ever been convicted of a felony? *	☒	☐
c. Have you ever been convicted of a drug-related crime? *	☐	☒
d. Do you have a valid driver's license?	☒	☐
e. Do you have any blood relatives employed by this company?	☐	☒

If yes, name of relative: ______________________________

Relation to you: ______________________________

(Company may have a nepotism policy that prohibits close relatives from working in the same department or division.)

f. Have you applied for employment with this company before? ☐ ☒

If yes, when Month ____________________ Year __________

** Conviction will not necessarily disqualify the applicant from employment.*

30. Additional information. Use this space to expand upon your answers to questions. Indicate item number.

Item Number	
21	*Was incarcerated in Virginia State Prison. Paroled on April 16, 2014.*
29	*Convicted of armed robbery, first offense. Served 7 of 10 year sentence. Released early because of exemplary behavior.*

31. Candidate statement: Use this space to communicate to the company any special information not listed in the application.

I used the time that I was incarcerated to re-evaluate my life and to learn ways to cope successfully in the world. I worked hard to obtain my GED and then when offered, get training as a truck driver. I am ready to make something of myself and only ask for an opportunity to prove my value to a company.

Notice: All information supplied by the applicant is subject to review and verification by the employer. Inaccurate information may result in rejection of the application or dismissal from employment.

"I certify that all of the statements made by me are true, complete and correct to the best of my knowledge and belief."

______________________________ Applicant Signature

______________________________ Date

HOW TO WRITE A RÉSUMÉ

A résumé is a one to two-page written summary of your unique combination of skills, experience and abilities. It has been described as an advertisement of the job seeker. Its sole purpose is to help you get a job interview. Since most employers are requesting that applicants submit a résumé, either a paper version or an online version, Returning Citizens need to know how to write a résumé.

The Résumé Is Used By:

The job seeker . . .

- To make a good enough impression on the employer to secure a job interview.
- To highlight unique and relevant skills and experience.
- For networking, phone contacts, cold calls and job fairs.

The employer . . .

- To screen out most job seekers.
- To identify candidates to interview who possess the skills the company desires.
- As an agenda for the job interview.

Résumé versus Job Application

Both the résumé and the job application are instruments to convey the same or similar information about the job seeker. The job application is in the format and content that the employer dictates, whereas the résumé's format and content is determined by the job seeker.

It is important that you complete the Career Success Guide: Sample Blank Employment Application and that you use the information in your Sample Completed Employment Application as the basis for your résumé.

There are many opinions about what a résumé should look like, what it should include and how it should be presented on the page. It is likely that no two people will agree on a résumé format when asked for advice. Therefore, you have to create a résumé that you are comfortable with.

What To Include In A Résumé:

- Name, address, telephone number.
- A clear and relevant job objective.
- All significant work experience.
- Education and training.
- Pertinent information about your skills.
- Details of past accomplishments.
- Military experience.
- Organizational/professional memberships.

What Not To Include On A Résumé:

- Irrelevant personal information (hobbies, marital status, children, age, Social Security Number, race, disability, height, weight, etc.).
- References: if employers want references, they will ask for them.
- Any negative information, including words, phrases or attitudes.
- Any handwritten or white-out corrections.
- Any reference to your conviction and incarceration.

There Are Basically Two Types Of Résumés:

Chronological

- Easiest and least time-consuming to compose.
- Lists previous experience in date (chronological) order, most recent experience first, followed by previous jobs.
- Most commonly used because this résumé format is the one most employers prefer, because it gives them all of the information they want to know in a job application format.
- This is the traditional résumé format, good to use if you have experience and skills similar to the ones needed in the job that you seek.
- It is difficult to hide your incarceration in this type of résumé.

Skills/Functional

- Is harder and more time-consuming to compose, but works well if you have problems in your work history such as gaps in employment, frequent job changes, limited experience, weak skills, etc.
- Some employers dislike this type of résumé because it can disguise a job seeker's faults.
- Organizes experience by key skills rather than by past jobs.
- Frequently used by professionals who want to emphasize a particularly strong or important skill area.

You can compose a résumé that uses a combination of the chronological and skills résumés. This format lets you combine the best elements of both your skills and your work history. Review the Career Success Guides: Components of a Résumé, Sample Chronological Résumés, and Sample Skills/Functional Résumés.

Choosing The Right Résumé Style For You

Look at the checklist below while considering your work experience, skills, abilities, education and training. The chart will help you decide which résumé style is the right one for you.

If you...	Chronological	Skills
have a poor work history, employment gaps or are unemployed		x
have education that is suited to the position desired	x	
have solid training for a specific job, but little paid experience		x
have a work history that demonstrates career growth	x	
are considering a career change	x	x
have had frequent job changes		x
possess related work experience	x	
have little or no related work experience		x
have an impressive work history	x	
lack education		x

Using Your Résumé in Your Job Search:

- Your résumé alone will not secure a job for you. Your job search strategy must combine an excellent résumé with targeted marketing, networking, follow-up and emotional support to be successful.
- Use your résumé for cold calls, when replying to help wanted ads or as a guideline for interviews.
- Follow up on all résumés that you have sent out preferably by telephone or personal contact.

Sample Résumés

Sample résumés can be found in the following Career Success Guides: Components of a Résumé, Sample Chronological Résumés, and Sample Skills/Functional Résumés.

Résumé Tips

- Limit your résumé to one page, if possible, by being brief, relevant, concise and specific. Never exceed two pages!
- Focus on what the employer wants to know and what you can offer the organization.
- Rewrite your résumé until you end up with simple, direct language that includes action words that create a positive impression. Review the Career Success Guide: List of Words to Use in Your Résumé.
- The résumé should be a brief advertisement, not a rambling history of your past. Omit long explanations.
- Proofread for accuracy, relevance, spelling, grammar or other errors.
- Update your résumé frequently, even if you are not looking for a job, just in case you need one quickly.
- Avoid using jargon, abbreviations, slang words and different verb tenses.
- When mailing a résumé, you should send it in a 9-x-12-inch manila-type envelope instead of folding it up in a letter envelope.
- Always include a cover letter when submitting a résumé (refer to the Career Success Guides: How to Write a Cover Letter and Sample Cover Letters).
- The résumé should have a clean, uncluttered appearance with the most important information at the top of the page.
- Your résumé should be easy to read with plenty of white space to break up the reading.
- Use good quality, plain white paper and a quality printer for the best appearance.
- Experiment with your résumé. For example, if your education is more relevant to the job than your experience, list education first on your résumé followed by experience, or vice versa.

Warning

All information on your résumé is subject to verification by the employer. Any discrepancies could be grounds for dismissal.

Internet Résumés

More and more employers today are requiring applicants to submit their résumé electronically. Résumés that are posted to the Internet are different in many significant ways from the traditional paper and ink résumés.

Because so many employers require applicants to submit their résumé electronically, it is important that the job seeker understand how to utilize this resource. For assistance in submitting an electronic résumé, review the Career Success Guide: How to Write an Internet Résumé.

COMPONENTS OF A RÉSUMÉ

There are two basic types of résumés: Chronological and Skills (sometimes called Functional). The components that are included in a Chronological Résumé can be found on this page and for a Skills Résumé on page two. Review the Career Success Guides: How to Write a Résumé, Sample Chronological Résumés, and Sample Skills/Functional Résumés.

Components of A Chronological Résumé

(1) **Joseph H. King**

(2)
1312 Monroe Street
Any Town, NC 99999

(999)756-9023
jhk@internet.net

Job Objective

(3) To obtain a position in sales utilizing my customer service skills and excellent communications and mathematical abilities.

Employment Experience

(4)
2005 - present — Library Assistant
Commonwealth of Virginia Prison System
Your Town, VA 99999

Duties: Assisted inmates in selecting reading material, cataloged books and periodicals. Taught remedial reading and writing.

1999 - 2005 — Sales Assistant
K and O Auto Parts
MyTown, MA 99999

Duties: Assisted sales staff with stocking, customer service and inventory.

Education and Training

(5) 1999 — High School Graduate, MyTown High School, MyTown,NC Certificate in automobile repair.

Skills

(6) Customer Service — General Automobile Repair — Auto Parts Sales — Database Teaching

1) **Name -** Use formal name, no nicknames; example, use Joseph H. King, not Joe King. Type your name in a larger font than the rest of the résumé. After all, that is what you want people to notice and remember: your name. Using a horizontal line under your name like the one in the example makes a nice appearance.
2) **Address/Telephone Number -** You should always use your complete, un-abbreviated address, including zip code. Use a telephone number that will be answered at all times - preferably your own, a cell phone or the phone of a friend who will take messages for you. Always include the area code. You may include your Internet e-mail address.
3) **Experience/Work Experience -** List most recent job first and then go backward. If work experience is slim, include any unpaid/volunteer experience. Cover gaps in experience with school/home, or whatever you were doing during this time period, rather than leaving it blank. Include dates of employment, job title, company name and location and description of duties performed. Use action words whenever possible to make a positive statement. Include any work performed while incarcerated.
4) **Education and Training -** If your education and training is more relevant to the job than your work experience, put this category first; otherwise put it after experience. Include any education and training that is relevant to the job including training while in prison.
5) **Special Skills/Abilities -** You can use this category to cover any other skills and abilities that you want an employer to know. Some examples are: good interpersonal/communication skills, attention to detail, require little or no supervision.

Components of A Skills/Functional Résumé

(1) **Monica L. Smith**

(2) 3344 Crown Avenue, YourTown, MO 99999 (999)825-3186
mosmith@Internet.net

Position Desired

(3) A challenging position as an Administrative Assistant using my exceptional clerical, organizational and communications skills.

Professional Skills

(4)
Organizational: Extremely well-organized work habits, detail oriented, decision-making and problem-solving skills.
Communications: Excellent oral and written communications skills.
Computer-Related: Proficient in Microsoft Word and Excel, Microsoft Windows and Internet Explorer. Knowledgeable of all office equipment.

Work History

(5)
1998 - Present Office Assistant to the Warden
Commonwealth of Virginia Correctional System, YourTown, VA 99999

1995 - 1998 Receptionist
Pikesville Furniture, YourTown, MO 99999

1989 - 1995 Professional Homemaker and Mother

1988 - 1989 Receptionist/Switchboard Operator
Buddy's Used Cars, Newton, SC 99998

(6) **Education**

A.A.S. Degree Office Systems Technology
YourTown Community College, OurTown, MO 99997

Graduate Newton High School, Newton, SC 99998

Bookkeeping 12-week course in bookkeeping. Career Specialists, YourTown, VA

(7) **Organizational Memberships**

None

1) **Name** - Use formal name. Do not use nicknames. For example use Monica L. Smith, not Mo Smith. Type your name in a larger font than the rest of the résumé. After all, that is what you want people to notice and remember: your name. Using a horizontal line under your name like the one in the example makes a nice appearance.
2) **Address/Telephone Number** - You should always use your complete, un-abbreviated address, including zip code. Use a telephone number that will be answered at all times - preferably your own, a cell phone or a phone of a friend who will take messages for you. Always include the area code.
3) **Highlights/Qualifications/Professional Skills** - Group all of your relevant skills and abilities into three or four categories sorted by skill area. Try to list these skills and abilities in order of importance to the position desired.
4) **Work History** - A brief history of your work experience including only dates of employment, job title, company name and location. Try to cover gaps in work history with something positive that you were doing during that time. Include work while incarcerated.
5) **Education** - Include any relevant education. This is usually listed after work history, but if education is more relevant to position desired, list education first on your résumé, followed by work history. Include any training while in prison.
6) **Organizational/Professional Memberships** - List any memberships or positions held with career-related organizations.

Hint: Complete the Career Success Guide: Sample Blank Employment Application before you start on your résumé. A completed application will help you organize the information that you need for either the Chronological or the Skills résumé. For assistance on completing your job application, review the Career Success Guides: How to Complete a Job Application, Sample Blank Employment Application, and Completed Sample Employment Application.

SAMPLE CHRONOLOGICAL RÉSUMÉS

Use the following two sample Chronological Résumés as a guide. Review the Career Success Guides: How to Write a Résumé and Components of a Résumé.

Mary A. Adams

127 Main Street
Anytown, Virginia 99999
(999) 555-0001
maa@internet.net

Job Objective

Customer Service representative with a retail or service company. A position utilizing leadership, communication and analytical abilities.

Summary of Qualifications

- Adept in areas of sales and customer service.
- Skilled in office procedures, filing and data entry operations.
- Proficient in the operation of office equipment and computers.
- Trained in Microsoft Word and Excel.
- Excellent oral and written communication skills.

Professional Experience

Bookkeeper/Administrative Assistant, Henry Construction Company, Anytown, VA, 2008 - 2012

- Maintained all financial records of company.
- Managed accounts receivable, payable, employee payroll and customer invoicing.
- Produced quarterly and annual financial reports.
- Implemented and operated computerized bookkeeping system.

Sales Associate, Yourtown Department Store, Yourtown, VA, 2002 - 2008

- Provided customer service to over 150 customers daily.
- Received inventory, stocked shelves and maintained records for reorders.
- Operated Hewlett Packard 1000 electronic register system.
- Organized all daily closing procedures for the department.

Newspaper Delivery Person, Yourtown Daily News, Yourtown, VA, 1999 - 2002

- Increased customer base from 65 to 250 people.
- Managed all record keeping and accounts for route.
- Opened new accounts and provided daily customer service.

Education

Associate Degree - Yourtown Business College, Yourtown, VA
Majored in business management, customer service and banking procedures.
Additional course work in accounting, customer relations and statistics.

Additional Skills and Accomplishments

Earned financing for education through part-time and summer work while maintaining 3.50 G.P.A. in school.

References available on request.

James R. White

134 Main Street
Yourtown, IA 99999
(999) 555-0009
jrw@internet.net

Job Objective

Truck driver, material handler or construction laborer

Work History

2006 - Present — Various Laborer Positions - North Carolina Correctional Institution, Anytown, IA 99999

- Provided janitorial duties such as cleaning bathrooms and showers, mopping floors and waxing floors.
- Responsible for two other workers.
- Food service worker. Washed dishes in main dinning room.
- Helped unload food products and other goods as needed.

1997 - 2006 — Truck Driver- Carson Industries, Yourtown, IA 99998

- Drove tractor-trailer daily between two major cities.
- Managed all required logs.
- Communicated with store managers to achieve customer satisfaction.
- Commended for safe driving record.

1990 - 1997 — Laborer - S & O Lumber and Hardware, Yourtown, IA 99998

- Loaded and unloaded trucks with building materials.
- Managed sales fulfillment, stocking and inventory control.
- Operated folk lift.
- Supervised three other laborers.

Education

GED, North Carolina Correctional Institution, Anytown, IA 99998
High School, OurTown High School, OurTown, NC

Special Skills and Accomplishments

- Received award from Carson Industries for safe driving record.
- Knowledgeable of laws and regulations for CDL drivers.
- Completed GED.
- CDL license

References available on request

SAMPLE SKILLS/FUNCTIONAL RÉSUMÉS

Use the following two sample Skills/Functional Résumés as a guide. Review the Career Success Guides: How to Write a Résumé and Components of a Résumé.

Before starting on your résumé, complete the Career Success Guide: Sample Blank Employment Application. This will help you organize the information you need to write your résumé.

Sample Skills/Functional Résumé

Mary L White

134 Main Street
Yourtown, FL 99999
(999) 555-1212
mlw@internet.net

Professional Objective

An administrative position with a social services agency that utilizes my excellent organizational and communication skills, and involves my knowledge of the judicial system.

Areas of Expertise

Organization:

- Coordinated a Child Protection Service (CPS) department servicing 475 clients annually.
- Assisted staff of 8 case workers.
- Assisted mid-level manager at large manufacturing firm.
- Re-organized small correctional center library.

Communication:

- Was initial contact for clients seeking assistance.
- Prepared monthly client flow information for staff.
- Prepared correspondence for small staff of managers.
- Taught inmates how to use the library facilities.

Knowledge of Legal System

- Involved as a participant in the legal system.
- Prepared briefs and other legal documents for self and other inmates.
- Counseled fellow inmates on legal options.

Experience:
Library Aide, Florida Correctional System, OurTown, FL 2004-2014
Administrative Assistant, ABC Manufacturing 1996 - 2004, YourTown, FL
Administrative Assistant, YourTown Department of Social Service, Yourtown, FL 1981-1993
Education and H.S. Diploma, YourTown High School

Licenses:
Clerical Training, Career Center

References available on request

Frank A. Adams
127 Main Street
Anytown, Maryland 99999
(999) 555-0002
faa@internet.net

JOB OBJECTIVE

Seeking job as a Carpenter Helper or General Laborer with a construction company.

CARPENTRY SKILLS

Skilled at using all of the tools used by carpenters such as power saws and power hammers. Knowledgeable of construction including framing and reading blueprints.

ROOFING SKILLS

Have experience and skill at installing shingles, asphalt and related types of roofing materials.

General Laboring Skills

Performed duties as general laborer and material handler. Am able to mix concrete and mortar.

Maintenance

Responsible for keeping floors in large area clean. Mopped, stripped and applied wax and buffed floors.
Assisted with the cleaning and sanitizing of restrooms and kitchen area.

EDUCATION

H.S. Attended AnyTown High School, Anytown, MD
GED Am enrolled in GED classes at AnyTown Vocational School. Expect completion in summer of 2014.

WORK EXPERIENCE

Maintenance Worker, Maryland Correctional System, Yourtown, MD 2002 - 2014
Roofer, Ourtown Roofing Company, Ourtown, VA, 1997 - 2002
Carpenter Helper, Ourtown Construction, Ourtown, VA, 1994 – 1997

INTERESTS

Sports, working out and music.

References furnished on request

HOW TO WRITE AN INTERNET RÉSUMÉ

Résumés that are posted to the Internet are different in many significant ways from the traditional paper and ink résumés. It is important for job seekers today to understand how to utilize this resource. The process of submitting an Internet résumé is no different for a re-entering job seeker than it is for anyone else. If you are only applying for entry level, unskilled jobs, then you most likely will not be asked to submit your résumé electronically. You may, however, be asked to complete an online application. Review the Career Success guide: How to Apply for a Job Online.

Electronic Résumés

Many job seekers make the mistake of thinking that an electronic résumé is nothing more than a traditional résumé that you e-mail to an employer. Eight years ago this may have been the case. Today employers either require applicants to submit their résumé electronically, or they convert the paper and ink résumé into an electronic document.

Why have employers embraced this media? There are two major reasons. First, it saves on paper and filing. Secondly, and most importantly, the electronic résumé allows the employer to use the computer to sort, categorize, screen and electronically file the résumés of applicants. By using this technology an employer can easily identify potential candidates. The employers simply ask the computer to list all candidates who meet certain criteria, mention specific skills and have a range of work experience or other criteria.

Job seekers need to create a résumé that gets the computer to include them whenever the computer lists possible candidates; therefore, the structure of the résumé must be computer friendly.

Because the Internet world is constantly changing, and this includes how employers utilize electronic résumés, it is advisable that you obtain the most current information about this topic. Check the following web site for the most up-to-date information: www.rileyguide.com.

Computer Résumé Tracking Programs

Initially only very large corporations had the capability to electronically record, sort and track résumés. With the advent of low cost software programs for personal computers, small companies have joined this electronic age. Electronic scanners are able to scan paper and ink résumés and convert them to readable formats. Most software programs also permit the employer to "cut and paste" e-mail résumés into their tracking programs. Job seekers need to be aware that even if they send a traditional paper and ink résumé to an employer, the chances are high that it will be scanned and converted to a computer file.

Internet Résumé Basics

- Always have two types of résumés available: a scan-able paper and ink résumé and a plain-text résumé (see description below).
- Use the chronological or skills résumé you created on your word processor as your "advertisement résumé" and submit it only if you are asked to submit a paper and ink résumé.
- Learn how to e-mail your résumé both as an attachment and as a part of the e-mail message.
- Know the format that the employer wants before you send a résumé to them.

Employers Prefer

According to surveys, employers prefer:

- E-mailed plain-text résumés that are embedded within the e-mail. Many employers refuse to open attachments from people they do not know.
- Scan-able résumés that are printed on white paper and mailed in a large, flat envelope.
- Scan-able faxed résumés. It must be a quality fax so that the résumé can be scanned.

Key Words

The power of the electronic résumé lies in the key words. The computer allows the employer to quickly evaluate every résumé to determine if the candidate possesses a set of specific skills and/or traits. Those candidates that mention the specific skills in their résumé will be listed in a key word search and may be invited to an interview. Résumés that do not mention the skills are kept in the database, but may not get selected.

You need to load your résumé with key words. They should be nouns and noun phrases, and industry specific. Try not to repeat key words and phrases since the computer only counts the inclusion once. Try to have as many as 75 such key words in your résumé. This is one time that more is better.

Types of Electronic Résumés

1. Plain-text. A plain-text, or ASCII résumé is an unformatted résumé without any special characters. It is a no-frills version of your résumé and contains no italics, underlining, bold, special fonts or bullets. Why plain-text? Because all computers can read and understand it. You will use this résumé 95% of the time. This type of résumé is scan- able and should be used if asked to send a scan able paper résumé.
2. Formatted. This résumé is created using a word processor like Microsoft Word. It can contain fancy fonts, underlining, bullets, etc. This type of résumé should only be sent if the employer specifically states that Word documents are acceptable. Do not assume that the employer can or will read a Word document. In order to send this type of résumé, you must attach the Word document to an e-mail. Be sure to alert the employer in your cover message that the document was created using a specific word processor.
3. Web Résumé. A web résumé is a résumé that you have placed on the web. If you have your own web page, or have access to a web page, you can post your résumé on the site and make the site known to employers.

Creating Your Electronic Plain Text Résumé

The plain text résumé is similar to your "advertising" fancy résumé without the bells and whistles. Because it will be read on a computer screen there are a few formatting tricks:

- Use your favorite word processor. Set your margins to allow only 60 characters per line (most computers read between 60-65 characters per line.) This way your text will not bleed over to the next line. Save your document using the ASCII Text option.
- Select a 10 or 12 point standard font like Times New Roman or Courier. Ten point will allow more text per line and page than twelve point font.
- Type in (or paste from your traditional paper and ink résumé) your résumé information, flush left. Do not attempt to center or indent any information because ASCII text does not recognize formatting. Do place parentheses around area codes so the computer can recognize the number to be a telephone number. Remember, keep it simple!
- Test to make sure it looks good. Save the completed résumé, again using the ASCII Text format. Close your word processor. Now reopen it and open your saved file. How does it look? If it changed how it looks, make your corrections and repeat this step until you get the résumé to look the way that you want. After you are satisfied with the résumé's appearance, send the file as an e-mail attachment to a friend. Have them open it on their computer. Don't be surprised if the résumé looks different on your friend's computer. Keep making changes until it looks good on the computers of several different friends.

Content of the Résumé

- The content and format of the electronic résumé differs slightly from the traditional Chronological Résumé:
- Heading. Place your name, address, city, state and zip code, telephone number and your e-mail address in descending order. You may highlight your name and major categories by using all capitals. Make sure each heading is left justified.

First 100 words critical

Many résumé tracking programs record only the first 100 words found in the résumé. These 100 words become the key word list. It is important that you get all of your qualifications mentioned early in the résumé.

- Job Objective. State what you want to do. Don't waste words. List the job title. If you are responding to an ad, make sure your job title matches the title used in the ad. This may require rewriting every résumé before it is sent to individual employers.
- Summary of Qualifications. This is where you list your qualifications. List the key words that match your qualifications and the requirements of the job. In preparation for writing your Internet résumé, you should compile a list of your skills and tasks that are relevant to the job sought.
- These skills need to be mentioned in your qualifications. Use short sentences filled with key words. For example: Able to use the following computer applications: Word, Excel, WordPerfect, PowerPoint and Dreamweaver.
- Experience. Begin your list of employers with your most recent employment. Be brief. When listing tasks performed and accomplishments, be mindful of key words. Employers are primarily interested in how your experiences match those of the job you seek.
- Education. List educational accomplishments. Be sure to mention relevant extra educational and training programs and certificates.

E-Mailing Your Résumé to Employers

E-mailing your résumé is the single best way to reach employers. It is fast and targeted; it reaches the person who has the authority to hire you. Review the Career Success guides: How To Make Cold Calls, Using Your Network to Locate Job Openings, and How to Respond to Newspaper Want Ads.

When responding to an ad or sending a cold e-mail, send only a plain text résumé that is embedded in the e-mail unless asked to send a formatted résumé.

- Copy your plain text résumé to the clip board. Your word processor program manual will explain how to do this. If you need help, ask for assistance from your local One-Stop Career Center.
- Create a cover letter e-mail. At the end of the message, paste your résumé from the clip board to the message.
- In the subject line of the e-mail, type Résumé of John Doe. Before you send the message make sure your e-mail program is sending the message as text and not the Internet language, HTML. Send the e-mail.
- If the employer has requested a formatted résumé, attach your résumé rather than embed the résumé into the cover letter. Make sure that you have told the reader in your cover message the word processor which was used to create the résumé.

Posting Your Résumé to a Database

This process is relatively simple. Follow the directions given by the site. Some will allow you to paste your text résumé to a database; others will have an online form to complete. If asked to complete a form make sure you include all of your key words from your résumé. Be wary of any Internet posting service that makes you pay for the posting service.

Posting To a Company Web Site

More and more companies allow applicants to submit résumés directly to the company on their web site. Check the company web site for directions. Some will ask you to e-mail your text résumé; others will have a form. Be sure to emphasize your key words!

The Electronic Cover Letter

Just as you shouldn't mail a résumé without a cover letter, you shouldn't send an electronic résumé without a cover letter. Review the Career Success Guide: How to Write a Cover Letter. The electronic cover letter is similar to the paper and ink variety except shorter. Remember, the cover letter is to be an introduction of you and a statement of why you are sending the résumé. Conclude the brief note detailing the next step. Examples include, I will call you next week to arrange an interview or I am looking forward to discussing possible positions with you.

LIST OF WORDS TO USE IN YOUR RÉSUMÉ

Your résumé must emphasize what you have done in an interesting and enthusiastic way. Use words that describe your capabilities, skills and accomplishments. Below is a list of action words. Check the ones you want to highlight on your résumé. Review the Career Success guides: How to Write a Résumé and Components of a Résumé.

_________ act

_________ adapt

_________ administer

_________ advise

_________ analyze

_________ arrange

_________ arbitrate

_________ assist

_________ audit

_________ Build

_________ calculate

_________ check

_________ coach

_________ communicate

_________ compile

_________ compose

_________ conduct

_________ compute

_________ contribute

_________ control

_________ consult

_________ construct

_________ coordinate

_________ counsel

_________ create

_________ deliver

_________ design

_________ detail

_________ detect

_________ develop

_________ diagnose

_________ direct

_________ discover

_________ display

_________ distribute

_________ dramatize

_________ draw

_________ drive

_________ edit

_________ enforce

_________ ensure

_________ establish

_________ evaluate

_________ examine

_________ execute

_________ express

_________ facilitate

_________ file

_________ fix

_________ follow

_________ generate

_________ give

_________ guide

_________ identify

_________ imagine

_________ implement

_________ improve

_________ improvise

_________ influence

_________ increase

_________ initiate

_________ inspect

_________ instruct

_________ install

_________ interpret

_________ invent

_________ investigate

_________ judge

_________ lead

__________ learn
__________ listen
__________ make
__________ manage
__________ memorize
__________ model
__________ modify
__________ motivate
__________ negotiate
__________ observe
__________ operate
__________ originate
__________ organize
__________ oversee
__________ paint
__________ perform
__________ photograph
__________ pilot
__________ plan
__________ prepare
__________ present
__________ print
__________ produce
__________ program

__________ promote
__________ provide
__________ publicize
__________ purchase
__________ raise
__________ read
__________ reason
__________ recommend
__________ reconcile
__________ recruit
__________ reduce
__________ relate
__________ reorganize
__________ repair
__________ report
__________ research
__________ resolve
__________ restore
__________ review
__________ risk
__________ schedule
__________ sell
__________ sew
__________ share

__________ sing
__________ solve
__________ speak
__________ start
__________ study
__________ supervise
__________ supply
__________ talk
__________ teach
__________ train
__________ transcribe
__________ translate
__________ travel
__________ tutor
__________ type
__________ understand
__________ unify
__________ verbalize
__________ utilize
__________ verify

TRULINCS Friendly! info@ReentryEssentials.org  www.ReentryEssentials.org  347.973.0004 2609 East 14 Street, Suite 1018, Brooklyn, NY 11235-3915

HOW TO WRITE A COVER LETTER

A cover letter is the letter that introduces you to a potential employer. Like a résumé, the cover letter gives you the opportunity to tell the employer why the employer should hire you. A properly crafted cover letter will entice the reader to not only examine your résumé, but to call you for an interview.

There Are 11 Basic Components to a Good Cover Letter

1) Every cover letter needs to have your address on it, either in a letterhead or typed at the top as shown. You may want to include your e-mail address.
2) The date you are writing is the next important part of the letter. Keep a copy of the letter so you can know when your first contact was made.
3) Always type the address just as it appears in the advertisement or job posting.
4) This is called the "salutation." Every letter should have one. It is your way of saying "hello." If you don't know a name, use the salutation shown.
5) The first paragraph is the statement of your purpose of writing. You need to identify the job you are applying for and say that you are interested in applying.
6) This is the "meat and potatoes" of your letter. This is where you explain why you are qualified for the position. Be sure to highlight the qualifications and personal attributes that match those requested in the advertisement.

(1) 45 Ace Drive
You're Town, NC 99999
(2) Today's Date

Acme Widget Company **(3)**
Personnel Department
123 Any Street
All town, NC 99999

Dear Sir or Madam: **(4)**

(5) I am writing in regards to your advertisement in the Sunday edition of the Times Herald. I am interested in the machine operator position. My résumé is enclosed for your review.

(6) As you can see from my résumé, I worked for two years as a press machine operator for a local automobile parts manufacturer. In that job, I was responsible for setting up the machine for each order, overseeing the machine's operation, maintaining the press in top working order and conducting quality control measurements.

(A) I would welcome the opportunity to discuss my qualifications with you.

(B) I can be reached by phone at (999) 555-4545 during the evening or by e-mail to msd@internet.net any time. If you do need to contact me during the day, I can be reached at my cell phone at (999) 555-1212.

(C) Sincerely,
Demeter Doe
Demeter Doe
(D)

Enclosure: Résumé
(E)

Review the Career Success guide: Sample Cover Letters

A. The next to last paragraph of your letter is where you try to "set the hook." One option is to state that you will be calling next week to see if an interview can be arranged. If you do this, be sure you do call exactly when you say you will or you will lose your credibility. If you don't feel comfortable cold calling the employer, use this paragraph to tell them you would welcome an opportunity for an interview.
B. Always include your telephone number. If possible, include a day time, an evening number and cell phone number. Be sure to provide a convenient time for them to call you.
C. This is the closing of the letter. Always use one. If you prefer a closing with more than one word (Very truly yours or sincerely yours), be sure you capitalize only the first word and always use an ending comma for proper punctuation.
D. Type your name here. There are always four lines between the closing and your signature line. Make sure you actually sign it in this area.
E. Be sure that you note on the letter that your résumé is enclosed. Don't forget to enclose it!

Should I Include Information About My Past In The Letter?

Unless you have submitted a résumé or job application that mentions that you are an ex-offender, the cover letter is not the place to talk about your past. If you have had to mention that you are an ex-offender, you can address this in a short paragraph following the same format you used in preparing your Summary Statement. For more information on the Summary Statement, review the Career Success Guide: How Do I Deal with Negative Information?

Setting the Stage...

The cover letter is often the first impression that the employer will have of you. Do not minimize its importance. Approach your letter with seriousness. It is as important as your résumé. You want the reader to be impressed with your cover letter. You want the reader to want to talk to you. There are books available in libraries and stores on cover letter formats. Check the Internet resources below for web sites that provide sample cover letters. You will want to also Google "sample cover letters" to get more samples.

Obtaining a Name...

It is best to have the name of the person to whom you are sending the letter. If you do not have a name, locate the phone number of the organization to which you are applying. Call and politely ask the person who answers the phone to give you the name of the person who is responsible for hiring for the position that is available. Make sure you get the exact spelling of the person's name and verify it. Also, ask for the title of the person, since titles vary from organization to organization.

Word Choices

How you word your letter is very important:

Don't just say...	When you can say this:
I ran a cash register.	I operated a cash register and was responsible for balancing the cash drawer at the end of each shift.
I babysat.	I was responsible for the daily care of two children. This included preparing nutritious meals, planning educational activities for them and providing a safe and enjoyable atmosphere.
I worked as a waitress.	I have experience hosting, as well as waiting tables. I am quick with my side work and had over a 20% rate of tipping.
I was a night manager at a convenience store.	As night manager at the convenience store, I was responsible for the total operation of the store including cash register operation, cash balancing, restocking, maintaining a neat and clean environment, dealing with vendors and ensuring friendly and prompt service to the customers.
I answered the phone.	I handled multiple phone lines, routed calls and took messages.
I can type.	I have experience with a number of common word processing programs and can type 50 words a minute.
I fixed cars.	I have experience trouble-shooting and repairing both domestic and foreign autos.
I was a receptionist.	As a receptionist, I handled multiple phone lines, transferred calls, took messages and made appointments. In addition, I received visitors, directed inquiries and ensured a smooth flow of office traffic.

Matching Your Qualifications to the Job

Are you qualified for the job? Employers often list the qualifications of the perfect person, hoping to find someone who comes close. Don't worry if you don't have every qualification listed. What you need to do is help the reader see that you are very close to that perfect person.

- Read the advertisement closely.
- Write down the qualifications listed by the employer on the left side of a piece of paper.
- On the right side, write down the qualifications that you have that closely match those requested.
- Use these items in your letter.

Qualifications:	Qualifications I Possess:
3 years' experience in an office setting.	I have 5 years of office experience.
Word processing experience.	I have knowledge of both WordPerfect and Microsoft Word.
Ability to handle changing priorities.	I handle pressure well, can prioritize and can adapt to a changing environment.

TRULINCS Friendly! info@ReentryEssentials.org  www.ReentryEssentials.org 347.973.0004 2609 East 14 Street, Suite 1018, Brooklyn, NY 11235-3915

SAMPLE COVER LETTERS

Include a cover letter with each résumé that you send to a prospective employer. Use the cover letter to highlight specific skills, experience or interests that match the description of the job for which you are applying. The cover letter should be 1) typed, printed or neatly written on the same type of paper as your résumé, 2) addressed to the same person to whom you are sending your résumé, 3) be short and 4) request a meeting to discuss the job opening. Use these sample letters as a guide. Be sure to review the Career Success guide: How to Write a Cover Letter to learn when you should not include information about your incarceration in the letter.

207 Oakhill Road
Any town, PA 01234
(999) 555-9999
February 2, 2014

Mr. William Saunders
Owner
Main Street Car Dealership
123 Main Street
This town, WV 00000

Dear Mr. Saunders,

I am writing in response to your advertisement in the February 1 issue of the Daily News for an automobile mechanic. I have had six years of experience as an automobile mechanic for a small-town automobile repair facility. I am confident that my training and skills will be an asset to your service center.

My current position is a general mechanic servicing all of the vehicles for a state run facility. My responsibilities have ranged from simple oil and tire changes to completely overhauling the engines of several vehicles. While serving in this position, I supervised three trainees.

I would welcome the opportunity to meet with you to discuss in greater detail my potential value to your service center. I have enclosed my résumé for your review. I will contact you later in the week to arrange a meeting at a time that is convenient for you.

Thank you for your consideration. I look forward to our meeting.

Sincerely,

Robert Morris

Robert Morris

Enc. Résumé

Sample Cover Letter #2 Using a Personal Letterhead

Karen Austin
132 Main Street
Any town, CT 99999
(999) 555-9879
March 6, 2014

Mr. James Benson, President
You're Town Department Store
426 Park Street
Your town, CA 99999

Dear Mr. Benson,

At the recent Job Fair in San Diego, your store manager, John Carson mentioned that Davis, Benson & Co., is looking for a sales associate in the women's clothing department. I believe I am an ideal candidate to fill the position for your company.

My background includes over ten years of experience in retail sales, customer service and stocking. I thoroughly enjoy interacting with customers in order to achieve maximum satisfaction for both the customer and the company. Because I am currently not employed, I am available to begin working immediately. As my résumé indicates, I am proficient with all types of cash registers. I am also able to do inventory control and stocking. I am interested in your position because it will allow me to use my sales expertise and to have the opportunity to return to women's retail sales.

I have been very impressed with the information that was provided at the Job Fair which named Davis, Benson, & Co., as one of the top ten retailers of women clothing in the state. It would be a pleasure to work with a company that fosters such high standards.

I have enclosed my résumé for your review. I will contact you early next week so that we can arrange a convenient time to meet in order to discuss the position of sales associate.

Thank you for your consideration. I look forward to meeting with you soon.

Sincerely,

Karen Austin

Karen Austin

Enc. Résumé

HOW TO OVERCOME CHALLENGES TO EMPLOYMENT

There are very few perfect candidates for any job. As a formerly incarcerated individual you obviously have some challenges to deal with in your job search or for a particular job that you desire. Some of the challenges come from your prior behaviors and some may come from the fact that you have little or no experience in the occupational area. How to overcome specific issues related to your incarceration are addressed in all of the other Career Success Guides. This guide will discuss some of the other more common challenges that may also impact your job search.

You Were Fired

The chances are good that if you were working at the time of your arrest and conviction, you were fired from that job. This may not have been the first time in your work history that you were fired. Being fired, however, can happen to anyone who has a job. You understand why you were fired from your job when you were incarcerated. What is most important, though is for you to understand exactly why you got fired the other times and decide if you can correct the cause. Some common reasons why people get fired are:

Poor Attendance Record – Determine if it was your transportation, personal schedule such as family obligations, or that you were not taking the job seriously enough.

Difficult Attitude – Ask yourself if you cooperated with your boss or co-workers, or did you feel that others did not like you or you did not "fit in?"

Not Following Policies or Orders – Did you have a hard time doing what your supervisor required because of what was asked of you, or because you just didn't care for your supervisor's personality?

When applying for a new job, you will have to deal with the fact that you had been fired from a job. Do not lie on an application or during the interview. On the application section, reason for leaving, leave it blank or put "dismissed." In an interview, be prepared to have a short explanation such as "I had problems with transportation, but I have solved that now."

It will help if you can find someone, like a co-worker at the prior workplace, who can describe your strengths at the old job, and use them as a reference.

Review the Career Success Guide: I Was Fired From Last Job.

Not Enough Experience

You will face this challenge every time you try to get a job that is new to you. You want a job to get the experience, but you do not qualify for the job because previous experience is required. This can be frustrating!

What you lack in experience can be exchanged for:

- Your eagerness to learn.
- Your willingness to work non-traditional hours like weekends, evening shifts and even split shifts.
- Your acceptance of an entry level wage with the understanding that as you learn the job, you will get appropriate wage increases.
- Your commitment to take classes and training to learn the skills needed for the job.

Transferable Skills

In order to convince a potential employer that you can do the job, you need to show that the skills that you have can be used on the new job.

These skills are called transferable skills. Transferable skills are skills that are used in a variety of jobs. A small sample of such skills are:

- Speaking and/or reading a foreign language
- Computer skills, including knowledge of software applications
- Organizational ability
- Interpersonal skills and the ability to relate to a variety of people
- Both written and oral communication skills
- Creative problem solving abilities

For a more comprehensive list of skills, review the Career Success Guides: SCANS Competencies and How to Determine You're Skills.

On your résumé include skills that you possess that are used in the new job. Review the Career Success Guide: How to Write a Résumé.

Job Hopping

If you have had more than four jobs in four years, you will probably be considered by employers to be a job hopper. Employers do not like job hoppers because they believe:

- They will lose their training investment in you, and
- You have not demonstrated that you are serious about working.

Here are some ways to defuse your job hopping:

- Explain that in each position you have held, you have gained more skills and training. This varied experience can be used on your new job.
- Tell the employer this time will be different because you have learned how to make a commitment to a job. You have become more mature in your goals.
- Emphasize the relationship between the tasks you performed in your previous jobs and the skills needed in the new job.
- If you have left a job or jobs for "good" reasons, such as to care for a family member or you were laid off, then state those reasons on your application and in the interview.

Lack of Transportation

Many employers say that dependability is the most important trait in an employee. You cannot be dependable if you don't have a way to get to work every day. Before you apply for any job, make sure you can get there. If you cannot afford to buy and operate a car, you must figure out how to get to work. The easiest way is to find work within a reasonable walking distance from your home.

The next easiest method is to use the public transportation system in your area. Find the routes for the bus or subway and then make sure the times for the stop locations fit your schedule for work. Finally, if you are going to rely on someone else, such as a friend or family member to drive you, then make sure you have a second or backup person for emergencies when the first person cannot give you a ride.

Dropped Out Of High School and Do Not Have A GED

Employers want educated employees who have achieved an educational level that matches the requirements for the job. A high school diploma or GED will give you many more opportunities for employment. Your wages will also be significantly higher than a non-high school graduate. If you have dropped out of high school, then get your GED as soon as possible. You can find out about getting a GED from your former high school or at your local One-Stop Career Center.

Even without your high school diploma or GED you will still be able to find jobs. They will be entry level jobs and will be primarily physical or menial labor. You will probably become frustrated with your lack of advancement and low pay. When filling our applications or during interviews, state that you are trying to get your GED. Then do it!

Review the Career Success Guide: Where to Get Job Training.

Other Challenges That Some Job Seekers Face

There are specific Career Success Guides that address other challenges that some job seekers face. These include:

- I Need to Change Jobs
- Job Search Tips for Ex-Offenders
- Tips for Offenders With Disabilities
- Job Search Issues For Women and Minorities

HOW DO I DEAL WITH NEGATIVE INFORMATION?

We all have things that we fear may negatively influence the hiring decision of a potential employer. Negative information, like being fired from your last job, lacking proper education or having a criminal record, must be addressed in your job search process. If you learn ways to deal with this negative information appropriately, you can minimize its impact when seeking employment.

How to Deal with Negative Information

On job applications:

You have three options:

1. Avoid applications altogether; seek jobs where they're not required (not easy to do), or;
2. Leave the offending question blank and explain the issue if you get an interview, or;
3. Tell the truth and trust that it will not eliminate you from consideration.

On résumés:

1. Select the form of résumé that will downplay your negatives. For example, if you have been out of work for more than 6 months, choose a format that emphasizes your transferable skills or your education.
2. Do not list jobs of very short duration (less than three months) to downplay an unstable work history.
3. Under no circumstances should you voluntarily put negative information such as an arrest or dishonorable discharge on your résumé. Never list your age or a disability. Negative information can wait for the interview, if it ever needs to come up at all.

During the interview:

1. If a negative subject comes up, assure the interviewer that the problem is in the past or that it will not affect your performance on the job.
2. Before you go to the interview prepare yourself to handle issues that might come up. Be ready to do damage control.

Are Your Ears Burning?

Is it possible that your former boss might be saying bad things about you? There are a few ways you can find out what your former employer is saying to potential employers:

- Ask them. If you are not convinced they will speak well of you, ask if there is someone else who can act as your reference when calls come in from potential employers.
- Ask a friend you trust to call your former employer. Your friend can simply say that you asked them to call your references to find out what they would say if a potential employer calls.
- If you are consistently being turned down for jobs, call the hiring firm and ask why you weren't hired. Ask if your references had anything to do with it.

THOU SHALT NOT LIE

Do not lie about your past or about negative issues. If the interviewer discovers you are lying, or even suspects it, you will almost certainly not get the job. If you do get the job, you could be fired at any time for lying to your employer.

Specific Negative Information - Damage Control

Fired - Admit you were let go (do not use the word "fired"). Explain the reason without getting defensive. Don't say negative things about your old boss or company. Explain that this was an isolated occurrence and that it will not happen at your new job. It may be possible for you to convince your previous employer to say something less damaging. Be sure that you and your former boss are saying the same thing. Review the Career Success Guide: I Was Fired From My Last Job. Now What?

Out of Work for a Long Time - Sometimes an employer will ask what you did while you were out of work. Rehearse your answer before you are asked the question in the interview. There must be something productive that you did while you were out of work. Possible answers include: I stayed home to care for my children, I took classes at the Community College, I have decided on a new career or focus, I took an extended vacation or trip, I stayed home to care for a parent or I was involved in a home improvement project. If you held a job while incarcerated, be sure to include that job in your application and résumé. This will fill in gaps in your employment history.

Not Enough Experience - Use relevant volunteer experience, education or hobbies on your résumé and job application. Focus on your readiness to apply yourself to your new career. Emphasize your transferable skills.

Lack of Education - Don't bring up the lack of a degree. Focus on your skills and abilities, your past experience, volunteer work and training. Don't lie if you are asked directly about completing your education.

Internet - "Google" your name to see what employers may find. Remove any compromising photos or information from your social networking profiles. Be ready to do damage control for negative comments people may have said about you.

Medical Problems/Disabilities - The Americans with Disabilities Amendments Act (ADAAA) of 2008 prevents employers from denying you employment based on a disability that does not affect your ability to do your job. Additionally, employers are required to make reasonable alterations to the workplace to accommodate an employee's disabilities. Explain to the employer that you are capable of doing the job and that your disability is not a problem. Be prepared to detail changes to the work environment that may be required to accommodate your disability...or, if none are required, be sure to emphasize that. Review the Career Success Guide: Job Search Tips for Offenders with Disabilities.

Criminal Record

- Plan on your employer discovering your conviction. Failure to reveal your conviction will most assuredly result in your being fired when your record is discovered. Be honest up front to avoid a later firing.
- If you were arrested, but not convicted, you are innocent and do not have to report your arrest to anyone. Leave all questions about arrests but not convicted blank on an application. Employers cannot legally ask about arrests, only convictions.
- If it was a major felony conviction, you might have to avoid applying for certain jobs. Jobs handling money or working with children or other jobs that require a high level of trust may not be the best choices for you. Jobs that require licensing or bonding may prohibit felons from employment. Your local One-Stop Career Center can assist you to identify employers who are willing to hire felons.
- You may want to bring up the issue yourself, if you feel the employer will encounter it during the employment process. This will give you the opportunity to explain the circumstances, that you have matured and that it will not happen again. It will also avoid the employer's discovery of the information later.
- Juvenile records are usually closed, so you don't need to reveal this information to potential employers.
- You and your employer may be eligible for special tax credits and bonding. This gives you added leverage when talking to a potential employer. Check with your parole officer and local One-Stop Career Center for information. For additional information, review the Career Search Guide: Job Search Tips for Returning Citizens.

When talking about your record here are some points to remember:

- Relax – Because if you are not comfortable talking about your conviction, your interviewer will be uncomfortable with your explanation. Practice telling your story until you are comfortable with it.
- Briefly explain your conviction in words that the interviewer will understand. Don't provide penal codes or legal jargon (the interviewer will only ask what they mean).
- Don't dwell on your conviction. Rather talked about your skills and what you bring to the company.

Two examples of how to respond to the interviewer asking, "I see from your application that you have been convicted of a crime. Will you explain this to me? Tell me about it."

"I'm glad you asked because I want you to feel comfortable about hiring me. It is embarrassing for me to talk about. I want to assure you that it had nothing to with my previous employers or work. I stupidly took some property that didn't belong to me and as a result, I was arrested, convicted and was incarcerated. I used my time in jail to not only reorient my life, but to decide what field I would like to get into. While in jail I was able to get training as a mechanic. You can see from my application and resume that I now possess the skills and training to do the job you require."

"When I was younger I got mixed up with the wrong crowd and got in trouble for using drugs. We all do things when we are young that we regret. I used the time in jail to my advantage by completing an air conditioning and heating training program and received my certificate. I've researched several air conditioning companies in the area and yours is well respected. I would really like to be a part of your team. I am more than willing to submit to a drug test."

Younger Workers: If you are relatively new to the work force, employers may be concerned about your lack of experience, possible immaturity and unreliability.

Explain that your youth is a benefit because you don't have bad habits to break. Your employer can train you to do things exactly as they want them done. If you are willing to put in extra time at work, mention this. Most of all, present yourself as a mature adult. On your résumé, focus on transferable skills and your education.

Gender - It is illegal for an employer to discriminate based on gender when hiring.

Men: Most people think that gender discrimination only happens to women. Men face similar problems when applying for traditionally female occupations. Direct the discussion to the skills and traits required to do the job.

Women: Most employers' concerns focus on your responsibilities to your family. It is illegal for an employer to ask you if you have children or to ask you about your plans in this regard. If you feel they are concerned about the issue, you might bring it up and assure them that your family responsibilities will not interfere with your ability to do your job. Review the Career Success Guide: Job Search Issues for Women and Minorities.

Sexual Preference - Employers may be afraid of the risk of HIV transmission to fellow employees. Additionally, there may be prejudice against gay and lesbian workers. As it does not affect your ability to do your job in any way, do not mention your sexual preference. There is nothing to be gained and it's irrelevant.

WHAT ARE PRE-EMPLOYMENT TESTS?

Many employers require all job applicants to take pre-employment tests. These tests are used to screen out unsuitable applicants and to validate information found on an employment application or résumé. These tests may include aptitude and personality tests, drug screening, honesty tests and medical examinations. Employers may also conduct background checks and contact references. Because an employer may try to verify the information you have given on your application and in your résumé, make sure that all of the information is correct. As a formerly incarcerated individual, you need to prepare to be tested by the employer before you are hired and perhaps even during your employment.

Aptitude and Personality Tests

Some employers use written tests, usually in a multiple choice format, to gain insight into your abilities and personality. There are four types of pre-employment tests which an employer may administer:

- General Aptitude Tests. General aptitude tests claim to measure a person's ability to learn.
- Specific Aptitude Tests These tests measure a person's knowledge or skill in a specific area. An example is a typing test which measures a person's typing speed and accuracy. Other tests may measure a person's eye-hand coordination, a person's knowledge of a foreign language (including English) or a person's knowledge of the required job tasks. The latter includes tests like the National Teacher's Examination.
- Personality Tests. Personality tests purport to measure the degree to which a person has certain traits. They are frequently used by the employer to predict the future behavior of the applicant. For example, the employer may want to know if the applicant has the personality for a management position. Personality tests are usually administered by psychologists. If you have a history of sexual misconduct and/or emotional issues such as anger management, employers may want evidence from a professional that these behaviors are no longer an issue.
- Integrity and Honesty Tests. These tests purport to predict the honesty of the applicant. Knowing this trait in an applicant is especially important to employers when the applicant will have access to money. It is common for retail employers to integrate this type of test into their application process. Often these tests are embedded (as a part of) other tests or interview questions. Do not attempt to be dishonest. Answer the questions honestly, even if you think such responses will disqualify you for the job. You can always explain your answers in the interview. For example, you may be asked if you ever took something from someone that did not belong to you. Answer it honestly and then explain the circumstances and that such behavior is part of your past, not your future.

Before an employer can use test results as a hiring criteria, the employer must prove that the results are valid. In other words, the employer must document that the test scores relate directly to the success or failure of employees. Pre-employment tests are not only valuable to the employer, they can be valuable to the job applicant. Studies have shown that one reason people quit a job is that they don't have the knowledge or ability to handle the work responsibilities. Pre-employment tests can help you find out if your qualifications are in line with what the company wants or needs.

Preparing For the Tests

Do not try to study for these tests. Try to be calm and take your time, if permitted. Some companies may have you complete a skills test as a part of your job interview. Come to the interview prepared to take a skills test related to the job you seek. Skills tests include typing, working computer software problems, or performing physical tasks such as sorting or lifting. It is important to do your best on these tasks.

Testing People with Disabilities

Employers cannot discriminate against people with disabilities. They must demonstrate that they are measuring an applicant's abilities and not the applicant's disability. The employer may need to make special accommodations for persons with disabilities. For example, the employer could provide the test in Braille or read the test items to the visually impaired applicant.

For Additional Information on Workplace Testing

If you want to learn more about workplace testing, read the U.S. Department of Labor: Employment & Training Administration Department's detailed report called Tests and Other Assessments: Helping You Make Better Career Decisions. You can access it for free on the department's web site: www.doleta.gov.

Background Checks

Employers will often use outside resources to get a better understanding of the applicant. If the information that the employer receives is negative, the employer will use that information to screen out the applicant. The amount of information that an employer seeks in a background check depends to a large degree on the sensitivity of the job. For example, someone looking for an unskilled position would be subject to far fewer requirements than someone applying for a job at a nuclear power plant facility or for the local police department. The company will either have you sign a separate statement giving them the right to conduct a background check or they will indicate on the company application that the company conducts background checks on all applicants. Your signing the employment application gives them the right to conduct the checks. Companies typically obtain and examine the following documents:

Employment Records - Employers will contact your former employers and, at a minimum, obtain your dates of employment. If they make a telephone call to your former supervisors, they will try to confirm the information that you gave in your application and résumé.

Criminal and incarceration Records - unless your criminal record was obtained as a youth, criminal records are public knowledge. Criminal background checks include only convictions. Assume that your employer will obtain a copy of your criminal record. Do not be surprised by what is in your record. Have your parole officer obtain a copy of your record before you start your job search and go over the record with him/her. Be prepared to explain each item on your record.

Litigation Records - Employers may want to know if you have filed suit against a former employer. This information is also public record, unless the court specifically sealed the verdict.

Education Records - Employers may check with schools to confirm that you graduated from a specific program.

Military Records - If the job you seek relates to your military specialty, the employer may seek confirmation from the military.

Social Security Number - Through the Social Security Administration and the Department of Homeland Security the employer will be able to confirm that you have the legal right to work in the U.S.

Driving and Vehicle Records - If you seek a job that requires a driver's license, then the employer can obtain a copy of your driving record from the state Department of Motor Vehicles.

Credit Report - If you seek a job that involves your handling money, the employer may want to get a credit report.

Reference Checks

Employers usually like to speak to the candidate's references in order to learn more about the candidate. You should have contacted all of the references you listed on your application. This will alert them that someone may contact them. Because personal references are not reliable sources of information about the candidate's work history, employers use the information to confirm personality traits noted in the job interview. More intensive reference checks can involve interviews with anyone that knows about you, such as teachers, friends, coworkers, neighbors, and family members. Employers use these in-depth checks when the applicant has applied for a job that has a security requirement.

Drug Screening

Congress passed the Drug-Free Workplace Act in 1988. Although the Act only applies to federal employees, many state and local governments adopted similar programs for state and local employees. Some governments only require drug tests for jobs involving public safety such as bus drivers. Some state and local governments require all employees to be tested. Private employers can make the candidate's passing a drug screening test a condition of employment. The employer should tell you if a drug screening test is going to be required. If this is the case, you may be asked to give your permission. If you do not give permission to be drug tested, you probably will not be offered the job. If you are taking prescription medicine or other drugs for a medical condition, you should tell the employer before your test. As an ex-offender, regardless of your crime, be prepared to be drug tested.

The basic drug test used by most corporate drug testing programs test for:

- Cannabinoids (Marijuana, Hashish)
- Cocaine (Cocaine, Crack, Benzoylecognine)
- Opiates (Heroin, Opium, Codeine, Morphine)
- Amphetamines (Amphetamines, Methamphetamines, Speed)
- Phencyclidine (PCP, Angel Dust)
- Benzodiazepines (Tranquilizers-Diazepam, Valium, Librium, Ativan, Xanax, Clonopin, Serax, Halcion, Rohypnol)
- Barbituates (Phenobarbita l, Secobarbitol, Pentobarbital, Butalbital, Amobarbital)
- Methaqualone (Qualuudes)
- Propoxyphene (Darvon compounds)
- Methadone

The employer may also test for:

- Ethanol (alcohol)
- Inhalents (Toluene, Xylene, Benzene)
- LSD
- Hallucinogens (Psilocybin, Mescaline, MDMA, MDA, MDE)

If there is a drug out there, there is a drug test for it!

WHAT ARE INTERVIEWERS LOOKING FOR?

No one can get a job without going through a job interview. Understanding what the interviewer is seeking from a candidate can assist you in answering the interviewer's questions. The interviewer has just a few minutes to decide if you are the right person for the job. Knowing specifically what the interviewer is looking for will help you shine in this most important part of the job search process. Returning Citizen, you must convince the interviewer that you are sincere, honest and will not be a risk.

Interviewers Are People Too!

You're probably not the only nervous one at your job interview. Interviewers are often uneasy during the hiring process because:

They're afraid to make a bad hire. The process of hiring and training people is expensive. An employer needs to make sure they've got the right person for the job before they put precious resources into training them. Also, if the other workers don't like the new employee, the interviewer will feel responsible.

They're not trained to interview people. Most interviewers are people who have risen into managerial positions. They don't have training in how to select new employees.

They don't want to have to turn people down. There are usually a limited number of open positions and a large number of applications. The interviewer doesn't like being put in the position of saying no to someone they really like.

They may be uncomfortable with people who have been incarcerated. As a Returning Citizen you will find that people who have never been incarcerated are uncomfortable with someone who has been incarcerated. This uneasiness comes from both their ignorance of ex-offenders and their curiosity. You may find that you will need to educate the interviewer and to convince the interviewer that you are not like the television stereotype. Do not be offended if the interviewer asks you questions about your incarceration and prison experiences.

At A Minimum, The Interviewer Is Looking To Discover The Following:

WHAT does the candidate want to do?

The interviewer wants to be sure that you will be happy performing the tasks required to complete the job properly. Few employers can afford to let new employees "try out" for jobs until they find one they like. Candidates need to be focused on what they want to do now and in the very near future. This job cannot be a stopping off point for the candidate.

CAN the candidate do what they say?

Interviewers try to discover how closely your knowledge, skills and abilities match those required for the job.

WILL the candidate actually do the job?

It is every employer's nightmare that they will hire someone who simply will not do the job. You must assure the interviewer that you will show up for work, will be on time and will put your best effort into the task at hand. The interviewer is also concerned about your personality. Will you be easy to work with? Will you cause morale problems among the other employees?

HOW MUCH will the candidate cost?

Do your salary and benefit requirements fit within the range that the employer has budgeted for the position? How long will it take the candidate to become productive?

First Impressions

Even before you say anything, the interview has begun. Your appearance, actions toward other people, hygiene and body language all make an impression on the interviewer. Think of how you will appear. The following are hints that can help you make a good first impression:

- Dress neatly in clean clothes that are appropriate to the job setting. For an office job, this may mean a suit for men and business outfit for women. For a construction job, less formal clothing makes sense.
- Be aware of your hygiene. Shower, brush your teeth, clean your nails and comb your hair before you leave for your interview. Bad hygiene can really turn off an employer.
- Start the interview before you walk in the front door. Don't be rude to anyone. If you are, word will get back to the interviewer.
- Pay attention to your body language. You need to smile, offer a firm handshake, stand or sit up straight in your chair (see the Career Success Guide: What Can I Expect During the Interview? for more body language tips).
- Don't smoke or chew gum at any time during the interviewing process. If you smoke, be sure to chew a breath mint before you enter the building.
- Mind your manners. Say please and thank you. If it's a mealtime interview, pay attention to your table manners.
- Be mindful of your mannerism and behavior. Remember you are no longer in prison. Mannerisms and behaviors that may be acceptable and expected while in prison may put off people who are unfamiliar with this culture.

The Ideal Candidate - You!

At the beginning of the hiring process, an effective interviewer will think about the open position and construct a profile of the ideal candidate for that job The closer you come to that profile, the greater your chances are of getting the job. The best way to discover what the employer is looking for is simply to ask them, before or during the interview, "Can you describe for me the ideal candidate for this position?"

If you don't have the luxury of asking this question, or if the interviewer hasn't thought about an ideal candidate, you'll have to figure the answer out for yourself. Before the interview, analyze any information that you have about the firm and the position. Want ads usually describe the knowledge, skills traits and experience necessary for the job. If you know someone who works at the company, ask them what it's like to work there. "What traits are rewarded or discouraged by the company?"

Review and complete the Career Success Guide: Ideal Job Worksheet.

We All Want To Be Liked

The interviewer wants to be liked, just as you do. Here are some ways to help you make a connection with the interviewer and make both of you more comfortable in the interview:

- Show an interest in the interviewer. Ask about something in the office - a photograph, poster or award.
- Follow the interviewer's lead and conversation style. Adjust your pace to theirs. Don't interrupt.
- Be courteous. Say please and thank you. Don't sit until asked to sit by the interviewer.
- Go into the interview with a positive attitude.
- Don't be negative about other people. This makes interviewers wonder what you'll say about them behind their backs.
- Speak openly and honestly about your incarceration. Emphasize the fact that you accept your punishment, that you learned from your mistake and that you took advantage of the opportunity to get training while incarcerated.

Some Of The Common Traits Interviewers Are Looking For:

- dedication to the job
- enthusiasm for the task at hand
- a pleasant personality
- honesty
- a positive attitude

Skills And Traits That Are Specific To Particular Jobs:

- knowledge of specific software programs or equipment
- professional degrees
- job-specific skills such as bookkeeping, carpentry or driving a bus
- licensing requirements such as a Commercial Driver's License (CDL)
- leadership abilities

Once you've discovered what the interviewer is looking for, highlight the parts of your training, experience and personality that fit the profile of their ideal employee. An employer needs to hire someone. They have a job that needs to get done. They would like nothing better than to discover that you are the perfect person for the job. BE THAT PERSON!

In Your Job Search...

- No one gets a job without an interview. It's an essential part of any job search.
- Realize that employers are people, too. Your interviewer may be just as nervous as you are.
- Preparing yourself for the interview ahead of time will put you more at ease on the day of the interview. Learn about the company, who you'll be meeting with and exactly where the interview will take place.
- Be prepared to not only speak openly about your incarceration, but to emphasize that you learned from the experience.
- The interview isn't just for the interviewer to get to know you, it's also for you to learn about the job, benefits, the company, and the people with whom you will be working. Feel free to ask questions that will help you evaluate whether you want to work there. Is travel required? Is overtime typical? Is there a dress code? What would a typical day on the job look like? Will you be working alone? Or as part of a team?
- Be positive about yourself, the job and the interviewer.

WHAT ARE THE DIFFERENT KINDS OF INTERVIEWS?

Most people think of the typical one-on-one type of job interview when they think of an interview, but there are many kinds of job interviews. Knowing what type of interview you will be having will help in your preparation. Re-entering Citizens will find that they are exposed to the same types of interviews that non-offenders face.

Types of Job Interviews:

One-on-One

This is the most common type of interview, where one person will be interviewing only you. See the Career Success guide: What Can I Expect During the Interview, which outlines exactly what will happen during a one-on-one interview and how to prepare for it. The interviewer may use one or all of the techniques detailed on the right. Most interviews for entry-level jobs are done by the manager or immediate supervisor and are this type of interaction.

Group

In a group interview, several candidates are interviewed at once. The purpose of this type of interview is usually to see how you act in a team situation and how competitive you are. Your group might be given a task to perform together. Those who contribute the most to the group will be considered first for open positions. There may be employees of the company mixed into your group, but you won't know who they are.

Team

In this type of interview you are interviewed by a panel of several employees of the company. The key to success in a panel interview is to interact with each member of the panel. Make eye contact. Answer questions asked by any of the members. Look for specific concerns from individual members and try to address them. Be aware that the team may play "good cop, bad cop." One may actually be confrontational while the second may appear to be your friend. Try to understand why they take this approach and respond appropriately.

Multiple

Often, several interviews will be set up with different members of the same company. If this happens, try to find out in advance what the schedule will be so that you will know how much time you have with each person. Use what you learn about the company and the tasks of the position in one interview to present yourself better in the next. Be sure to get the business card of each interviewer so you can send them all thank-you notes.

Second Interviews

If you are invited back for a second interview, it usually means that you are one of a few final candidates for the position. It often also means that the decision-maker either has not interviewed you or still must be convinced. Approach this interview with the same enthusiasm, knowledge and care as you did the first.

Techniques Used By the Interviewer:

Question and Answer

This is the typical interview format. Questions may be straight-forward, or they may be tricky. The interviewer directs the interview. As you answer each question, be sure to highlight your strengths (see the Career Success Guide: Common Interview Questions).

Non-Directed

Not everyone is a skilled interviewer. You may find yourself in an interview where the employer is unprepared or seems unsure of what questions to ask. In this case, you will have to do your best to keep the interview focused on your interests and abilities and to find out what you need to know about the position being offered. If you are well-prepared, and you know what you want to communicate, you can use a non-directed interview to your advantage by communicating exactly what you want and avoiding topics that might not cast you in a favorable light.

Behavioral

In this type of interview, you will be asked questions about how you acted in a specific situation. Questions might include: Describe a situation where you had to resolve a conflict or describe a situation where you used creativity to solve a problem. In these interviews, the interviewer is looking for responses that demonstrate a specific skill that is used on the job. You may also be asked to describe a situation where you were not successful in solving a problem and what you did about it.

Here the interviewer is looking for evidence of accountability and the ability to learn from mistakes. Prepare for this type of interview by taking each task that the job will entail and identifying a situation in which you performed that task.

Traveling Tips

After screening interviews given on campus, at job fairs, or over the phone, companies often will invite the top few candidates to their company headquarters for further interviews. If you are not interested in working for the company, or if you have no intention of moving, thank them politely and decline the interview. On the other hand, if you are interested, set up the interview.

Arrangements must be made prior to your trip. Will you fly there? When? How should you get from the airport to the office? Where will you be staying? Knowing ahead of time your schedule and what will be reimbursed will allow you to be more relaxed during the trip. Usually, the interview will consist of multiple interviews and probably a mealtime interview.

Screening Interviews:

Screening

These are shorter interviews, usually performed by a member of the Personnel Department. Standard questions are asked, usually designed to weed out unqualified applicants. The interviewer may not know a lot about your field. Give them plenty of reasons to pass you on to the next step and try not to give them reasons to exclude you. Emphasize your experience and education. Treat this interview as you would a typical one-on-one interview.

Campus and Job Fair Interviews

Campus interviews are a form of screening interview. They are shorter, usually one-on-one interviews and are designed to allow a recruiter to see a large number of applicants on a single trip. Most college and university career placement offices have procedures for scheduling these interviews, which are typically with large corporate employers. Follow the procedures established by the placement office or job fair sponsor, or you might miss out!

Campus recruiters are trained interviewers. You should prepare for these interviews thoroughly. A recruiter is looking for the candidate who is alert and well-presented and who comes to the interview with knowledge about the company. Your placement office can help you gain this information. If you are successful at the interview, you may be asked to an on-site interview at the company. Don't forget to write your thank-you note. It might help you stand out from the rest of the crowd.

Telephone Interviews

Telephone interviews are often used to evaluate an applicant before paying for them to visit the company. Usually, a time for the interview is set up in advance, but not always. Some employers simply pick up the phone and call the candidate. Be ready for the call.

Make sure that you have no distractions, such as children or dogs. There are some advantages to the telephone interview. Obviously, you don't have to get dressed up, and you can have your résumé and information about the company right in front of you while you talk to the interviewer. For more information, review the Career Success Guide: How to Ace Telephone Interviews.

Other Types of Interviews:

Meals

Sometimes an interview will take place over lunch or dinner, or a series of interviews will include lunch. Dining with your interviewer is a great opportunity to develop a more comfortable relationship. BEWARE! You are still on an interview. Do not forget this! Resist the urge to become overly familiar with the interviewer. Remain professional, and remember your table manners: no elbows on the table and don't speak with your mouth full. Order something in the mid-price range on the menu, but nothing messy, like spaghetti. Avoid alcohol and don't smoke. Your host will almost always pay the bill but you should offer and be prepared to pay for your meal.

Informational interviews

These interviews are not about employee selection at all. If you are considering entering a new field, you can use an informational interview to find out about what that field is like from someone in that line of work. First, compose some questions you would like to ask. What is a typical workday for you? What are the educational requirements for this type of work? What's the best way to get into the field? Next, call your contact and ask them for fifteen minutes of their time. This is important. Be sure to ask them first, and do not go over fifteen minutes! At the end of the interview, thank them for their time and end the conversation politely. This type of interview is not about job openings. Resist the urge to ask about open positions.

For more information, review the Career Success Guide: How to Acquire Job Information by Interviewing.

Spouses

Occasionally, you will be asked to bring your spouse with you, especially if the job involves a relocation. Remember, your spouse is also being evaluated! Many companies encourage family values and evaluate how the candidate and their spouse interact.

WHAT CAN I EXPECT DURING THE INTERVIEW?

Everything that you have done in your job search has been designed to get you an interview with a potential employer. Now that you have that interview scheduled, it is important that you prepare. There is a natural flow to most interviews. Knowing what is going to happen will help you prepare for this important part of the job search process. Remember: No one gets a job without interviewing.

1. Preparing For the Interview

Before the big day, find out as much as you can about the company and the job. Your local One-Stop Career Center, library and Chamber of Commerce can help you. Look for the company's website and do an Internet search for articles about the company. You can ask a librarian to help you find articles in national magazines, too. If you know someone who works at the company, talk with them. Check Internet networking sites such as www.linkedin.com to find contacts. Review the Career Success Guide: How to Research the Job & the Employer. Also if you obtained the job interview or contact from an organization that assists Returning Citizens, then contact your representative. He or she will be able to give your insight and information on the company, their attitude toward hiring job seekers with criminal justice involvement and what to expect in the interview.

Prepare for some of the questions that you think you might be asked. The Career Success Guide: Common Interview Questions, lists some of the major questions that interviewers ask. Be prepared to tell the interviewer:

- Why you want this job with this company.
- What your knowledge, skills and abilities are as they relate to the position you seek. Be ready also to talk about examples of past successes that prove you can do the required tasks.
- That you are ready and willing to do the job.
- About your incarceration.

Find out where the interview is and determine how long it will take you to get there. You might want to make a practice run so that you don't get lost on the day of the interview. Be sure to bring copies of your résumé and your completed job application.

2. In the Waiting Room

The interview begins before you even meet the interviewer. It is very important that you make a good first impression. Do this by being on time or a few minutes early, dressing appropriately (review the Career Success Guide: How to Make a Good First Impression) and presenting a positive, friendly attitude. Be courteous to everyone you meet in the building. If you are rude to someone, you can be sure that this will get back to the boss. Remember, many non-Returning Citizens have pre-conceived attitudes about formerly incarcerated individuals. Make sure you do not exhibit any of these stereotyped behaviors. And don't forget to turn off your cell phone!

3. Meeting the Interviewer and Making a Connection

Body language is important (see sidebar). Stand when the interviewer comes into the waiting area. Shake the interviewer's hand when it is offered to you. Your handshake should be firm, but not bone-crunching. Look the interviewer in the eye and don't forget to smile! The first few minutes of the interview are usually spent on small talk and may actually be the most important few minutes in the whole interview. This is the time that you might want to search for a connection to the interviewer. Comment on a painting in the office or the golf trophy on the desk. Don't get too personal or friendly, however. Remain professional. Let the interviewer set the pace of the interview.

Body Language

During the interview, how you act is almost as important as what you say. Your posture and facial expressions can tell the interviewer a lot about you. Unfortunately many non-Returning Citizens expect reentering individuals to exhibit the same behaviors that they have seen on TV and in movies. Not demonstrating any of these stereotyped mannerisms and behaviors will greatly enhance your image in the mind of the interviewer.

- Look to the interviewer for cues. Shake hands when one is offered. Wait to be told where to sit.
- You want to appear relaxed, but attentive. Sit up straight. Look the interviewer in the eye, but don't scare them down.
- Gestures that make you appear open and flexible include showing your palms, keeping your arms relaxed at your sides and uncrossing your legs.
- Closed or defensive gestures include folding your arms across your chest and tightly crossing your legs. Placing your hands on your hips or crossing your hands behind your head may indicate inappropriate dominance and should be avoided.
- Everyone has habits in their body language. Try to learn what yours are and control them. Typical nervous behaviors include tapping a foot, nail biting, fidgeting, excessive arm waving or gesturing.
- Many people pepper their sentences with "You know" or "like" or say "um" before every sentence. Try to limit or remove these expressions from your conversation. Raising your voice in pitch at the end of each sentence makes it sound as if you are insecure and seeking approval. Audio or video taping yourself talking with friends may reveal these speech patterns so that you can learn to avoid them.
- Don't get too hung up on body language. If you try to control your actions too much, you will appear stiff or nervous. Take it slow and easy to show that you are confident but respectful.

4. Getting Down To Business

After you have chatted for a short while, the interviewer will probably begin to ask you questions or will tell you about the company or the specific job for which you are applying. This is where your preparation pays off. You should already know what you want to communicate to the interviewer: the reason why you want this particular position, that you are capable of doing the job and that you will be a good employee who can be counted on to perform the work. Additionally, you want to convince the interviewer that the issues that resulted in your conviction are no longer issues.

Questions asked by the interviewer may be designed to discover these things, or they may not. Practice all of the questions listed in the Career Success Guide: Common Interview Questions. Be courteous throughout the interview. Don't get defensive or be apologetic. Follow the interviewer's lead.

5. Time to Go

Most interviews last about an hour. Again, follow the interviewer's lead to know when the interview is coming to a close. In the last few minutes, try to emphasize the following points: State that you are still interested in the position; summarize the major points of the interview, including your applicable strengths; and, if the interviewer raised concerns about you during the interview, state why these concerns are not problems. At this point, ask when a decision will be made about the position. This way you will know how long to wait before calling to find out if you got the job. Shake the interviewer's hand and leave, making sure that you haven't left anything behind.

Asking Questions

You will also want to ask questions about the job or the company. Have these in mind, or even written down, when you go into the interview. Refer to your notes during the interview, if you like. You may also want to jot down some information, so have a pen and paper handy.

Find out from the interviewer what knowledge, skills and abilities their ideal candidate has. Frame your answers around their description of the ideal candidate. For more information on the ideal candidate review the Career Success Guide: What Are Interviewers Looking For?

6. After the Interview

Send a thank you note within one day of the interview (Review the Career Success Guide: How to Write a Thank You Note). You may even want to fax or email it, depending on how soon the decision about the hire will be made. Thank the interviewer for their time and state again that you are very interested in the position. This is important. One company gives a second interview to anyone who sent them a thank you letter. Sending a letter shows that you are interested, responsible and organized. Be sure to check the spelling of names, if possible, to avoid misspellings in your letter.

7. Salary Negotiations

Only discuss salary after you have been offered the job. (See the Career Success Guide: How to Negotiate a Fair Salary.) Try to avoid being the first person to state a number. If they ask you about salary before they have offered the job, make the best of it, but avoid stating a salary. If you do, chances are your number will either be too low, and you will have lost money, or too high, reducing your chances of getting the job. Try starting with the following: Before I answer your question, could you give me an idea of the salary range for other people who are doing work similar to what I would be doing?

8. The Job Offer

Occasionally, an employer will offer you the job during the interview. Before accepting any offer of employment, consider the following:

- Make sure you want the job. Remember, the employer is hiring you, but you are also hiring the employer. Do you want to work for the company? Will you be doing what you want to do? Are you being paid what you feel is a fair salary? Have you thought through all of the positives and negatives?
- It is best not to accept an offer if it is given during the first interview, because you have not had ample time to review the pros and cons. Indicate that you are flattered by the offer and that you will give them a decision within 24 hours.
- If an offer is not made during the interview, and it usually isn't, review the pros and cons of working for that employer after the interview. Then you can be prepared to give an answer when you are offered employment.
- Review the Career Success Guides: Pre-Interview Checklist, Post-Interview Checklist, and How to Respond to a Job Offer.

9. Congratulations!

Accepting an offer means understanding and accepting the terms of your employment. Before you accept, your salary should be settled. You should ask about benefits, health insurance, holidays, vacation and sick time, and more basic things like when you will begin work, where to report and whether there are any dress requirements for the company. Many companies will put the terms of employment into a letter. You might want to request this, even if they don't offer it, so that everyone is clear on what is expected.

HOW TO PREPARE FOR THE INTERVIEW

Being well prepared for a job interview will increase your chances of receiving a job offer. When you are prepared for the interview, you will come across as self-confident and assured. Preparation lets you take care of the details ahead of time, minimizes the effects of Murphy's Law ("Whatever can go wrong, will go wrong") and allows you to focus on the task at hand - landing that job. Since it may have been years since you last applied for a job, it is doubly important that you take the time and effort to prepare for this event.

Preparing In Advance Gives You An Edge By:

Eliminating the Fear Of The Unknown

When giving a speech, it is often helpful to overcome your anxiety and fear of "freezing" by writing it out and practicing it ahead of time. Why not apply the same technique to the interview process by writing out and practicing your responses to the most frequently asked interview questions?

Reducing the Element of Surprise

If you prepare properly by taking care of the logistical details of getting to the interview and anticipating questions you'll be asked, you will reduce your chances of being surprised and caught off-guard.

Increasing Your Self-Confidence

Employers look for applicants who are confident in their ability to do the job. Knowing you have prepared thoroughly in advance only adds to your confidence level, an attribute that comes across loud and clear to the interviewer.

Allowing You to Focus On The Interview Itself

As you get ready the day of the interview, you won't be bothered trying to remember the details. Since you already will have taken care of them, you'll be able to review your responses to the anticipated questions.

Preparation Falls into Several Categories

For more in-depth information about these, refer to the appropriate Career Success Guide on each topic.

Know Yourself

Know your career goals, skills, interests and aptitudes, strengths/weaknesses and value that you would add to the company. See the Career Success Guide: Ideal Job Worksheet.

Practice Your Interviewing Skills

Anticipate common questions that could be asked, and know your answers to them; practice responses to difficult questions; and use videotape and/or mock interviews to practice your skills. See the Career Success Guide: Common Interview Questions.

Leave Your "Street" Attitude at Home.

The job interview is not like many of the "interviews" that you experienced while incarcerated. The job interviewer is not trying to trick or intimidate you. Rather he or she is only trying to determine if you are the right candidate for the job. Try to relax, not be defensive and fearful that you will say the wrong thing. The only thing bad that can happen to you if you blow the interview is that you will not be hired.

Research the Job and the Company

This high-value activity can pay off handsomely. The more time you spend here, the less time you waste later. Not only will you avoid wasting time on a job you don't really want, you will impress an employer during an interview by taking the time to find out about the organization and its competitors. The employer's assumption is that your thoroughness here will also show up in your job performance. See the Career Success Guide: How to Research the Job & the Employer.

Preliminary Activities

Know where you're going:

- Being late is the kiss of death! Employers assume that if you are late for an interview, you will be late for the job.
- Find out the exact address, building, floor and room number. Don't be late because you've been wandering around an office complex or a large building looking for the right place.
- Get directions to the interview when you are contacted for the interview or by using the Internet mapping service such as Google Maps (http://maps.google.com/maps) or MapQuest (www.mapquest.com).
- Decide on the best route. Find an alternative route in case rush hour traffic or construction interferes with your timetable.
- Arrive at least 10 minutes early so you can catch your breath and visit the restroom to check out your appearance and make any last minute adjustments.
- If your interview is being conducted by telephone or video, be sure you are familiar with the procedures and any video/virtual meeting software that might be used. You may need to download and install free video conferencing software. Familiarize yourself well in advance of the interview with the software. If you need assistance, seek help from your local One-stop Career Center.

Know who is conducting the interview:

- From the person who contacts you for the interview:
  - Find out the name and title of the interviewer(s) and write the information down. Don't rely on your memory.
  - Make sure you know how to pronounce and spell the name correctly.
  - If a group or panel will be interviewing, find out the number of people and their job responsibilities.
- Have enough résumés for everyone on the panel plus yourself.

What to Do the Day before the Interview

Think about your agenda

Know what points you want to get across. You don't want to take over the interview, but make sure they know what you can bring to the job as well as the value you can add to the company.

Fuel Up

Put gas in the car. Have a map of the area handy in case you are forced to take an alternate route. If using public transportation, make sure you have change or tokens, and a schedule.

Get Your Money Together

Have enough cash for parking, public transportation and snack machines.

Pick Out Your Clothes

Decide on the outfit you will be wearing to the interview. Choose conservative clothing. Make sure your clothes are clean, fresh and pressed. Don't forget to shine your shoes. Lay out clothes and shoes the night before.

Set Your Alarm Clock

Synchronize your alarm clock and watch with the correct time, then set the alarm. Use a wind-up, or battery powered alarm clock or your cell phone's alarm function as a back-up in case you lose electrical power during the night.

Get A Good Night's Rest

You'll want to be at your best for the interview, so a sound night's sleep will ensure that you are clear-headed.

Assemble Your Materials

Organize the materials you'll be taking with you.

- Use a clean folder for:
  - Résumés - Have enough copies for the interviewer or interview team, plus one for yourself (even if you submitted your résumé electronically)
  - Letters of recommendation/references
  - Copies of your completed Sample
  - Employment Application (see the Career Success Guide: Sample Blank Employment Application).
  - List of questions you want to ask
- Memo pad
- Business cards - You can print your own business cards using your computer. Office supply stores have blank business cards on which you can print your name, address, telephone number and e-mail address.
- Portfolio, if one is necessary for the job
- A pencil and two pens

The Day of the Interview

Personal Hygiene

Shower, shave, use deodorant and clean your fingernails. Avoid excessive amounts of aftershave or perfume. Also, do not drink alcohol or eat unusual or garlicky foods before the interview. Take along some breath mints that you can chew 15 minutes before the interview.

Review your Materials

If it has been awhile since you have looked at your résumé and other materials, do so. It can be embarrassing to forget something you included in your own materials. This will also help you present your qualifications succinctly and accurately.

Relax

Listen to your favorite music, take a deep breath or use relaxation techniques to stay calm and collected and put yourself in a positive frame of mind. You want to appear calm, confident and self-assured.

Review Your What, Can, Will and How Much

Take some time before the interview to review what it is the interviewer is looking for. Review the Career Success Guide: What Are Interviewers Looking For?

WHAT: How does the job for which you are interviewing match what you really want to do with your life at this time? Prepare three or four examples of how it matches.

CAN: Jot down at least three skills that you believe a person in this occupation should have. Inventory your skills and compare them with these skills. Prepare at least two examples of how you have successfully used each of these skills.

WILL: Identify at least 3 traits that successful people in this occupation have. Prepare examples that illustrate that you possess these same traits.

HOW MUCH: Do your homework to determine what people in this occupation earn, especially at the company in question. Know what you are worth and what you are willing to accept. Don't be in the position of having to make that decision for the first time when the question is asked during the interview!

TRULINCS Friendly! info@ReentryEssentials.org **www.ReentryEssentials.org** **347.973.0004** **2609 East 14 Street, Suite 1018, Brooklyn, NY 11235-3915**

HOW TO ACE TELEPHONE INTERVIEWS

Telephone interviews are very popular today. Employers use telephone interviews as a cost saving alternative to having every candidate interviewed at the employer's place of business. Telephone interviews are different from face-to-face interviews. They are usually very short and structured. The questions asked are intended to assist the interviewer to determine if the candidate should be invited for a more thorough interview. If you contact a potential employer before you are released, you most likely will be screened via a telephone interview.

Telephone Interviews

Both large and small employers are using the telephone interview as an effective screening tool. After generating an applicant pool based on the applications and résumés received for the open position, the employer identifies qualified applicants. Often the recruiter needs to further narrow the applicant field so the recruiter conducts a telephone interview with each selected applicant. Applicants that successfully pass the telephone interview are then invited to the company office for a face-to-face interview.

While Still Incarcerated

Highly motivated soon-to-be released inmates start their job search before they are released. If you plan to make contacts with prospective employers while still incarcerated, you need to arrange ahead of time with the prison officials what you need to do to conduct a telephone interview, should you be contacted by a prospective employer. Each correctional facility has their own rules and procedures. Be sure to find out what these rules and procedures are before starting your job search.

Be Prepared

It is important to prepare for a telephone interview every time you apply for a job.

When Making A Cold Call

Frequently when you make a cold call to a prospective employer, the employer will begin interviewing you during the call. Unlike the employer who calls in response to a submitted application or résumé, the cold call employer knows nothing about you. In the brief time available, the employer will ask questions to determine if the employer is interested enough to have you submit an application or résumé.

When you make a cold call, be prepared to give the following information:

- The type of job you seek.
- A very brief history of your experience and education as it relates to the job you seek.

Since the employer may ask you to elaborate on your work experience and education, have a copy of your résumé and completed job application (see the Career Success Guide: Sample Blank Employment Application) in front of you. Conclude the call by asking to whom and where you could send a résumé. For more information on making cold calls, review the Career Success Guide: How to Make Cold Calls.

After Submitting a Résumé or Job Application

Expect to receive a phone call from every employer to whom you submitted an application or résumé. Make sure that you have included contact information on every application that you complete, on your résumé and in the cover letter. If you are still incarcerated, you need to obtain the contact information from your prison officials. They will give you an address and telephone number where prospective employers can contact you. Be sure to change this information once you are released. Conclude every cover letter with the following, *I can be reached during the day at (999) 123-4567 and in the evening after 6p.m. at (999) 987-6543. My cell phone number is (999) 123-0987. My e-mail address is myname@internet.net. I check my e-mail several times each day.*

When the Call Comes

When recruiters call, they will introduce themselves and ask if this is a convenient time to talk. Be honest in your reply. If you are prepared to spend the next five minutes to as much as one hour with a recruiter, indicate that you are prepared. If you are not prepared to spend the time, give the recruiter a convenient time to call you back. Confirm the telephone number with the recruiter, especially if it is different from the one that was used on your résumé.

Approaching the Telephone Interview

It is easy to underestimate the importance of the interview because it is being conducted over the telephone. You must, however, approach the interview with the same frame of mind and professionalism as you do any face-to-face interview. The telephone interview is the second step in the recruiting process for many recruiters. They are checking to see if you can support what is in your résumé or on your application. The recruiter is evaluating you against the same criteria that has been discussed in the Career Success Guides: What Do Employers Expect from Their Employees? And What Are Interviewers Looking For?

Telephone Interview Tips

Answering Machines and Voice Mail

Nearly everyone today has either an answering machine or voice mail. Put yourself in the shoes of the recruiter calling you. What will be the impression of the recruiter when the recruiter gets your answering machine or voice mail message? What may be appropriate for your family and friends may leave the recruiter with the wrong impression. Remove all music from the message. Limit your message to giving your name and asking for the caller's name, a brief message and the caller's telephone number. It is acceptable to add that you can be reached at a different telephone number, if that number is also monitored by you. Check the messages on your telephones (business, home and cell) at least every two hours while conducting your job search.

When the Phone Is Answered by A Family Member

Make sure that everyone in your household is aware that you are looking for work and that prospective employers may call to schedule an interview. Place a pad of paper and a pencil next to the home telephone. In the event that you are not home to answer the telephone, ask your family members to record on the pad of paper the following information from the employer: company name, person's name, telephone number and the best time for you to call back.

Anticipate the Call

Because you may have given a number of employers your résumé and completed applications, it is easy to lose track of your contacts. It is embarrassing to have an employer call and you have no recollection of having applied for employment with that employer or any information on the job. This is why it is important that you complete a Help Wanted Response Form for each employer that you contact. This form is found in the Career Success Guide: Help Wanted Response Form. Keep a copy of this completed form next to the telephone.

Also, keep a copy of all completed Post Interview Forms (Career Success Guide Post-Interview Worksheet) next to the phone in the event that the employer calls you for more information or a job offer.

Some Do's And Don'ts

- Find a quiet place to take your phone calls. Check to make sure that the telephone sounds clear (some phones sound tinny).
- Alert everyone in the house of the importance of quiet and that you are not to be disturbed during the call. Arrange to have someone care for children and pets so they are not a distraction. Turn off all televisions and radios.
- Your voice should sound enthusiastic, upbeat and confident. Although you want to relax during the conversation, you do not want to sound casual. Standing up and smiling during the phone interview can help you keep a professional tone in your voice.
- Don't chew gum, eat, drink or smoke while on the phone. Avoid words such as: "err", "huh", "like" and "yeah".
- Although the interviewer cannot see you, they are usually trained to pick up nervous voices and can tell if you are disorganized or unprepared. Keep all of your job search records in a specific location so you can find them easily and keep them in front of you during the interview.
- Do not start the conversation with, "Now what job is this? I have applied to so many." Instead, say, "Thank you for contacting me."
- Listen to what they are saying. Always ask what the next step in the hiring process is and what the time line will be for this job.

Immediately After the Interview

Before the interview concludes, make sure that you obtain the name and mailing address of the person who conducted the interview. Send a thank you note to this person. Use the same format found in the Career Success Guide: How to Write a Thank You Note. In the letter include any information or materials that the interviewer requested. Complete a Career Success Guide Post Interview Worksheet.

Possible Questions

Be prepared to answer the same questions that you may be asked in a face-to-face interview. Review the following Career Success Guides: Common Interview Questions, What Can I Expect during the Interview? and How to Prepare for the Interview. Most interviewers will begin by asking you to elaborate on the information that you provided in your résumé and application. Have both in front of you during the interview.

COMMON INTERVIEW QUESTIONS

You cannot get a job, any job, without going through an interview. Whether the interview is a lengthy process or short and informal, employers need an opportunity to find out who you are. An employer knows you only by what you presented in your job application or résumé and now in the interview. Understand what an employer wants to know, and use the interview to show them that you match the job.

What Employers Want To Know

Employers need information in order to make decisions about hiring employees. Employers structure all interview questions in order to gain information about a potential employee in four basic areas. These areas are:

What do you want to do?

Employers need to know whether your interests and abilities match those needed to do the job. It is important for them to know that you enjoy the type of work for which you are applying. Employers want to know whether the job is an appropriate step for you so that you will meet your goals and stay committed to the work.

Can you do the job?

Employers need to know whether you have the skills, education and aptitude to do the job for which you are applying. They want to know how your education and previous work experiences relate to what is needed in the job. Before the interview, research the job for which you are applying. You need to identify your skills and abilities in order to determine whether you are suited to the position.

Will you do the job?

Employers want employees who are motivated to do the job and are responsible and dependable. They want to know whether you have the personal traits required for the job. The ability to interact effectively with others, to resolve problems when they arise and to approach a job with enthusiasm are important traits that employers look for in employees.

What will it cost to hire you?

All employers work within budgets. When considering a new employee, employers need to evaluate the cost of hiring that employee in order to determine whether the cost will fit into their budget. Employers need to determine the training an employee will need and what salary and benefits are appropriate for the employee.

The Ideal Candidate

All employers are looking for the ideal candidate for the job. Employers have a set of traits they believe an ideal candidate should have. They envision what such a person would be like. During the interview the employer is listening to see how close the skills, abilities and personal qualities of the candidate come to those traits of their ideal candidate. The employer makes comparisons between the current candidate and the ideal candidate based on how those being interviewed respond to questions and present themselves. Review and complete the Job Search Guide *Ideal Job Worksheet*. As you respond to interview questions, remember to present: 1) your desire to do the job, 2) your ability to do the job, 3) your willingness to do the job and 4) a realistic assessment of your value to the company. If you keep these four factors in mind, you will answer questions effectively and present yourself well. Responding to questions in this way will illustrate whether or not there is a match between you and the requirements for the job. This will increase your chances of being hired for a job that is right for you.

The Most Frequently Asked Interview Questions

During an interview, you must be ready to answer any question that you are asked. Prepare yourself for a job interview by becoming knowledgeable about the information employers seek, commonly asked interview questions and the appropriate responses. The more you prepare yourself, the better you will do in your interview.

The Biggest Question

Every formerly incarcerated person dreads the inevitable question, *Tell me about your criminal record*. How you answer this extremely important question will determine whether or not you will be considered for employment. Here are some guidelines for how you should answer this question:

Be honest. Background checks are simply too easy to do these days to run the risk of being dishonest. And even if you don't get caught right away, if your employer finds out later it will be grounds to fire you.

Take responsibility. Simply put, you have to admit your conviction and not make excuses. In some instances all you have to say is, yes, I was convicted of a felony and give the reason (my judgment was clouded by...immaturity, drugs, financial stress, poor values, hanging with the wrong crowd, etc.) Because of mitigating circumstances of your offense you may feel compelled to identify the offense. Just remember to keep it brief, look the employer in the eye and beware of providing too much information. The interviewer does not need to know the details about the arrest, trial and incarceration.

Move on. Now you want to talk about how you have improved yourself and turned your life around. Be specific: While in prison I got my GED, I completed a drug program, I am pursuing further education and training, etc. Mention anything that shows steps you have taken to change and better your life.

Acknowledge the employer's concerns. Say something such as, I understand how you may be hesitant or you may have concerns, BUT, I want to assure you that I will do a great job for you. As uncomfortable as this may be to acknowledge, it shows the employer that you are sensitive to his/her concerns and determined not to let your past interfere with your work life.

Make your pitch and close. End by reiterating that you have the skills and attitude for the position and that you will do a great job.

A Sample Response to the Question, "Tell Me about Your Criminal Record"

"When I was younger and very foolish, I was convicted of a felony. I absolutely regret my actions and have committed myself to changing — which I have. Since that time I have taken courses, received my GED, had excellent job reviews and become focused on where I want to go with my life. I am never going to make those kinds of choices again. I understand you may have concerns about this, but please be assured that I have left those poor decisions in the past. I am committed to doing an excellent job for you. I have the skills required for this job, and I hope you will consider me for this position."

Frequently Asked Interview Questions

"Tell me about yourself."

This question is often used as an "icebreaker" and gives you an opportunity to make a connection with the interviewer. Answer this question by giving a brief history of what you have done, emphasizing your experience, training and interests that relate to the job for which you are applying. Point out specific personal qualities that make you a good candidate for the position.

"Why do you feel that you are the best candidate for this position?"

This question gives you the opportunity to match yourself to the ideal candidate. Relate your skills and experience to those that the job requires. Show that you are motivated to perform the job, that you have the desire to do the job well and that you have a positive attitude about work in general. Present yourself in the most positive light.

"Tell me about your work and school experiences."

Describe your experiences (both paid and unpaid), education and training that relate to the job. Don't forget to include training and work experience you received while in prison. Point out specific work projects or training programs that are particularly relevant. Explain the reasons for any gaps in your work history. Show the employer that you have appropriate training and experience, as well as a willingness to learn new skills as needed.

"Describe your strengths and weaknesses."

Identify your greatest strengths. Relate them to the job requirements. Point out specific examples of how you have used these strengths and what you have accomplished by using them. Be honest about your weaknesses. Illustrate how you are overcoming them or improving in those areas.

"Where do you see yourself in five years?"

Describe your career goals. Show the employer how the job is an appropriate step for you in order to reach your goals. Express a commitment to the job, for yourself and for the benefit of the company. Emphasize your commitment to the non-criminal career that you have chosen.

"How would others, especially former supervisors and fellow workers, describe you?"

In response to this question, be positive about yourself. Take responsibility for your actions. Do not speak negatively about former work experiences, supervisors or co-workers. If a situation did not work out well, either omit talking about it or describe what you learned from it. Talk about your contributions to previous work environments.

"What do you know about us?"

Before the interview you need to find out as much as you can about the company. Based upon your homework, briefly tell them what you know about the company. This will communicate to the interviewer that you are interested enough in the position to have taken the time to do research ahead of time.

"What are your salary requirements?"

Answer this question realistically. In order to do so, you need to know what a reasonable wage is for the position. Comparing your training and experience to others in similar positions will help determine a salary. There may be certain benefits that are important to you; thus, it is appropriate to also inquire about benefits packages at this time.

"Who may we contact to find out more about you?"

Have a list of references ready to give the employer. Each reference should include the name, address, phone number, email address and a brief identification of their relationship to you (i.e., former supervisor, co-worker, etc.). If possible, give local references. If you have letters of reference, offer copies of these to the employer. Be sure to contact all your references ahead of time for permission to use their name.

For further information about job interviews review the Career Success Guides: What Are Interviewers Looking For? What Can I Expect During the Interview? How Do I Deal with Negative Information? And How to Negotiate a Fair Salary.

Questions for You to Ask

An interview is not just a time for an employer to ask you questions. It is also a time for you to gather information in order to determine whether your skills, abilities, values and needs match those of the job for which you are interviewing. During the interview process it is appropriate for you to ask questions. The interviewer will invite you to ask questions, usually after they have concluded their questions.

- What would my job responsibilities be?
- Could you describe your ideal candidate for this job?
- Will you tell me a bit about your workplace?
- What is the salary range and what is the benefits package for the job?
- May I meet the person for whom I would be working?

TRULINCS Friendly! info@ReentryEssentials.org www.ReentryEssentials.org 347.973.0004 2609 East 14 Street, Suite 1018, Brooklyn, NY 11235-3915

HOW TO MAKE A GOOD FIRST IMPRESSION

Studies have shown that people form initial impressions of strangers in the first 30 seconds of the encounter. First impressions are based almost exclusively on the appearance and behavior of the person. This Guide gives information on how a job seeker can make a positive first impression both in the job interview and on the job. Those who have been incarcerated need to pay particular attention to how they are perceived by employers. Behaviors, mannerism, dress and language of the prison culture are not only foreign to most employers, but will serve to turn them off toward you.

At The Job Interview

Job interviewers have only a few minutes to decide whether you are the right candidate for the job. They have reviewed your application or résumé and determined that you have the skills, values and experience that may match the job. The interviewer must now decide if you are the right person for the job. This process begins the minute that you arrive for the interview, continues through the interview and concludes with the follow-up contact. Your task as the job seeker is to make sure that nothing you do before, during or after the interview disqualifies you for the job. How you present yourself to the company and the interviewer significantly influences the interviewer's decision. Remember, the interviewer most likely will have a preconceived idea of what to expect from a formerly incarcerated individual. It will be your task to present a different picture. The following are areas that you need to address to assure that you make a good impression on the company and the interviewer.

Appearance

As stated above, people make an initial decision about a stranger based almost exclusively on appearance. Here are some actions that you can take that enhance your chances of making a good impression:

Dress. Nothing says more about how serious you are about the job than the way you dress. Dress casually and you communicate that you do not take the job seriously. Here are some dos and don'ts:

- Jeans, t-shirts, shorts or any clothing that has writing on it are definitely not acceptable.
- Men should dress professionally. Regardless of the job for which you are applying, wear a conservative suit or sports jacket. If applying for a professional job, wear a tie.
- Women should wear a conservative dress or business pants suit.
- Never wear anything that is sloppy or revealing to an interview.
- Bare midriffs, short skirts, see-through clothing, swim wear or low-cut necklines should never be worn to an interview.
- Tuck-in your shirt, wear a belt and make sure that your pants are pulled up.

Shoes. Both men and women should wear dress shoes. Do not wear tennis, running or walking shoes. Wearing high heeled shoes for women is optional. If you do wear high heeled shoes, they should be conservative. Make sure that your shoes are clean and polished.

Body Appearance.

- Absolutely no body piercing. Although wearing numerous earrings, nose studs or tongue piercing makes an individual statement, they are not appropriate when looking for a job. Only one set of earrings is acceptable.
- Cover all body art. If you have tattoos on your arms, wear a long sleeve shirt. Try to cover all ink on your neck.
- Avoid any jewelry that represents a religion, group or any organization. Men should avoid wearing any jewelry.
- Use only a moderate amount of make-up. The tones of the make-up should be natural. Be sure to check your make-up just before you enter the place of business.
- Get a professional haircut before the interview. Your hair should look natural. Like the prohibition of body piercing, your hair style should be conservative.
- If you use perfume or after-shave lotion, use it in moderation.

The Day of the Interview

The day of the interview you need to:

- Bathe, wash your hair, clean your fingernails, brush your teeth, shave and comb your hair.
- Apply an antiperspirant and groom your hair.
- Make sure your clothes are clean and pressed. Have your clothes professionally cleaned after every interview.
- Avoid smoking after dressing. Tobacco is easily absorbed by clothing. If you do smoke, smoke in the open air, not in your car.
- Either brush your teeth or use a breath mint before you enter the building.
- Have someone look you over before you leave the house.

Your Behavior Says a Lot about You

Remember, you are being evaluated by everyone in the company from the moment that you arrive for the job interview until you leave. The following are some suggestions that will help you leave everyone with a good impression of you:

- Arrive 15 minutes early for the interview. This will give you time to settle your nerves and check your appearance in the washroom.
  - Greet everyone with eye contact and a smile. It is not only engaging, it is polite.
  - Greet everyone with a handshake. Make sure your grip is firm but not bone-crushing. Pump your hand a couple of times then remove the grip.
  - Monitor the tone of your voice. People tend to raise the pitch of their voice when they get nervous. Try to speak in your normal voice. If you speak loudly, you may be perceived as being aggressive. Speaking too softly may be interpreted as your being timid.
- Do not smoke even if offered. Also do not chew gum or breathe mints at any time during the interview process.
- Be mindful of your language. Avoid using the following phrases: "you know," "uhh" or "like."

Send a thank you note to everyone who interviewed you. This will definitely leave a positive impression.

Make a Good Impression at Your New Job

Your first few days on a new job can set the tone for how your supervisor and co-workers will feel about you. It is important, therefore, that you make a good impression. In addition to the suggestions offered in the Career Success Guide: What to Do When Starting a New Job, the following are some ways to make a good impression when starting a new job:

Have a positive attitude. Nothing will endear you to your supervisor and co-workers more than having a positive, upbeat attitude.

Be a team player. Ask for assistance from co-workers and be willing to give assistance when asked.

Learn co-workers' names. Until you can remember the names of your co-workers, keep a diary. Each time you meet a new person, write down the person's name and add a brief statement that will help you remember the person. For example, Bob Smith, has a grey beard. Each evening review your diary until you can name all of your co-workers.

Learn everything you can about the company. Study the company handbook. Become an expert on the company's employee policies. By knowing what the company policies are, you can avoid violating one that may get you terminated.

Come each day prepared to work. It is best to establish a habit of arriving to work at least ten minutes early. Make sure that your transportation to work is reliable.

Leave your personal life at the front door. Do not let your personal life interfere with your work life. Avoid taking personal phone calls at work.

Avoid gossip. Most work environments are fertile ground for rumors and gossip and it is easy to get caught up in it. Try not to associate with those employees who tend to thrive on gossip and rumor. If a rumor directly affects you (for example, there is a rumor that your division is to be shut down), go to your supervisor and ask if the rumor is true.

Get organized. Being organized assists you to be more productive. For suggestions on how to get organized, review the Job Search Guide How to Effectively Manage Time at Work.

Keep your skills and knowledge current. Do not assume that the company will provide the training that you need to stay current in your occupation. It is your responsibility to maintain and upgrade your skills and knowledge. Check with your supervisor to see if the company will provide financial assistance for training that you schedule.

Keep your supervisor informed. Do not assume that your supervisor knows everything that you are doing. Schedule meetings with your supervisor to discuss your performance and to help establish a positive relationship. Use these meetings to express an eagerness to advance your skills and to move ahead in the company.

TRULINCS Friendly! info@ReentryEssentials.org www.ReentryEssentials.org 347.973.0004 2609 East 14 Street, Suite 1018, Brooklyn, NY 11235-3915

PRE-INTERVIEW CHECKLIST

Because an employer may call at any time to schedule a job interview, you need to be prepared. Keep copies of this checklist next to the telephone so when an employer does call, you will be able to record and organize the information you need. Once you have concluded the phone call, use this Pre-Interview Checklist to prepare for the next important phase of your job search, the interview. Make at least 10 copies of this checklist.

Record the following information from the caller:

Date of the call: ______________________________

Company Name: ______________________________

Person who called: ______________________________

Date of the interview: ________________ Time: ________________

My interview will be with: ______________________________

Location of the interview (building and room): ______________________________

Address: ______________________________

City: ______________________________

Where should I park? ______________________________

Interviewer's telephone number: ______________________________

Do I need to bring anything to the interview? ________ No ________ Yes, What ________________

Between now and the interview date, prepare the following for the interview:

A. Try to find out as much as you can about the employer. Review the Job Search Guide How to Research the Job & the Employer.

________ I have re-read the Career Success Guide: How to Research the Job & the Employer.

________ I have researched the employer on the Internet and completed The Company Worksheet that is a part of The Career Success Guide: How to Research the Job & the Employer.

________ I understand the main business of the company.

B. Here are five skills that I have that match this job:

1. ______________________________
2. ______________________________
3. ______________________________
4. ______________________________
5. ______________________________

C. I have reviewed my résumé and job application and can support everything on both.

Yes ____________ No ____________

D. Here are three things I learned in school that help prepare me for this job:

1. ______________________________
2. ______________________________
3. ______________________________

E. Review the common interview questions found in the Career Success Guide: Common Interview Questions. Practice answering each question as it relates to this job. If possible, have a friend or relative ask you the questions. Repeat your answers until you feel comfortable with your responses.

_________ I have practiced answering the common interview questions.

F. I have the following ready to take to the interview:

_________ Four copies of my résumé.

_________ Two copies of my completed Career Success Guide: Sample Blank Employment Application.

_________ A list of my personal references.

_________ If the interview came from a cold call contact and you completed the Career Success Guide: Cold Call Telephone Log for that job, bring a copy of your completed Log.

_________ A copy of the Career Success Guide: Post-Interview Worksheet.

G. _________ I have checked the route that I must take to get to the interview.

H. _________ I estimate that it will take me _________ minutes to get to the interview. In order to arrive at least 15 minutes early I need to leave home at _____________ (time).

The day of the interview:

_________ My clothes are clean and pressed. My shoes are polished.

_________ I have bathed, brushed my teeth, combed my hair and used deodorant.

_________ I have sufficient change to pay for parking, bus or subway.

You have prepared, so on the way to the interview, relax. Good luck!

TRULINCS Friendly! info@ReentryEssentials.org www.ReentryEssentials.org 347.973.0004 2609 East 14 Street, Suite 1018, Brooklyn, NY 11235-3915

POST-INTERVIEW WORKSHEET

Most job seekers have several job interviews before they are offered employment. It is important, therefore, to keep a record of each interview so that you remember the important details about the job and the company. Immediately after each interview, write down what you learned from the interview. Record your impressions of how the interview went and any further steps that you need to take with the employer. Use the form below to keep track of the results of your job interviews. Make at least 10 copies of this form.

Post-Interview Worksheet		
Name of Company:	Date of Interview:	
Name(s) of interviewer(s):	Title:	Phone #:
Describe the general tone of the meeting or the feeling between you and the interviewer:		
In what ways do you match the needs of the employer?		
What information about yourself did you not convey clearly that you would like to emphasize again?		
What could you have done to improve the interview?		

Post-Interview Worksheet Side Two

What did you learn about the job and the company?

What questions do you still have about the job and the company?

The probable start date for the position:

If salary and benefits were discussed, you said your requirements are: They said:

How did the employer describe the position? What kind of person are they looking for?

What materials did you leave with the employer?

What materials do you need to send to the employer (résumé, references, etc.)?

What would you like about this job?

What might you dislike or find challenging about this job?

Additional follow-up steps that are needed:

Thank you note sent? ☐ yes ☐ no Date sent:

HOW TO WRITE A "THANK YOU NOTE"

The "Thank You" note is written to the employer immediately following the interview. In the note you should again highlight the match between you and the job. A courteous and enthusiastic note leaves a lasting positive impression. Your pursuit of the job does not end with the interview; therefore, it is essential that you stay in touch with the employer until a hiring decision is made.

(1) Susan Peters
1920 Mountain Road
MyTown, OH 12345
(999) 555-1515
sp@internet.net
(2) March 27, 2014

Ms. Jane Willis (3)
Carlson Construction
124 9th Avenue
MyTown, OH 12345

Dear Ms. Willis: (4)

Thank you for your time and attention during our meeting yesterday. I remain very interested in your position as a framing carpenter. I was impressed with Carlson Construction's commitment to building quality homes at an affordable price. I am confident that this commitment will be well received in the home-buying market for years to come. (5)

My background in construction and training in carpentry makes me very appreciative of the value of your product. Prior to my incarceration I worked as a framing carpenter for a small construction firm. Here I learned from two seasoned employees the value of providing quality work and a strong work ethic. (6)

As I said in the interview, I am ready to put my past behind me. I used my time incarcerated to get my GED and obtain further carpentry training. I was able to apply these skills as a maintenance assistant. I would very much like to continue my career as a framing carpenter with Carlson Construction. (7)

I look forward to hearing from you next week. (8)

Sincerely,

Antonio Peters (9)

Antonio Peters
(10)

(1) Include your name, address, phone number and e-mail address on all correspondence.
(2) Mail the letter the next business day after the interview.
(3) Be sure to spell all names correctly.
(4) Letters go to all interviewers and the hiring authority.
(5) Be courteous. Restate your interest in the position.
(6) Emphasize your knowledge, skills and experience. Show a match between you and the job.
(7) Again express your interest in the job. Close on a positive note.
(8) Use 12-point, easily readable font. Reiterate time-frame for the next contact.
(9) Include a closing.
(10) Sign first and last name.

Additional Information:

During the interview, if the employer requests additional information from you, or you feel supporting documents will be helpful, include these documents in your "Thank You" note. Add a paragraph to the note like: "Enclosed you will find a copy of my high school diploma as you requested." Another example of a note you may add to the letter: "In the interview you asked about the Federal Bonding Program. I am enclosing information on this important program."

"Thank You" Note Helpful Hints

- Keep the "Thank You" note focused and brief - 1/2 to one page.
- Mail the note the next business day after the interview. Do not e-mail the note unless you are asked to use this medium.
- Write the note on paper that matches your résumé. Mail in a matching envelope.
- Maintain a consistent style and tone in all written correspondence.
- Use a computer printer. If you hand write the note, print neatly.
- Proofread the note carefully, and then have someone else proofread it.
- Obtain business cards from everyone with whom you interview, including the secretary and/or administrative assistant. Having the names of the interviewers makes follow-up contacts easier and more business-like.

Email "Thank You" Notes

Is it acceptable to send an email "Thank You" note after your job interview? Yes. In this age of electronic communication, most employers are used to thi form of communication. Email "Thank You" notes are especially appropriate when the hiring decision is to be made quickly. It is important, however, tha you also send the employer a paper thank you note. The email "Thank You" note should be sent immediately after the interview. Email "Thank You" note should take on the same form as the paper thank you note.

Follow-Up—Keep in Contact

An employer knows you only by what you show about yourself. It is important to stay in contact with the employer until a hiring decision has been made Polite persistence can pay off. Following-up with the employer enables you to:

- Create a lasting positive impression.
- Emphasize that your skills, interests and experience match those of the desired job.
- Show that you are well-organized and can follow through.
- Demonstrate your good written and oral communication skills.
- Show that you are interested in the job.
- Reemphasize or correct a point that was made during the interview.
- Stand out among many applicants.

Preparing for Follow-Up: Information You Will Need

Listen carefully during the interview. Immediately after the job interview complete the Career Success Guide: Post-Interview Worksheet. Do not rely or your memory; be sure to include the following information:

1. The name, title and address of the person(s) who interviewed you. Get their business card if possible.
2. Specific skills or background experience that you have that will match the job.
3. The employer's time-frame for making a hiring decision.
4. The personal qualities that the employer is looking for in an employee.

The Interviewer May Not Have Hiring Authority

In most companies, the person who will be your immediate supervisor has the ultimate hiring authority. If the person with whom you interviewed is no the hiring authority, get the hiring authority's name. Write a letter to both the interviewer and the hiring authority. Express your interest in the job, anc close the letter to the hiring authority with," I look forward to meeting with you."

Phone Calls

If you do not receive a response in the time-frame discussed in the interview, call the interviewer or hiring authority. Use the call to express your continuec interest in the job and to inquire if a hiring decision has been made. If a decision has not been made, follow up in another week with a second phone ca or email. It is important to stay in touch, as new job openings occur frequently. Remember to inquire as to convenient times for the employer to receive your call.

What if I don't want this job?

If, after the interview, you have decided, for whatever reason, that the job is not for you, you should immediately remove yourself from consideration Write a brief note or email to the hiring authority, stating that you would like to remove your name from consideration. You may indicate the reason(s why, provided that the reason is not negative. An example response may be, "I am looking for a position that better matches my current interests. Thank you for considering me." In the future, you may want to reapply or need this person as a contact in the industry.

HOW TO NEGOTIATE A FAIR SALARY

Successful salary negotiation occurs after the job applicant and the employer share a common understanding of the job. Once the tasks and responsibilities of the job are clearly articulated and understood, the two parties can establish a monetary value for the job. At the beginning both the applicant and the employer have an opinion of the monetary value of the job which may not be the same. Negotiating is the process of both parties coming to an agreement on the value.

Ideal Salary Agreements:

- Are based on mutual respect.
- Create gain for both parties.
- Lay a firm foundation for a good working relationship.

Successful Salary Negotiations:

- Are neither adversarial nor antagonistic. The employer and the applicant are not enemies.
- Gives both the employer and the applicant the feeling that they've won.

You're ready To Negotiate When:

- You've gathered information about the labor market and you know how much your job typically pays.
- You've determined your needs and wants.
- You've gathered sufficient information about the employer, the work, the environment and the people with whom you will be working.
- You've done all you can to convey your willingness and ability to do the job and the employer has all the information needed to reach a decision about you. Typically, salary negotiation occurs toward the end of the interview or after the applicant receives a job offer from the employer.

What Is The Job Worth?

The relationship between the employer and the employee is a business relationship. Typically, employers analyze the dollar amount they invest in an employee and forecast the financial return they are likely to receive from the employee.

- Employers know that new employees usually cost more than they return in productivity. In time, however, new employees become experienced and more productive. It is not until then that the employer breaks even and finally returns a dollar for each dollar of effort by the employee.
- Savvy job hunters know how long it will take to bring them up to the point when they are making money for the employer. Their salary demands are based on that knowledge.

When Should You Discuss Salaries?

Mentioning a specific salary early in the employment process can eliminate you from consideration even before you've had a chance to demonstrate that you are the best candidate.

- Answer any salary question on the application form with "Negotiable."
- Never put a salary request on your résumé.
- At the job interview, let the interviewer be the first to mention salary.

Wait until you know more about the job and the employer, and the employer knows more about you, before you price yourself too low or too high. If the employer begins discussing a salary in the early part of the interview, postpone negotiations by saying something like, "If you don't mind, I'd like to wait to discuss salaries after I have learned a little more about the job."

It Pays To Increase Your Negotiating Power

Your negotiating power reflects how much you're in demand. You have more room to negotiate when:

- You work in a fast-growing field in which there are many job openings with few skilled people to fill them.
- You can demonstrate unique skills that few applicants have.
- You have job offers from more than one company, and you let potential employers know that you are in demand.
- You have a job or you have savings reserves to fall back on, and you're not feeling financial or psychological pressure to take the job.

Help for Employers Who Hire Formerly Incarcerated Individuals

There are several federal programs that can benefit employers for hiring Returning Citizens. Several of these programs actually subsidize the employment. These subsidies may assist you in getting the salary you seek.

- DOL's Federal Bonding Program provides fidelity bonds to employers hiring at-risk individuals at no cost to the employer. The bonds guarantee honesty for "at-risk," hard-to-place job seekers and cover the first six months of employment. To determine your eligibility, contact your state's bonding coordinator. For more information, go to
  www.careeronestop.org/businesscenter/recruitandhire/hiringadiverse/workforce/ex-offenders.aspx#sthash.2SmcV0im.dpuf
- Employers who hire people with felony convictions can benefit through The Work Opportunity Tax Credit (WOTC). The credit allows eligible employers to reduce their federal tax liability by up to $9,600 per new hire. The credit applies to temporary, seasonal, or part-time and full-time workers. The employer should contact their state WOTC Coordinator at:
  www.careeronestop.org/businesscenter/recruitandhire/hiringadiverseworkforce/ex-offenders.aspx#sthash.2SmcV0im.dpuf

Know Your Needs

How much salary do you need to support yourself and your family?

- Determine the minimum income you need by completing the worksheet found in the Career Success Guide: What Are Your Salary Needs?
- If the salary offer doesn't cover your needs, you can:
  - Accept the job and find other work to supplement your income.
  - Walk away from the job offer because the salary is insufficient and non-negotiable.
  - Negotiate a higher salary.

Know Your Wants

What extras would you like to afford, beyond your basic needs? Perhaps you want a better car, an annual vacation abroad or to save for early retirement. Determine what salary would let you afford the 'extras' that you want.

What You Need To Know Before You Start The Salary Negotiations:

- What you will be required to do on the job.
  - Analyze the job description and other information you have been given by the employer.
- The typical earnings for the job according to industry standards.
  - Examine The Department of Labor statistics at your local One-Stop Career Center.
  - Write or telephone trade associations.
  - Talk to local employment agencies.
  - Ask the reference librarian at your public library.
  - Search the job banks on the Internet for comparable jobs.
  - Conduct informational interviews. Review the Career Success Guide: How to Acquire Job Information by Interviewing.
  - Check the web site www.indeed.com/salary. This web site provides average wages for occupations by location.
- What are the typical earnings of the company and how do they compare to the industry?
  - Find out the name of the company's closest competitor and ask what they would pay. It's likely to be similar.
- Find out if there are many other applicants.
  - How do they compare with you? This may be difficult to investigate, but employers will sometimes provide this information.
- Find out how long the position has been open.

After You Receive a Job Offer Is When You:

- Have the most negotiating leverage.
- Step back from the situation and evaluate the offer.
- List the pros and cons of accepting the offer as it stands.
- Determine what is acceptable and what could be better.

When You Accept An Offer, Do It Graciously And Get Everything In Writing.

Applicants should give serious consideration before accepting a salary that they feel is too low so that they do not feel that they have been cheated.

Making a Counter Offer

Many companies and governmental agencies have a published salary scale or range. Salary ranges allow for differences between candidates' skills, qualifications and the amount of training they will need. If the job you seek is covered by a salary range your goal is to show that you have the strengths, skills, job history and enthusiasm to merit a salary near the top of the range.

If the salary offer is low, make a counter offer. When you make the counter offer make sure that you:

- Compare it to industry norms.
- Compare it to past work you've done that is similar and for which you were paid more.
- If you have a higher offer from another company, this is the time to mention it.

Notice that in each case you link your counter offer to a real-world example of higher earnings. State your case simply without being arrogant.

If the employer won't raise the starting salary and you still want the job:

- Ask the employer to describe the conditions under which the employer would be willing to pay more.
- Focus on how you can either save the company money or generate more revenue for the company.
- Negotiate a contingency that your salary will be increased in three to six months if your work meets mutually agreed upon criteria. Get the agreement in writing in case the person who hires you leaves the company.
- Are there other benefits or conditions of the job that you can negotiate? For instance, could you have three weeks of paid vacation instead of two weeks, fewer hours for the same pay, flexible time or additional benefits?

HOW TO RESPOND TO A JOB OFFER

The culmination of your successful job search comes when you receive a job offer from the employer. Although it is tempting to immediately accept a job offer, it is important that you give thought to your decision before you answer. There are many factors to consider when assessing whether to accept or not accept the offer.

Evaluating the Job Offer

Salary and Benefits

When the employer makes the job offer, they will provide you with information about your salary and the benefits that the company offers. You need to do some research before you can determine if the salary that is offered is fair and consistent. The following guide will assist you in making this determination:

- *What Are Your Salary Needs?*
- *What Are Employee Benefits?*
- *How to Negotiate a Fair Salary*

The Company

Before you accept the job offer, you need to be confident that the company is a good place for you to work. Factors to consider are:

- How stable is the company?
- Is the product or service that it provides in demand and will it continue to be in demand?
- What is the company's philosophy and attitude toward employees? Is there high turn-over of employees?
- Is it a good work environment for me? Will I be exposed to the same environment and people that contributed to my incarceration?

The Job

Unless you are being hired to do the exact job that you did previously, it is important that you determine if the job is appropriate for you. Trying to assess whether or not you will like the new job is not easy. Here are some questions to ask yourself:

- Does the job match my interests and make use of my skills? Review the job duties and the description that was provided at the job interview.
- How important is the job to the company?
- Am I comfortable with the job schedule? If I am required to travel or work split schedules, will this interfere with my personal life?
- How long do people tend to stay with the company? High turn-over may signal low morale.
- Will the environment and fellow employees help me avoid situations similar to those that led to my incarceration?

Size and Age of The Company

How will the size of the company affect you?

Large firms usually offer more training, varied career paths, managerial advancement and employee benefits than do smaller companies.

Small companies give employees more responsibility, a closer relationship to management and the chance to participate in company decisions.

How long has the company been in business? New businesses have a high failure rate. Working for a new company, however, can be exciting because you are contributing to the creation of a new business. If the new business is a success, you also have an opportunity to share in the financial rewards. If you are not a risk taker, seek work at established, successful companies.

Your Boss and Co-Workers

Hopefully during the interviewing process you had an opportunity to spend time with your immediate supervisor and to visit the work site. If you didn't, ask to interview this person before you make your decision to accept the job. Also, ask if you can observe and talk with potential co-workers.

Ask yourself:

- Can I be happy working for this individual? Is the chemistry good between us?
- How does the supervisor treat and interact with co-workers?
- How do co-workers interact? Do they appear to have a good relationship with each other?
- Can you see yourself fitting in with your potential co-workers?

Where is the job located?

If the job is located in another part of the country, you need to consider the cost of living, availability of housing and transportation and the quality of education and recreation in the area. Review the Career Success Guide: How to Relocate to Another Community. If the job is local, you need to assess the time and cost of commuting.

When a Job Offer is Made

Since most job offers are made over the telephone, it is important that you be prepared for the telephone call. When the employer calls with the good news, make sure you are clear on the offer. Although the caller may give you the following information when the offer is made, be sure that you write down the information. It is easy to forget what is said in the excitement of getting the job offer. If something that is important to you is not mentioned, it is acceptable to ask about it. Even though this information may have been discussed during your job interview, it is important that you obtain or confirm the following information:

- Date that the employer wants you to start work.
- Time and place that the employer wants you to report. Are there any special dress requirements?
- Name of your immediate supervisor (be sure you get the proper spelling).
- Salary details. What is the probation period? When will you have your first performance and salary review?
- What are the benefits? Confirm amount of vacation time, insurance and other benefits.

Complete the call by stating that you are excited about the offer and that you will give them an answer within 24 hours.

Accepting a Job Offer

You have done your homework, talked with your relatives and friends about the offer and are ready to say, "Yes." The best way to convey your acceptance of the job offer is to respond to the offer in writing. The letter permits you to reiterate the employer's offer. Review the following sample acceptance letter

Jerry Smith
123 Any Street
You're Town, OH 99999

John Doe, Manager
Acme Company
987 State Street
Our Town, OH 99999

April 11, 2014

Dear Mr. Doe:

It is with pleasure that I accept the position as a machinist at the Acme Company.

As we discussed, my starting salary will be $15.50 per hour and I will be eligible for health and life insurance benefits. My work day will be from 8:00a.m. Until 5:00 p.m. per day, Monday through Friday. My work performance will be evaluated in 90 days and, based upon my evaluation, I will be eligible for a salary increase. After nine months of employment, I will be eligible for one day of vacation for each month worked.

I look forward to starting my new position on Monday, April 23, 2014. I am to report to my supervisor, Carl Jones at the Acme Company building. If you need additional information, please feel free to contact me at 999-123-4567 or by email at jsmith@myprovider.net.

Thank you,

Jerry Smith

Jerry Smith

Within 24 hours of receiving the offer, hand deliver the letter to the employer. Also, notify all employers with whom you are corresponding that you have accepted another position. Thank them for their consideration.

Rejecting the Offer

If you have issues with the offer, consider a counteroffer. Review the Career Success Guide: How to Negotiate a Fair Salary for suggestions on how to make a counteroffer.

Compose and hand deliver your rejection letter within 24 hours of the job offer. The letter should be short and not include details as to why you are not accepting the employer's offer. "Thank you for offering me the position as a machinist at the Acme Company. After careful consideration, I find that I cannot accept the offer."

Career Success Series
Guide 59

WHAT TO DO WHEN STARTING A NEW JOB

Congratulations! Your hard work has paid off. Your focus must now, however, switch from looking for a job to becoming an effective employee. You will need to use the same commitment to preparation that you did in your job search to make the transition a successful one. The first week in your new job will set the stage for how you will function in your new position. There are a few unique issues that you may encounter as a returning citizen. You need to be prepared for these situations and plan what you will do and/or say when the issue is present. This guide provides many helpful hints as to how you should approach your new job.

It is understandable if you have a bad case of the jitters. You want to start off on the right foot. Here are some suggestions that will help you transition into your new job. These suggestions apply to everyone starting a new job:

The Day Before You Start the New Job

Determine when & where you report to work.

It is probable that when the employer called and offered you the job, the employer indicated when and where you report to work. In the excitement of getting the job, however you may have failed to note this important information. Do not assume that you know this information. Call the person with whom you interviewed and ask them. You may tell them that you were so excited to get the job that you failed to write down the information.

Most companies will have you report to the main business office. If it is a large company with a Human Resources office, you may be directed to that office to receive an orientation before you report to your supervisor. Be sure you know where the Human Resources office is. Here are some additional questions you need to ask:

- Should I bring lunch or is there a company cafeteria?
- Where should I park?
- If the work site is secure (all employees and visitors must go through security), will the security officer have my name?
- What documents do I need to bring with me?
- If you are unsure of the dress code, ask, "What is the employee dress code?"

Who will be your supervisor?

This may or may not have been mentioned in the interview. It is possible that you may have been interviewed by your supervisor's supervisor, or even someone in the Human Resources office and not have met your actual supervisor.

Transportation

How do you plan to get to work? Are you going to drive? If so, have you mapped how you will get to your place of work? This is especially important if the place where you are to report is different from the place where you interviewed. For example you may have interviewed at the business' home office but you are to report to a construction work site, a branch office or a separate plant. Make sure your car is filled with gas and is ready to make the trip.

Get your paperwork together.

Sometime during the first day your employer is going to ask you for some documents. You need to bring the following with you:

Social Security Card. You need to have the original card that was supplied to you when you applied to Social Security and were given a Social Security number. If you do not have an original card, you need to immediately contact the Social Security Administration. Your employer will not be able to accept Social Security cards that are laminated in plastic or have the words printed, "Not Valid for Employment." If you do not have a valid Social Security Card, you can present one of the following documents to your employer as proof of your citizenship: a passport, a certified birth certificate or the appropriate immigration status documents.

Proof of your identity. You need to have a government issued document, like a valid driver's license, that has your picture on it and includes a physical description such as age, gender, height and weight.

Review your paperwork.

Take time to review your résumé and job application. Reread your job duties and the job description. If you were given any materials by the employer such as an Employment Manual, read it carefully. In the event that you do not understand a policy, mark it in the Manual so that you can ask your supervisor about it.

Clothes

Set out your clothes the night before. Make sure they are clean and pressed. Don't forget your shoes. Are they polished? You need to be as mindful of your appearance as you were when you were going to an interview.

Get a good night's rest.

Tomorrow is going to be a big day. Plan on it being exhausting, exciting and stressful. It is important, therefore, that your mind and body are ready for the experience. Try to relax the evening before. Limit your alcohol intake. Get at least eight hours of sleep. Set your alarm to give you sufficient time to prepare.

Your First Day on the Job

Your first day on the job will set the tone for the rest of your time at this company. It is important to make a good impression. Review the Career Success Guide: How to Make a Good First Impression. Here are some suggestions to make your first day productive:

- Bathe, shave, brush your teeth and comb your hair before leaving home. Women should apply minimal make-up and no perfume. Remove all body piercing.
- Plan to arrive at least 15 minutes before you are expected. If it is possible that you could be delayed by traffic or public transportation, then plan to arrive 30 minutes early.
- Leave your cell phone at home or in your car. This will remove any temptation to call someone or have them call you at work.
- Come prepared. Make sure you have all of the paperwork that you assembled the day before (Social Security Card, driver's license, etc.).
- Carry at least one ballpoint pen and one pencil. Have a small note pad handy.
- Leave your smoking materials in your car. Also, do not chew gum.
- Be humble. It is natural to be nervous your first day on the job.
- Don't be afraid to ask questions.

Making a Good Impression

In order to have gotten the job, you were successful at impressing the employer with your knowledge, skills, abilities and willingness to work and be a team player. It is important that you continue impressing your employer, supervisor and co-workers. Here are some suggestions:

Communications

Each new person that you meet is going to formulate an impression of you. Although you will be nervous, try to relax and have your body language match what you are saying. As you meet co-workers:

- Be an active listener. Maintain eye contact.
- Speak clearly. Don't mumble.
- Shake the person's hand confidently.
- Smile!
- Remember, you are no longer in prison. Your fellow employees are friends and equals. You do not need to impress them or try to intimidate them as you may have done with fellow inmates. Such behavior in a work environment is unacceptable.

Be Eager

Be eager to learn as much as you can about the company, the products and your area of responsibility. Be open to learning new skills.

Remember Names

You will be meeting a lot of new people during the first week of your employment. It is unrealistic to expect that you will remember the name of everyone you meet.

- Ask for a business card from everyone you meet. On the back of the card make a note that may help you remember the person. For example, you might write, "Lives in my neighborhood".
- Keep a note pad handy. If you didn't get a business card, jot down the person's name, title and something to help you remember that person.
- Don't be afraid to ask a person their name even though you know you were introduced to them early that day or a few days ago. Simply say, "I am sorry I forgot your name. I have met so many people the past few days that names are starting to blur."

Bury the past

Do not discuss anything related to your conviction or incarceration even if asked. Fellow employees, mainly because they are curious, may query you about your prison experiences. Simply say, that part of my life is in the past and I would prefer to keep it that way.

All Those Forms

One of the tasks that you will need to complete the first day of your employment is filling out a number of forms. Many of these forms are required by state and federal governments and others are required by the employer. In order to accurately complete these forms you will need to have available the documents mentioned earlier. Having a copy of your completed Career Success Guide Sample Blank Employment Application will also help you to complete the forms.

Employment Eligibility Verification (I-9 Form)

The federal government requires employers to verify that the worker is legally entitled to work in the United States. To complete the Form I-9, the employer must examine two kinds of documents: proof that you are a US citizen and proof that you are who you say you are. A valid Social Security card or a document verifying your immigrant status is required for proof that you have the legal right to work in the U.S. A government issued document like a driver's license is needed to prove your identity. Once the employer has examined the documents and completed the I-9 Form, you will be asked to verify the information by signing your name.

Employee Withholding Allowance Certificate (W-4 Form)

The W-4 Form is used by the employer to determine how much tax should be withheld from your paycheck each pay period. The amount of tax that is withheld depends on the number of dependents you claim as well as the amount of your pay. The form can be confusing, so be sure to ask for assistance from your employer to complete the form correctly. If you do not complete the form correctly, your employer may withhold too much from your paycheck or not enough. If not enough is withheld you will be subject to taxes when you file your yearly tax return. Note that a similar form will probably be required for your state government's taxing agency.

Other Forms

Your employer may also have you complete additional forms. Make sure you understand what you are completing and that the information you supply is accurate. You may be asked to complete your time sheet or time card, insurance forms, an employment contract, permission to deposit your pay check into your bank account and to verify that you received the Employee Handbook.

HOW TO KEEP YOUR JOB

Now that you have secured a job, it is important that you do the things that will insure you're keeping the job. Because you are someone who has been impacted by the criminal justice system, employers will be especially vigilant of your behavior and attitude. This guide will give you suggestions on how to stay on the positive side of your employer and, enable you to keep your job.

Being a Good Employee

Review the Career Success guides: *What Do Employers Expect from Their Employees*? and *What to Do When Starting a New Job*. Since the employer decided to hire you, they must think that you have the traits and qualities that they was seeking. The following are things that you can do to improve your value to the employer and assure your success on the job.

Be At Work on Time, Every Day

You cannot be a good employee if you don't show up for work. Your employer needs for you to be at your work station on or before the specified start time every day. That is why you were hired. When you do not show up, for whatever reason, it requires your coworkers to not only do their job but also yours. If you have to miss work for a legitimate reason, call your supervisor as soon as you realize that you will either be late or not able to work. Let them know why.

Properly Present Yourself

Think of every work day as an interview. That means that you need to shower, shave and use deodorant every day. Wear clean, appropriate clothing. How you appear says a lot about you and your attitude toward the job.

Be Ready To Work

The employer expects you to be able to give 100% of yourself to your job. This means that you cannot come to work tired, preoccupied with personal problems, hungry or hung-over. Get a good night's rest, eat breakfast and leave personal problems at home.

Improve Your Skills

Although most employers will provide on-the-job training, you can improve your value by constantly trying to improve your skills. Ask your supervisor about ways that you can learn new skills. This may mean reading a manual on a new piece of equipment or attending special training classes. Be open to new learning opportunities.

Have a Positive Attitude

Nothing can get you terminated quicker than having a bad attitude. Although you may not like everything about your work, how you deal with the negatives of your work says a lot about you. Be creative and find ways to liven up boring, unpleasant or routine tasks. Remember, employers have a preconceived notion of how formerly incarcerated individuals behave. Do not display these behaviors and attitudes if you want to keep your job.

Respect your Employer

Employers expect you to treat their property at work with the same care and respect that you want someone to treat your property. Don't assume that it is okay to "borrow" items from your employer because "the employer will not miss them." The truth is that employers are sensitive to any "borrowing because it is theft. Employers expect all employees to be honest. Violation of this rule will result in immediate termination.

Remember, that while you are on the time clock, the employer expects you to be engaged in work activities. Goofing off, using the telephone for personal business, non-business related conversations with co-workers, surfing the Internet and any activity not related to business are not considered acceptable by employers.

Be Flexible

One of the most important players on a baseball team is the utility player: the person who can, at a moment's notice, perform any of a variety of tasks. That player is flexible. Even in the most routine employment environments, things happen that interrupt the routine. Flexible employees are able to respond to problems and change.

Know the Rules

Every workplace has a written, as well as unwritten, list of rules. These rules detail acceptable and unacceptable activities and behaviors. They also describe company policies and procedures.

Many rules are common to all workplaces. These include policies on drinking, using tobacco, drugs, firearms and weapons and aggressive behavior. These rules are printed in a company manual. If you have not been given one, ask your supervisor for a copy. Don't assume a particular behavior is okay because it was acceptable by your previous employer or workplace.

Getting Along With Co-Workers

How you feel about your co-workers is a major factor in job satisfaction. If you cannot get along with your co-workers, not only will you be miserable, your co-workers will have little to do with you. It is essential, therefore, that others see you as being cooperative, friendly and a hard worker. The following are suggestions on how to get along with your co-workers:

Know your Co-workers' Names

Everyone wants to be called by their given name. In the first few weeks you will meet many new people. Keep a pad of paper handy and jot down names and something about each person. "Jane Doe, janitorial supervisor." They will not be offended.

Compliment Coworkers

Everyone loves a compliment. Go out of your way to recognize others and what they do. Look for things to praise. "You really did that job fast." Don't feel as though you need to be competitive with your coworkers. You are part of a team.

Control your Anger

It is human nature to occasionally get angry at work. A customer may have insulted you, or a coworker said or did something to offend you. Rather than losing your temper, walk away for a few minutes. It is better to "lose face" than to lose your temper and get fired. In the prison culture, being "dissed" frequently results in a confrontation and/or violence. Be mindful that people usually say and do things that are not intended to be disrespectful but you may perceive to be so. Just do not react as you may have done while incarcerated.

Don't Gossip

Never gossip or say unkind things about co-workers at work. If you need to talk about how you feel about a co-worker, talk in confidence to a close friend. Sometimes just talking about a situation will reduce your anger.

Accept Criticism

Don't get offended by criticism. None of us likes to have a fault pointed out. We must, however, be willing to learn from our mistakes. This means that we need to listen to constructive criticism and be open to correcting our deficiencies. Don't hesitate to ask your supervisor for assistance and suggestions.

Don't Cover for Co-Workers

Covering for a co-worker can get you into trouble with your supervisor. For example, if asked to clock-in for a co-worker respectively decline.

Don't Forget Your Manners

Phrases such as "thank you," "please," and "have a good day" not only are good manners, they convey respect for others.

Watch your Language

The use of swear words or sexually explicit language is a part of the prison culture. Such language is not acceptable in the work place.

Dealing With Conflict at Work

On most jobs you will, at some point, experience conflict with a co-worker or supervisor. Before you do something that gets you into trouble, talk to someone. If the problem is with a fellow worker, talk to your supervisor. If the problem is with your supervisor, talk to your supervisor's supervisor. If a resolution to the conflict cannot be resolved at this level, request a transfer to another area in the company or a change in shifts.

Remember, you do not lose face when you compromise. If, after discussing the issue with your supervisor, there appears to be little opportunity for resolution, compromise. This may mean that you have to give a little to get a resolution. The next time a conflict occurs, you have a greater chance of success. There will be times, however, when you are not willing to compromise your values. In these cases, you will be respected for standing your ground.

Getting Along With Your Supervisor

- Supervisors have a job to do. Like you, they make mistakes, have good days and bad days. You don't have to love, or even like, your supervisor in order to get along with him or her.
- Analyze your supervisor. Get to know their strengths and weaknesses, what sets them off and what gets you praise.
- Understand your supervisor's job responsibilities. If you can, help your supervisor realize his or her job goals and objectives. You will be perceived as a team player.
- Don't compete with your supervisor. If the supervisor thinks that you are vying for that job, you will no longer get along. Let your supervisor know that you do not want their job.

Stress on the Job

All jobs have stress. Stress is not always bad. In fact, many people use stress to stay focused and alert on the job. Professional athletes and entertainers thrive on stress. It is when stress becomes incapacitating that stress is bad. You need to recognize the signs of disabling stress and take measures to reduce it. Talk to your supervisor or a professional counselor and see if there are ways to reduce the workplace stress. These may include a restructuring of your job tasks, change in shifts, relocation or time off. The Job Search guide, *How to Handle the Stress of the Job Search* provides suggestions as to how to deal with stress.

Sexual Harassment

Sexual behavior of any sort in the workplace is not tolerated by most employers. In fact, such behavior may be illegal and grounds for immediate dismissal. Forbidden behavior can range from suggestive remarks or jokes to actual physical contact. As one employer states in their Employment Manual, "Treat everyone in the workplace as though the person is your mother or father."

TRULINCS Friendly! info@ReentryEssentials.org 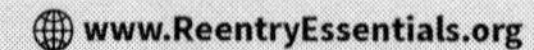  www.ReentryEssentials.org 347.973.0004 2609 East 14 Street, Suite 1018, Brooklyn, NY 11235-3915

HOW TO SET GOALS AT WORK

In order to succeed at work, you need to have clear goals. These may be goals your boss has set for you or ones that you have set for yourself. Setting goals is a great way to motivate yourself and to turn your wants into realities. If you are not used to setting goals, use the suggestions below to create a process to set goals for your work and personal life. As a Returning Citizen, it is critical that you set the following as one of your primary goals: I will avoid those behaviors that led to my incarceration.

Why Set Goals?

Most of us know what we want for our future (job satisfaction, a comfortable economic life-style, satisfying personal relationships, etc.). Unfortunately these personal desires often get lost as you struggle with daily issues, especially unemployment. It is essential, however, that you not lose sight of your goals. By setting goals you force yourself to pursue your dreams and stay motivated.

By Setting Goals For Yourself You Will:

- Achieve more.
- Provide a road map to help you clearly see what the future can hold for you.
- Keep your mind and body sharp.
- Be able to identify and overcome obstacles that hinder your attaining your goals.
- Improve your self-confidence and motivation.
- Inspire others to excel and perform better.

Achieving Goals Doesn't Happen By Accident

Achieving your goals can be difficult. You can accomplish them, however, if you focus and have a clear idea of what is required to meet each goal. The following are steps that can help you identify and attain your goals.

- Determine your goal and write it down. You can visualize your goals better if you write them down. Eventually, you can post them on your refrigerator door, your computer or any place you look at regularly. Imagine yourself achieving everything on your list and be sure to view it on a regular basis.
- List the reasons you want to achieve your goal. Write down at least 3 reasons why the goal is important. You will stay motivated if you are reminded why you created the goal in the first place. Also, write down what will happen when you get off course. You are more likely to stay on track if you have a back-up plan.
- Be specific. Here is an example of a vague goal statement: I want to control my consumption of alcohol. This is not specific enough. Goals must be time-specific and deadline-oriented. A better goal statement would be: I will limit my drinking to only one drink per day and will not frequent any bars starting today. Goals without deadlines usually do not get met.
- Break down your goal into measurable steps. Work backwards from your goal. Create the action steps you need to reach your goal. Each step needs to have a weekly or monthly time line. For example:
  - My goal is to sell 1% more of the product per month.
  - In order to achieve this goal, I will need to contact all of my customers from last year.
  - Therefore, this week I need to create a list of all of last year's customers.

  By writing out the steps needed to reach the goal, you can stay on track with your original goals and see the progress you are making over a specific amount of time.
- Use trusted co-workers to keep you focused. Motivate each other by talking about your successes, your challenges and your goals. Make yourself accountable by telling others of your plans. Choose your support group wisely. People who are not very goal-oriented may be unsupportive or try to distract you from your goals.

Setting goals is essential for all aspects of life, from running a business, supervising employees, losing weight, controlling the consumption of alcohol, earning more money, maintaining a relationship ... no matter what you do, setting goals helps ensure you will excel, rather than just get by.

Commitment to Your Goals

For any goal to be achieved, there must be a commitment to make the effort to accomplish the goal. Perhaps you have heard someone say that they have given their 100% commitment to make a relationship work, such as marriage. You may also have heard the coach of a sports team say that all the players made a commitment to give their best efforts to achieve the team's success. There is no doubt that the greater your level of commitment to achieving your goals, the greater your chances of success will be.

Ways To Help You Stay Committed To Achieving Your Goals:

Give yourself pep-talks.

If you plan to increase sales, say to yourself, I love our product; it really helps people. I am good at helping people buy this. It's best to say these statements out loud so that it reinforces the goal in your mind. It will also help you achieve the goal much faster. Turn your most important goal into one or two sentences that you can remember, especially when you find yourself getting off track.

Do it daily.

Many of the daily duties of your work can limit you from having enough time to devote to your goals. You can easily get caught up in just getting your job done each day at work. One method to help you to stay focused is to set aside a specific time each day for you to evaluate how you are doing. Many successful people use the last 15 minutes of each work day to review the day's events and relate these events to personal and work goals. They conclude by making plans for the next work day.

Take action.

Don't procrastinate. Just planning will not help you achieve your goals. You must take action. Once you have determined a goal for yourself, take your first step, no matter how small, within 24 hours.

Re-evaluate your goals.

At some point, you may need to change your goals or some of the steps you have planned. Do not think you have failed if you are falling behind in your plan. Just taking time to adjust either the goal statement or the steps will help you achieve your ultimate goal. Remember, you are either moving toward or away from your goals.

The Number One Cause Of Failure Is...

Too often we believe that we are not capable of achieving the same success as others. It is easy to believe that successful people have had an inherent advantage (they were born into money, were smarter, more talented, etc.) that we have not had. The simple truth is that most successful people did not have this inherent advantage. They achieved based upon their effort.

The number one cause of failure is lack of action! Unless you are willing to risk taking the first step, you will never move forward. In the absence of action your dreams will remain just that ... dreams. Everyone knows that action is required for success. Unfortunately, not everyone believes that it applies to them.

Reward Yourself

If you find yourself wondering if all your effort is worth it, then you probably should reward yourself along the way. These step rewards do not have to be huge; they just need to be some kind of recognition OF YOU! The following techniques can be very useful in setting up your step rewards.

- As you plan your individual goal steps, create a specific reward for each step you complete.
- Your reward should be equal to the amount of work. For example, how you reward yourself at the end of the month should be more significant than your reward at the end of the week.
- Be consistent about rewarding yourself for every accomplished step.
- Take the time to acknowledge the fact that you accomplished your goal.

TRULINCS Friendly! info@ReentryEssentials.org www.ReentryEssentials.org 347.973.0004 2609 East 14 Street, Suite 1018, Brooklyn, NY 11235-3915

HOW TO EFFECTIVELY COMMUNICATE AT WORK

Unless you are working alone on a deserted island, much of your day is spent communicating with coworkers, customers, colleagues and the general public. Communication is two way... you are trying to convey your message to another person and you hope that the other person understands what it is that you are saying. Communication can take many forms: it can be verbal, non-verbal, written or electronic. To be an effective employee you must be able to communicate clearly and concisely in all of these forms. This guide offers some strategies to help you communicate better in the workplace.

Can the Prison Slang

Every prisoner quickly learns that there is a language spoken by prisoners. These slang expressions convey many meanings that are not understood by people who have never been incarcerated. Most prisoners, when speaking to fellow inmates and guards, use these slang expressions. Unfortunately, once you become comfortable using this language, it may be difficult talking to others without using prison slang. This slang includes inappropriate words and expressions (commonly referred to as swearing), racial terms and voice inflections that could be construed as threatening.

Like retiring military personnel who are used to speaking "militarese", a language filled with acronyms, the formerly incarcerated must can the slang and jargon of the yard. This is one of the most difficult things that you must do in their transition to civilian life. You will never be able to effectively communicate with non-ex-offenders if you cannot stop using prison-talk, especially in the workplace.

The Process of Effective Communication

In simple terms, communication occurs when one person tries to convey his or her thoughts to one or more other people. It is not easy, however, to convey thoughts in such a way that the other person or persons completely understands what has been communicated. There are a number of barriers that can block effective communication:

1. The person initiating the communication has not thought through what it is that he or she wants to say. If you cannot put into words what it is that you want to say, it is impossible to expect the listener to understand.
2. If you and the listener do not speak the same language, then communication becomes difficult. Sometimes you may be speaking the same language, but you are using jargon, slang or acronyms that are not understood by the listener.
3. The listener does not give you feedback that they understood what you just communicated. We all look for acknowledgment from the listener that they heard and understood the message. Feedback usually comes in the form of non-verbal clues like a smile, head shake or a look of puzzlement.
4. The setting or context of the conversation can affect our ability to hear what is being said. Communication can be difficult in a noisy environment, such as on a factory floor. Not being able to clearly hear what is being said can lead to mis-communication and misunderstanding.

The following are suggestions for ways that you can overcome these communication barriers while at work.

Be Clear and Concise

At work, you will need to communicate accurately and efficiently. This may be different from the way you are used to communicating at home, in school or with friends. Communicating at work is more formal and less emotional.

- If you are excited or upset, calm down before you communicate with your boss, coworkers or customers. It is very difficult to express thoughts and ideas when you are emotional, especially when you are angry.
- Time is valuable. Get to the point quickly. It is easy for the message to get lost in long-winded stories.
- Communicate to solve problems. Although it is appropriate to provide information on a problem, it is important that you communicate a solution to the problem.
- Praise co-workers and others often and sincerely.
- Don't gossip. Not only is gossip unproductive, it usually ends up hurting someone.
- Ask for feedback. Because evaluations are usually stressful, it is important that you confirm with your supervisor what he or she says to you. If possible, take notes so that you can accurately reflect back on the conversation.
- Keep confidences secret.

How You Say It

Perhaps you have heard the expression, "It is not what you say; it is how you say it." In order to get feedback we focus on the listener's voice, mannerisms and body language. Here are a few hints for communicating at work.

- Slow down – People will think you are nervous or unsure of yourself if you talk rapidly.
- Liven up – Avoid speaking in a monotone voice. Your voice should convey emotion and be expressive.
- Enunciate your words – Speak clearly. Don't mumble.
- Use appropriate volume – Lower your speaking volume when you are physically close to the person with whom you are speaking
- Pronounce words correctly – Mispronounced words lead to miscommunication and misunderstanding.
- Use the right words – Learn the key words and phrases of your workplace and industry. This will help you communicate with coworkers who share the same jargon, phrases and acronyms.
- Make eye contact –Don't look away or down when speaking.
- Body language – Your body language should match your message.
- Customer conversations – Keep a friendly and helpful attitude when talking to customers.

Written Communications

Many people are intimidated by writing. Your job may, however, require you to write memos, letters, reports or other formal communications. Here are some basic tips when writing:

- Avoid the use of slang words.
- Try to avoid the use of abbreviations or acronyms unless you know the recipient of the memo or letter is familiar with the abbreviation.
- Take special care in spelling the names of people and companies. Double check when possible.
- Numbers should be expressed as words when the number is less than 10. The number 10 and any number above 10 should be expressed as a figure.
- Keep your sentences short.

Because written communication is permanent, it is critical that the writer be mindful of grammar, spelling, punctuation, writing style and wording. Use a computer word processing program whenever possible. These programs can check for spelling and grammar; however, they are not 100% accurate. Many computer programs have trouble when there is more than one correct spelling (like the words, too, to and two) and will not indicate that the word is misspelled. It is always prudent to have your memos, reports and letters proofread by a coworker. Even the most successful people have their writings proofread.

Electronic Communications

If you work in an office setting you will be required to use email to communicate with your co-workers and possibly with customers. Here are some rules to remember when you are conducting electronic communication:

- Always use spell check and proper grammar.
- Indicate in the email message if you are including an attachment.
- Do not send or receive personal emails at work.
- Be aware that no emails are permanently deleted.
- Do not forward jokes, videos, chain letters, or private documents.
- Respond to all emails within one day.
- Preview your messages before sending.
- Be friendly but professional – no smiley faces or graphics.
- Always include a subject line.
- Do not send an email if you are angry.

What Did You Say? – Listening Skills

You can think faster than others can speak. That's one reason your mind may tend to wander when people are talking to you. Here are some suggestions that may help you keep your mind focused on what is being said to you.

Treat listening as a challenging mental task. Active listening requires you to stay focused on the person who is talking. One suggestion to help you stay focused is to pretend that you will be required to repeat the conversation to someone else. Keep telling yourself, what was just said? How will I accurately repeat it?

- Focus on the idea being expressed, not on the delivery of it. Try to block out the speaker's accent or the tone of voice.
- Control your emotional involvement. This is one of the reasons why conflicts develop and arguments occur. If you feel your emotions are on edge during a conversation, take a five minute walk or distract yourself. Sometimes getting your mind off the subject is enough to calm you down.
- Listen to what the person is saying and try not to think about what you want to say next. Once you start thinking about your response, you will stop listening to what the person is saying.
- Try to remain objective and open-minded. Try to understand not only what the person is saying, but why they are saying it. Is there an emotion behind the words?
- If you cannot understand the person due to a noisy background or other distractions, ask to move to another location.

HOW TO EFFECTIVELY MANAGE TIME AT WORK

Do you ever wonder at the end of the work day what you have accomplished? Do you begin your work day feeling you will never get your work done? Many workers have these feelings. If you frequently have these feelings, you probably are not managing your time efficiently. This guide offers some proven methods for improving your work flow and helping you manage your time at work.

From Authority Regulated To Self-Regulated

Recently released ex-offenders often find that they have difficulty regulating their time and schedule. Ever since the arrest and incarceration, time and schedule becomes regulated by the prison authorities. Prisoners have little or no control over their time.

Additionally, there was a set routine to each day and each day of the week. Again, the prisoner had no control over their routine. Once released, the ex-offender has the freedom to make scheduling decisions. This means that they are responsible for routine activities such as when to get up in the morning, what they eat, when they go to bed at night and everything in between. In other words, you are now responsible for managing your time as well as your activities. Even though this guide focuses mainly on managing your time at work, the suggestions are also applicable to managing your time away from work.

Managing Your Time

Managing time is a skill that is learned. It does not come naturally to most people. Some people learn to be organized, whereas others never do. It does not matter how skilled you are, if you procrastinate you will have trouble getting your work done. As an ex-offender, you need to get a handle on managing your time, especially managing your time at work. When you manage your time effectively, you improve both the quality of your work and your life. You reduce work and life-related frustration because you are organized. Time management will increase your energy level and reduce stress and anxiety; you will be achieving more while expending less effort.

How Do You Spend Your Usual Day?

Before you can start managing your time at work, you need to have an idea of how much time you spend doing all of the tasks that the job requires. For a period of one week, make a list of everything you do during the day. Your list will probably include:

- Reading. Identify what you read (mail, emails, memos, reports, etc.) and from whom (co-workers, supervisors, customers, personal etc.).
- Writing. Identify what you write (mail, emails, memos, reports, etc.) and to whom (a co-worker, supervisor, customer, personal, etc.).
- Talking on the phone. Identify with whom you talk (a co-worker, supervisor, customer, personal, etc.) and the nature of the conversation (casual, order taking, discussing a work project, etc.).
- Other activities such as taking breaks, eating, attending meetings, receiving training, training others and operating office equipment such as a copy machine, etc.

Note how much time you devoted each day for each item listed. Add the time. At the end of the week, total the amount of time that you spent for each category. Make a new list using the same categories. On the new list enter the amount of time that you want to spend each week in each category. By comparing the "actual time spent" with the "ideal amount of time you want to spend," you can identify the activities where you need to devote more time and those where you need to reduce your time.

You may want to also share this information with your supervisor. Your supervisor may not only have an opinion on how you should spend your time, but also have suggestions on ways that you can more effectively manage your time.

Suggestions for Getting More Out Of Your Day

Managing emails. A major portion of correspondence in today's office environment is transmitted electronically in the form of emails.

- Organize your email folders. Create a folder for each subject or sender. Give the folder a name that describes the folder content (Some examples; August, 2009 Sales Meetings, Mary Smith and Personnel Memos).
- Only look at your email or regular mail once. If it is an important message, print it.
- Immediately after reading the message, decide to respond to it, file it away or delete it. If the message is appropriate for more than one folder, copy it to all appropriate folders. Do not leave messages in your Inbox; otherwise, your Inbox will become cumbersome, especially when trying to locate a message. Always copy the message to the appropriate folder.
- Create a "Respond to" mail box and move all emails that need to be answered at a future time into that box. Check this mail box daily.
- Once you have responded, move the message to the appropriate folder.
- Use a spam filter to filter unwanted messages. If you use a spam filter, check the spam folder at least every other day. An important email may have been inappropriately placed into this folder. Delete all spam emails.

More Suggestions

Do not multitask if you can help it.

Multitasking occurs when you try to do more than one task at a time. For most people multitasking does not come easily and will decrease your productivity. Unless you know that you are skilled at multitasking, do only one thing at a time. If this is not possible, then limit yourself to doing only two activities at once. Doing two things at once, however, means neither task gets your full attention. For example, if you try to read a report while you are on the telephone talking to a customer, then you might not hear what the customer is saying, or you might not understand the contents of the report. Be careful about doing multiple tasks if one of them requires your entire attention.

Complete a task before moving to another.

Most tasks have a beginning, a middle where most of the work is done, and an end. We use the beginning to organize our thoughts and the end to confirm and correct what we did. Interruptions during the process often require us to go back to the beginning and try to remember where we were in the process. This not only wastes time, it increases the opportunity for errors. It is better, therefore, to schedule taking a project from beginning to end with no interruptions.

Generate a "To Do List" at the beginning of each day.

If you don't know what you should be doing, how can you manage your time to do it? Each morning review your list from the prior work day. Identify tasks that were not completed. These should be the items that you tackle first. Next, add items that you know need to be addressed. Finally, add items to your list as the day progresses. Prioritize all items, then assign a time in the day when you will perform each task. This may seem obvious, but think about how many times you've put off an important task so you could do something else that really didn't need to be done at that time. Do the most important things first.

Don't wait.

If you find yourself waiting for a reply or a decision so you can continue with a task, move on to another task and return to the first task after you get the required information.

Group similar activities together.

Make all your phone calls at once. Check all of your email messages at one time.

Check your email on a schedule.

If you are using email at work, people understand they may not always get an immediate response. You can answer most e-mails by checking your emails only a few times each day.

Take breaks.

Taking a five or ten minute break can re-energize you and improve your efficiency at work. Stand up and stretch at least once each hour.

Find a good place to work and make sure it is organized and neat.

Clutter is not good for time management. A cluttered desk prevents organization and wastes your energy trying to find important papers. Keep your desk clean and use a good filing system. Before leaving at the end of the work day, arrange the papers on your desk in the order that they need to be addressed the next day.

Know when you work best.

Each person has a most efficient time of the day. You can discover your by monitoring your productivity over a period of time. Use thi information to manage your schedule, keeping your best work time fre for your most important work.

Learn to say no.

It is not easy to tell a supervisor or a co-worker that you cannot hel them. If you are unable to spare the time, or are on an urgent deadline ask your supervisor to prioritize your schedule. It may be possible t adjust the due date for a project. Most work settings require you to b flexible and to be able to set aside a task in order to work on a unexpected project.

Identify and avoid activities that waste time.

We all have distractions that waste our time. Co-workers can easil involve you in time-wasting activities such as unnecessary persona conversations, and you can also allow your personal issues to occup your thoughts. Review the Career Success guide *How to Communicat on the Job* for suggestions on ways to deal with coworkers.

Identify and avoid distractions.

Some people are able to work with music on, while others find distracting. Most people require an environment with few distraction when they are trying to concentrate. Eliminate distractions when yo need to get high priority tasks completed. If possible, avoid takin telephone calls, answering emails or receiving visitors when you have project with a tight deadline.

Don't procrastinate.

If you postpone starting a task, assess what you are being asked to do You may find that you lack clear goals or you have underestimated th difficulty of the task. If you are uncertain about a task, discuss the projec with your supervisor.

TRULINCS Friendly! info@ReentryEssentials.org www.ReentryEssentials.org 347.973.0004 2609 East 14 Street, Suite 1018, Brooklyn, NY 11235-3915

Made in the USA
Columbia, SC
15 July 2024